INTRODUCTION

Any successful course is a special mixture of the instructor's teaching style and competencies, the students' interests and abilities, course requirements, time strictures, and choice of text. This Instructor's Manual for *Looking Out/Looking In* is a compilation of various materials we have found useful in teaching our basic interpersonal communication courses. We offer these suggestions with the hope that they will help you develop your own successful blend of ingredients.

You might use the teaching strategies given here in the way a good chef uses recipes. Although they're a starting point, your own special talents and the needs of the specific classroom may call for an adaptation of the basic formula—or even the creation of a new approach. You'll find that the format of *Looking Out/Looking In* will allow this kind of flexibility. The text is organized into ten chapters, each covering material available for one unit in a course. Chapters Two through Seven are written so that they may be arranged in any sequence that suits your needs.

This Instructor's Manual, the separate Activities Manual, and the text itself provide more exercises and activities than you can probably use in a one-semester course. Once again, we have offered this abundance so that you may pick and choose from among the exercises the ones that will work best for you. We're sure you have many of your own favorite exercises to add to the blend as well.

The Instructor's Manual is organized into four parts as follows:

Part I provides general suggestions concerning course format and grading options. A detailed course syllabus is included to illustrate how to organize a course using the text, the Activities Manual/Study Guide, and the Instructor's Manual. New to this edition of the Instructor's Manual are lists of Internet sites that relate to chapter material. Instructors can easily find links to journals, publications, collections, bibliographies, teaching strategies, and other course-related materials such as audiotapes and videotapes.

Part II contains chapter objectives. Notes for class and student activities in each chapter are found here. Exercises found in the text are listed in boldface type by title in the index of *Looking Out/Looking In*. Activities from the Activities Manual/Study Guide are listed by number (e.g., 1.4 for the fourth activity in Chapter One).

Part III is a test bank of over 1000 questions and answers keyed to each chapter. They are organized by chapter and then by question type (T = true/false, M = multiple-choice, Matching = matching, and E = essay). In addition, you will find that each question is referenced to the text page(s) on which it can be found and by cognitive type. Thus, each question looks like this:

How many parts are there in this Instructor's Manual?

    a.   four
    b.   three
    c.   two
    d.   one
    e.   This Instructor's Manual is not divided into parts.

Answer: a   **Type: M**   **Page 123**   **Knowledge**

Please note that the cognitive type identifiers will help you construct quizzes or exams that are easier or more difficult, depending on your purpose. The cognitive types are:

KN = knowledge (remembering terms, facts, or theories)

CO = comprehension (understanding, summarizing material)

AP = application (use of learned material in new and concrete situations)

AN = analysis (understanding content and structural form by differentiating, inferring, or outlining)

SY = synthesis (categorizing, combining, or organizing parts to form a new whole)

EV = evaluation (judging, comparing, or contrasting the value of material for a given purpose)

Starting with the Ninth Edition of the test bank, we added one more category of test item:

RE = recall (simple recall of reading—no course content)

We include this category for instructors who like to give simple quizzes on the chapters to check that their students are keeping up with the reading. Other instructors prefer not to use these types of questions because they do not test course concepts. By separating out this category, and grouping the questions together at the beginning of the true/false and the multiple-choice sections, instructors who want these questions can find them easily and those who don't want to use them can skip over them quickly.

The test bank is available on computer disk for adopters of *Looking Out/Looking In.*

Part IV contains interpersonal communication exercises specific to such occupations as nursing and computer programming. These exercises can be copied and given to students majoring in these particular occupations or they can be used as models for creating your own occupation-specific exercises. Our thanks to Ruth Tangman and the professors at Albuquerque Technical-Vocational Institute who created these exercises and allowed us to use them.

CONTENTS

PART FOUR: INTERPERSONAL COMMUNICATION EXERCISES FOR SPECIFIC VOCATIONS   251

PART ONE

GENERAL SUGGESTIONS

THE INSTRUCTOR IS THE MAIN INGREDIENT

It is our belief that instructors of interpersonal communication have a particularly rewarding but difficult job. In addition to dealing with the problems faced by all instructors in the classroom, the interpersonal communication teacher faces the challenge of being the model interpersonal communicator in the classroom. In recognition of this role, we strongly suggest that as instructor you actively participate in class exercises. Although there will be many times when you must play a specialized role to facilitate an exercise, we encourage you to interact with the student whenever you can. Our involvement has paid dividends in three ways.

1. It encourages participation from our students. When they see that we are willing to discuss our own experiences, they seem to be encouraged to do the same. Student comments support this assertion.
2. Giving something of ourselves seems to increase our interaction with the group. Although it may sound paradoxical, we've found that we have been most successful when we've taken the risk of participating and making mistakes.
3. Our participation gives us a good perspective on the student's experience in the class. We sometimes discover that what appears to be a simple exercise to us is actually quite challenging; and on the other hand, activities that appear valuable in theory may prove to be dismal failures in practice.

STUDENT FEEDBACK

So that you may discover how students perceive the class, we suggest that you ask your students to make periodic formal evaluations of the course. We found that using a form encourages more specific responses that are the most useful to us. You will probably find that allowing students to respond anonymously works best, although you might allow students to sign their names if they wish. You can design the form to fit your particular situation.

Here is a sample form we have found useful:

1. What expectations did you have for this course (unit)? Has the course (unit) met your expectations? If not, why not?
2. Do you find the workload too light, too heavy, or just right? Were there any specific assignments on which you'd like to comment?
3. Do you think that the grading has been fair? If not, why not?
4. What do you think of the classroom atmosphere? How would you like to see it change?
5. Have the readings (text and outside) been satisfactory? Please give specific examples.
6. Is the teaching style satisfactory? What do you like about your instructor's style? What do you think should be changed?
7. Please make any other comments you feel might be helpful. Do you have any suggestions for improvements? Is there anything you feel we ought to continue doing?
8. What was one thing you learned today?
9. What thing(s) was (were) unclear?
10. What question(s) do you have?
11. What would you like to discuss next time?
12. Do you have any relevant examples or experiences you'd like to share?

THE IMPORTANCE OF EXERCISES

Our unshakable belief is that complete learning takes place only when the student understands a concept on an affective as well as a cognitive level. For example, we consider ourselves to have failed if by the end of the semester a student can list all the factors necessary for effective listening but cares no more about being attentive or understanding than when he or she began our class.

This commitment to encouraging our readers to examine everyday behavior explains the number of exercises you find in *Looking Out/Looking In* and the Activities Manual. We have purposely supplied more than you'll need for a one-semester course. Our hope is that you can find exercises that work for you for each unit you cover in your interpersonal communication course. We've taken this extra step because we expect that participating in exercises, both group and individual, will make a personal application of the subject almost inevitable. Each activity is designed to lead the reader beyond talking about how people communicate and to ask the question "How do I communicate?"—and further, "How can *I* make my communication more satisfying?"

This emphasis on self-examination necessarily involves asking your class to examine (individually and as a group) feelings and behaviors that often aren't revealed in academic settings. Although we've found that very little growth comes without this kind of examination, it's absolutely essential not to push too hard, not to demand more self-disclosure or risk than the group is ready to volunteer. And always, we respect a student's right to pass or to carry out an alternate task in place of a given exercise. Despite our best efforts, we are often unaware of the personal anguish that some of our students suffer that they would prefer to keep private.

You'll find that the text exercises start by asking for very simple contributions and progress gradually to relatively greater amounts of self-disclosure. We hope that this pacing will prevent any anxiety on the part of your students; but in any doubtful cases, we urge you to move at whatever pace seems right for your situation.

ACTIVITIES MANUAL/STUDY GUIDE USE

The **Activities Manual/Study Guide** is a valuable student aid for the course.

Activities Manual

In addition to the many exercises in the text, the Activities Manual has 68 individual and group skill builders and invitations to insight that focus on written and oral interpersonal communication skills. Two *new* additions to the Tenth Edition of the Activities Manual involve students with one another to a higher degree. Short case studies for each chapter focus on ethics, competence, and adaptation to situation; they are referred to as *Your Call*. Technology influences on interpersonal communication are analyzed in each chapter of the Activities Manual; they are referred to as *Mediated Messages* and invite students to adapt their knowledge of interpersonal communication to mediated situations.

Study Guide

The Study Guide section contains over 500 puzzles and test questions with answers that enable students to test themselves on the many concepts and skills contained in the text. In addition, extensive outlines help students check their reading or follow classroom lectures. Students using the Study Guide aids in the Activities Manual/Study Guide should understand class material more readily, guide themselves through skill development more easily, and score higher on exams.

The Activities Manual/Study Guide is an invaluable complement to the text. *The publisher makes the text and Activities Manual/Study Guide for* Looking Out/Looking In *available in a shrink-wrapped package for a reduced price.*

CLASSROOM ENVIRONMENT

Although many of the exercises and activities in this book suggest particular arrangements, we feel that some general notes on the design of the classroom may be in order. If we expect our students to interact with each other, it becomes very important to create the best environment possible to promote this development. Knowing that we all work within certain limitations, we'd like to mention some of the items we have found helpful. Chapter Six speaks directly to this subject.

1. Arrange the classroom seating so that all members of the group can see each other. If the room plan will allow it, a circle is the most useful arrangement.
2. If possible, choose comfortable chairs or small table-armed desks that can be easily rearranged into large groups, small groups, and dyads. Vary the arrangement of the classroom to meet the needs of lecture, discussion, and group work.
3. Regroup students frequently. This allows them to get to know many more people and to get new perspectives on communication behavior.

Another way to set up a good classroom environment is to set up expectations about attitude and behavior in one of the first classes. Two methods that address this are the "contract" and the "standards for student success."

Bill Edwards of Columbus State University in Georgia offers this version of an instructor/student "contract" that he and his students adapted from Melanie Booth-Butterfield at West Virginia University.

I divide my class into two groups. One group will rewrite the contract for the professor and the other group will rewrite the contract for the students by accepting, revising, adding, and omitting contract items.

Instructions: Read the following contract. Revise the contract in any way you see fit. Your goal is to design a good contract which each party will sign. You can omit, revise, or accept any item. You can create new items.

INTERPERSONAL COMMUNICATION PROFESSOR'S OATH

As your professor I pledge that I will do the following appropriate teacher behaviors:

I will strive to be on time for class and to dismiss the class in a timely fashion when I have finished, so that you don't have your time wasted.

I will offer you an opportunity to ask questions and make observations.

I will respect you and treat you as an adult.

I will try to always be fully prepared and well-organized in class.

My material will be up-to-date and contemporary in hopes that it will apply to your life.

I will attempt to be unbiased and reasonable in my approach to the material.

I will always be available to talk to you during my office hours.

I will try to be energetic, encouraging, and enthusiastic, because I like the material and I hope you do too.

box continued

None of the assignments will be busywork. Each will have direct relation to class goals.

I will prepare you for assignments and exams.

I will provide quick feedback on written assignments and exams.

I will put forth effort in teaching this class.

Signature: _____

INTERPERSONAL COMMUNICATION STUDENT'S OATH

As a student in this course I pledge to do these appropriate student behaviors.

I will be actively involved with the class and its activities, asking questions, providing examples, etc.

I will smile and nod at my professor a lot, because I know this encourages the teacher to do his/her best.

I will not read newspapers, have side conversations, wear my headset, have my beeper turned on, pack up early during class because I know that it hurts my learning and my teacher's feelings.

I will be on time for class on a regular basis.

I will not attempt to cheat on exams, copy others' assignments, turn in others' work as my own, etc. All work that I do in this class will be my own original work.

I will be polite and cooperative with my teacher and classmates. I won't try to put anything over on them, or ask them to make exceptions for me.

I will try to always stay awake during class.

I will endeavor to keep my mind open to the ideas presented and really consider how they affect my life.

I will put forth effort in taking this class.

Signature: _____

A second way of setting up a positive classroom environment comes from the Communication faculty at Santa Barbara City College. They put the following "Standards for Student Success" in all course packets and review the expectations at the outset of each semester:

STANDARDS FOR STUDENT SUCCESS IN COMMUNICATION DEPARTMENT COURSES

To Our Students:

Welcome to the Communication Department! Your instructor may choose to share the ten following expectations with you. These standards or norms for success address attitudes and behaviors beyond the good practices you have already acquired in your years of experience in educational environments. Some of these are givens that fall under the heading of routine but sometimes unstated premises that operate in healthy classrooms. We believe that noting expectations early in the semester will help you to be a successful learner, provide benefits for other students in the class, save time, and assist your instructor in conducting effective class sessions that offer every student the opportunity to be heard and acknowledged as a productive course participant.

Your instructor will discuss variances in the expectations with you. We are, after all, individuals whose standards may differ. We hope you will talk to your instructor about your expectations as well. The most constructive classroom environment will be one that encompasses the best that everyone—instructor and students alike—can offer to produce a positive learning experience . . . and that is what Santa Barbara City College is all about.

The Communication Faculty at Santa Barbara City College

1. **Attend classes regularly, be on time, and stay for the entire class period**. In most courses, students receive attendance credit/points but the points are less important on a day-to-day basis than what you will miss by unnecessary absences and what your classmates will lose in not having your discussion contributions. Latecomers are a distraction to everyone. Anticipate challenges and try to plan for them. For example, it is well known that finding a parking spot at 10:00 A.M. is difficult. Plan your schedule with enough flex time to accommodate circling the lots until you find a slot.

2. **Participate in class discussion**. Some courses have participation points and others do not. Your discussion contributions are important in either case. Be a positive force in your classroom interaction. Ask questions, express your opinions, and make yourself known as someone who is actively involved.

3. **Use the instructor's office hours**. This time is set aside explicitly for you to talk with your teachers. You don't have to come with a monumental issue or problem (although these are good times to drop by). Students often use office hours to:

   a. introduce themselves to the instructor.

   b. provide important information about unique challenges such as learning disabilities, child care issues, and potential conflicts with work responsibilities outside the college. Crucial factors known in advance are likely to be better accommodated than last-minute surprises.

   c. ask questions about course material and/or discuss individual problems. In many cases, the instructor will never know your concerns unless you speak up.

   d. pass the time of day sharing insights and observations. The office hour is yours. A casual and nontask-oriented visit may produce positive results on both sides.

4. **Avoid speaking with your instructor about significant issues immediately before and after class** as s/he is trying either to get everything ready for one class or prepare for the one starting in 10 minutes. Use office hours, e-mail, or telephone messages to contact the instructor on important items. The SBCC voice mail allows you 24-hour access. We will return calls promptly if we are not in when you call. (Leave your name and phone number.)

5. **Understand that instructional memory is not flawless**. Many of us have 150 students and more. It is hard to recall all the details of your class performance without help. If you want to discuss, for example, your progress from one assignment to the next, bring along instructor critiques and any other helpful notes to the meeting with your instructor. Be prepared to explain your issue or complaint. If videotape is available, review it before discussion with your instructor. If you have questions about a grade, write out your reasons so your teacher can see the specifics.

6. **Take notes in class**. Informed discussion is far more likely to arise from documented notes than hazy recall. Notes will also aid study for exams.

box continued

7. **Read assignments in the text and comply with homework expectations on the dates assigned.** Bring materials required (Scantron answer sheets, pencils, etc.) when needed. Don't expect others to bail you out if you neglect your responsibilities.

8. **Review the syllabus periodically**. Ask questions if you have them. Know what is expected. If you don't know, ask.

9. **Participate in class activity appropriately**. This involves such disparate behaviors as listening to others and acknowledging opposing viewpoints, choosing language that avoids uselessly antagonizing others (obscenity, personal attacks, hostile or sarcastic comments, etc.), blatantly reading *The Channels* or some other noncourse-related text while class matters are in progress, talking with other students while someone else (who has the floor) is trying to speak, and taking a nap during class. Some of these negative behaviors may seem barely worth mention but they do occur and they do influence classroom interaction. Most of the courses in the Communication Department are relatively small. One person's distracting behavior can have a larger impact than you might imagine. For the student or students trying to present a speech, a group project, a review of the literature, and so forth, audience members who appear to be dozing or paying no attention whatever, present an extremely bothersome problem. Your responsibility as a student of Communication theory and practice includes being an open, alert, courteous, and receptive listener, as well as a competent presenter.

10. **Take responsibility for your education**. Excuses and rationalizations should be eliminated from your academic repertoire. Know that your instructors are human and predisposed to trust rather than doubt you. If you get away with a faked illness or fabricated emergency, you may find that the inevitable result hurts you more than anyone else. In one recent course, the instructor distributed a take-home quiz with instructions to use the text as a resource but work alone in discovering the answers. A student inquired, "How will you know if we cheat?" The teacher responded, "I probably won't ever know... but you will."

Learning is not a game or a contest to discover who is most adept at bending/breaking the rules to suit individual needs. It is an opportunity to prepare for life, professional requirements, and individual success—both as a singular human being and a contributing member of an enduring social network. You are attending Santa Barbara City College in the interest of your own professional advancement and the enhancement of the society in which you live. We are here to help you give both of these aims your best shot. Help us, and we will do our best to help you.

METHODS OF EVALUATION

A good evaluation system should serve at least two purposes:

1. It should give the student feedback on his or her mastery of the skills under study—to answer the question "How well do I understand the subject?"
2. It should give the instructor feedback on how successful he or she has been in communicating the subject matter to the students—to answer the question "Which areas have I taught successfully and which do I need to cover in greater depth or in a different way?"

At the same time, a good system of evaluation should avoid the trap of inviting and rewarding unproductive behaviors—busywork, deceit, and "shooting the bull."

At first, we despaired of finding a useful system of grading that would help rather than hinder students and teachers. But experience has shown that there are several good alternatives. In addition, we have found that no matter which grading system we used, it was very important to delineate clearly the method of grading, the student assignments, and the assignment due dates at the outset of the course. We've also found it important to collect work on the assigned date. These practices seem to reinforce the seriousness of the work involved, increasing respect for the instructor and the course.

A number of grading alternatives follow, which can be used either singly or in combination. For each, we have listed both advantages and disadvantages.

Traditional Examinations

The biggest advantage of traditional examinations is the greater likelihood that students will read and study the text with care. We have found that giving a quiz before the discussion of each chapter works well. Test questions are for checking comprehension after the unit has been studied. We have included over 1100 questions in true/false, multiple-choice, matching, and essay formats. The questions appear in print in this manual, and on computer disk (in either PC or MAC formats) for adopters of *Looking Out/Looking In*.

The principal disadvantage of a grading system based only on tests is that it may not actually measure the most important goals of the class—namely, improving the student's everyday communication behavior. For example, it is entirely possible for a student to describe in writing a number of effective listening behaviors, but he or she may never practice any of them. Thus, tests may measure skill in taking tests about communication and little else.

Practice tests can be a good study aid for students. With the large number of test items available in this test bank, it is relatively easy to create short exams for practice. Whether you do it in class or a laboratory situation, students can grade themselves and review items to prepare for the graded exam.

Student-Planned Examinations

In this procedure, students split into small groups, each of which submits several possible examination questions. All questions are then displayed to the entire class, with the understanding that the instructor will select several of them for the actual test.

Although this method carries the same disadvantage as the traditional method just described, students do study the material more intensively as they select and draw up questions. Another challenge is students' lack of familiarity with writing exam questions; it can take some time before items of quality emerge.

Written/Oral Skill Assignments

In this approach, emphasis is placed on performance of the skills introduced in *Looking Out/Looking In.* After the presentation of material in class, students use many of the exercises from the Activities Manual to practice the concepts in class. Then, written and/or oral exercises are assigned as tests of the skills introduced.

A major advantage of this approach is that instructors can evaluate the student's ability to put into operation the skills introduced. Both written and oral abilities are assessed, and students who score poorly on objective tests can often demonstrate their knowledge in essay and oral formats. Another advantage is the amount of involvement students feel in the class when they see one another performing the skills they have studied; this also serves to help students to individualize the skills, to make them realistic by noting real-life situations in which they are used, and to move toward integrating the communication skills into their everyday lives.

A disadvantage of this approach is that it can take a lot of class time. Any videotaping facility on campus can help here by allowing students to practice oral skills and tape them for playback in class. A communication laboratory with videotape cameras and communication tutors can ease the burden on the instructor.

Student-Instructor Contracts

In this system, students and instructor develop a specific program of study that the students agree to undertake, in return for which they receive a predetermined grade. Contracts can cover work corresponding to units of study, or they can be written for term projects, which may take the place of a final examination. Projects can take many forms—research papers, interviews, dramatic productions, surveys, journals.

There are two advantages to such a plan. First, it demands student initiative in proposing a course of study—a pleasant contrast to more passive types of assignments in which students play less creative roles. Also, such a format allows students some latitude in choosing how to channel their energies. Research and experience show that the quality of work and motivation are higher when students work on subjects with a high degree of personal interest.

Two disadvantages often occur in the contract method. First, some tasks that students choose may not focus on concepts that the instructor deems most important. However, this difficulty can be remedied by defining acceptable areas of study—for example, "Develop a project demonstrating three factors influencing perception and communication." The second disadvantage lies in the inability of some students to be self-motivated scholars. After being trained for twelve or more years in the passive art of test taking, it is difficult to suddenly have to define and pursue one's own course of study.

Journal (Diary) Assignments

In place of examinations, some instructors substitute journal assignments in which students reflect on how topics under study apply to their personal lives. Journals may either be graded or returned to the student for revisions until they are satisfactory.

The advantage of such an approach to evaluation lies in extending the concepts discussed in the classroom into the student's everyday relationships. The value of such applications is obvious in a course designed to improve the participant's communication skills.

One potential disadvantage lies in the failure of journals to focus clearly on key concepts discussed in class. We think this problem can be remedied by assigning journals that concentrate on specific topics—for example, "Record the number and types of destructive styles of conflict you use during the next week." Many assignments in the Activities Manual follow this method; a collection of these from each chapter would make a substantial journal. Most of the exercises labeled "Invitation to Insight" in the Activities Manual/Study Guide are useful as journal entries.

Book Reports/Exercises

Book reports may be assigned to students to encourage more in-depth study of a particular subject.

The greatest disadvantage of book reports as a method of evaluation is that students often prepare reports that only regurgitate what was said in the book. To overcome this disadvantage, when assigning book reports, we have asked students to create an activity from the book they have read. The activity should be designed to teach others in the class one important thing (cognitive or affective) that the student gleaned from the book. We suggest that students look in the text for model exercises. Then we periodically set aside a class session for students to work out their activities with their classmates. Class members are asked to give feedback evaluating each student's exercise. The book report/exercise method seems to reinforce learning of the basic tenets of each book, and most students seem to enjoy sharing discoveries with their classmates.

Self-Evaluation

This method operates on the assumption that in many respects, the student is in the best position to judge his or her own progress in the course. Instructors who use self-evaluation systems ask each student to select a grade that reflects that person's effort and gain in understanding key ideas. Usually, the student is asked to write an explanation for the chosen grade.

The first advantage of this approach is its emphasis on self-judgment. It demonstrates that the student is responsible for his or her own growth and that whatever grade appears on the transcript is merely a symbol of that growth. Second, asking a student the question "What grade do you deserve?" often generates much more self-reflection about effort expended than any other system of evaluation.

The most obvious disadvantage is the potential for abuse. There is no guarantee that a lazy student will not take a high grade. A second shortcoming is the absence of any feedback from the instructor, who presumably has some valuable information about the student's progress. A remedy is to have the instructor reserve the right to give the final grade.

Peer Evaluation

In this system, the students assign each other individual grades based on the assumption that in a communication course, the perceptions of one's peers are a good indication of improvement and mastery of skills. The most efficient method of peer evaluation we've discovered involves reproducing the names of every class member, four to six names to a page. The names are equally spaced down the left side of the paper, and horizontal lines are drawn to separate the area on the paper that will be used to write comments to the student named there. (The back side of each student's space may also be used if the writer needs more room.)

Copies of this special evaluation roster are then distributed to everyone in the class. Each student records a grade and a statement of specifics that supports the assigned grade for each classmate. Ample time should be allowed for this assignment. In-class time seems to result in the best feedback.

The completed pages are collected. Like pages are stapled together and then cut with a paper cutter into individual packets. At the first opportunity, these packets are returned to the individual student. If all has gone well, the student will receive a sheaf of papers containing a grade and an evaluation from every member of the class.

The greatest advantage of peer evaluation is the feedback each student receives. If the class has been successful, students should know each other well enough to make many valuable comments. Assuming that class members are a representative sampling of the general population, the comments should be a fair reflection of the way a student is perceived outside of class.

The biggest disadvantage of this method is the desire of students to be nice to avoid any negative feedback—thus turning the exercise into an experience reminiscent of signing high school yearbooks. On the other hand, there is always the danger (although experience shows it to be extremely rare) that some unfavorable feedback can be psychologically damaging to the student.

GRADING SYSTEMS

Recognizing the strengths and weaknesses of each method of evaluation, you may want to combine several of them to suit your needs. Several possible grading systems follow as illustrations. We have successfully used each of these systems. You'll find that we have personalized each system by choosing to emphasize different areas. In addition, each grading system also posits a slightly different type of student-teacher relationship.

Grading System Option 1: Activities Manual/Study Guide Emphasis (Examinations, Quizzes, Attendance, Written and Oral Exercises)

Objective This grading system places added emphasis on the individual student's involvement with the various units covered in the course. It asks that students demonstrate their knowledge on traditional exams and quizzes and also in written exercises or oral skill checks from the Activities Manual. The philosophy underlying this approach suggests that communication skills should be studied and practiced and then performed orally to demonstrate knowledge of the material. It is believed that students will be more likely to use communication skills in their personal lives that they have practiced in a number of ways in class.

Examinations	35% of the final grade
Quizzes	10% of the final grade
Oral/Written Assignments	40% of the final grade
Attendance	10% of the final grade
Participation/Extra Assignment	5% of the final grade

Here are the points you will need to earn the grade of your choice:

A = 900–1000
B = 800–899
C = 700–799
D = 650–699

Here are the activities that will earn you points:

100 points   Attendance. Everyone will start with 100 points. You are entitled to a certain number of absences without penalty (3 for classes that meet 3 times a week, 2 for classes that meet 2 times a week, and 1 for a class that meets only once a week). Beyond these, each missed meeting will cost you points (correspondingly 6, 9, and 18), on the assumption that you need to be present to learn and practice the skills introduced in the course. Anyone who drops below 75 points in this area may be dropped from the class.

50 points Class Activities. Fifty points are available here for quality of class participation, extra assignments, or other activities assigned by the instructor.

100 points Quizzes. There will be ten brief quizzes, designed to check your reading of the text. These quizzes are simple recall quizzes and are aimed only at being sure you've read the assigned pages. To take the quizzes, you'll need a packet of Scantron teststrips—the 15-question size. (10 quizzes × 10 points = 100 points)

350 points Tests. There will be two 100-point midterms and a 150-point final exam. These exams will consist of objective questions (multiple-choice, true/false, and matching). For the exams you will need a packet of 100-item Scantron test strips. (100 + 100 + 150 = 350 points)

200 points Written Exercises. Written exercises from the Activities Manual will help you apply course information to your own life. Entries will be assigned periodically, and selected assignments will be collected and graded. Exercises turned in late will be penalized for each class session they are overdue. (5 exercises × 40 points = 200 points)

200 points Oral Skill Demonstrations. These dyadic exercises from the Activities Manual will help you orally practice the skills covered in class by applying them to your experience and receiving feedback from a partner. Anyone not in class when these exercises are conducted forfeits the points. (5 exercises × 40 points = 200 points)

NOTE: Some exercises may need to be videotaped in class or in the communication laboratory. You will be able to review videotaped oral skills after they are graded by the instructor.

Grading System Option 2: Attendance, Tests, Quizzes, Papers, Projects, Book Reports

The grade you earn in this class will depend on the amount of work you choose to do as well as its quality. Following is a list of activities, each of which will earn you a number of points. None of these activities is required. You choose the grade you want and pick the tasks that look most appealing that will earn you that grade.

Here are the points you will need to earn the grade of your choice:

A	=	420–500
B	=	340–419
C	=	220–339
D	=	180–219

Here are the activities that will earn the points:

100 points Attendance. Everyone will start with 100 points. You are entitled to a certain number of absences without penalty (3 for MWF classes, 2 for TTh classes, 1 for evening classes). Beyond these, each meeting you miss will cost you points (10 for MWF classes, 15 for TTh classes, 30 for evening classes), on the assumption that you need to be present to learn and practice the skills introduced in this course. Anyone who drops below 50 points in this area will be dropped from the class.

150 points Tests and Quizzes. There will be seven brief 10-point quizzes, designed to check your reading of the chapters of *Looking Out/Looking In*. These quizzes will be simple and are aimed only at being sure you've read the assigned pages.

In addition, there will be a 40-point midterm and a 40-point final examination, designed to test your understanding and your ability to apply the information discussed in this class.

150 points Papers. You will be given a number of opportunities to write papers throughout the semester. You may write on up to six of the topics presented. Each paper will be worth 25 points.

These papers aren't tests. Their purpose is to help you see how the ideas we discuss apply to your everyday life. They will lead you to think about the way you presently communicate, offer you some alternatives, and invite you to try these alternatives to see if they help.

100 points Projects and Book Reports. The project gives you an opportunity to focus on whatever area of interpersonal communication especially interests you. It might take the form of an experiment in which you try out different behaviors to see which work best, a research paper in which you explore an area of personal interest, or a questionnaire or survey to learn how other people see you or deal with a situation similar to yours. You may want to keep a journal to record certain kinds of communication, which you will then analyze.

In any case, if you are interested in doing a project, you will need to complete and turn in a contract form by _____. It will include a description of the area you want to explore, why that area interests you, how you plan to work on that area, and what you will hand in. In addition, it will indicate how many points you want to work for on your project. The instructor will look over your contract and either sign it or negotiate revisions with you. After signing it, the contract becomes the standard against which the quality of your work will be measured. All projects must be typewritten and are due no later than _____.

Book reports may be done on any book in the bibliography you will receive in class or on any title you clear with the instructor in advance. You may write up to two reports, each of which will be worth up to 50 points.

Your reports must be typewritten and should include a chapter-by-chapter discussion of the book in which you (1) describe the author's ideas in the chapter and (2) discuss how these ideas relate to your life.

Finally, you should write a conclusion in which you summarize your opinions of the book and how it relates to your own life.

Optional Paper Topics The following paper topics are designed to help you see how the ideas discussed in class apply to your own life. These papers aren't tests. Their purpose is to help you think about the way you presently communicate, offer you some alternatives, and invite you to try out these alternatives to see if they help.

You can earn up to 25 points for each paper you write, and you may write as many as six papers. (In addition to the papers described on this sheet, you may propose in writing any other paper assignment that you believe will help you apply the concepts discussed. With the instructor's approval, such assignments will substitute for one or more of the papers.) In each case where there is more than one paper described for a chapter, you may do only one of the papers described. The last dates each paper will be accepted will be announced in class, and no work will be accepted after those dates.

The format for each paper involves:

1. Following the instructions in the text.
2. Writing a summary that describes
   a. What (if anything) you learned about yourself in following the instructions.
   b. How you feel about this learning (satisfied, indifferent, depressed, resolved, etc.).
   c. Anything you want to say about the exercise (suggest changes, describe difficulties, etc.).

Paper Topics

Chapter 1: A First Look
1. Expanding your Communication Effectiveness (1.2 in Activities Manual/Study Guide)

Chapter 2: Communication and Identity: The Self and Messages
2. Who Do You Think You Are? (2.1 in Activities Manual/Study Guide)
3. Reevaluating Your "Can'ts" (2.4 in Activities Manual/Study Guide)

Chapter 3: Perception: What You See Is What You Get
4. Pillow Method (Shifting Perspectives, 3.3 in Activities Manual/Study Guide)
5. Your Call—Perception (3.8 in Activities Manual/Study Guide)

Chapter 4: Emotions
6. Recognizing Your Emotions (text, p. 143)
7. Disputing Irrational Thoughts (4.5 in Activities Manual/Study Guide)

Chapter 5: Language
8. Examining Your Language (5.5 in Activities Manual/Study Guide)
9. Your Call—Language (5.7 in Activities Manual/Study Guide)

Chapter 6: Nonverbal Communication: Messages Without Words
10. Evaluating Ambiguity (6.3 in Activities Manual/Study Guide)

Chapter 7: Listening: More than Meets the Ear
11. Responses to Problems (7.2 in Activities Manual/Study Guide)

Chapter 8: Communication and Relational Dynamics
12. Discovering Dialectics (8.1 in Activities Manual/Study Guide)
13. Relational Stages and Self-Disclosure (8.6 in Activities Manual/Study Guide)

Chapter 9: Improving Communication Climates
14. Understanding Your Defensive Responses (9.1 in Activities Manual/Study Guide)
15. Your Call—Climate (9.6 in Activities Manual/Study Guide)

Chapter 10: Managing Interpersonal Conflicts
16. Writing Clear Messages (10.2 in Activities Manual/Study Guide)
17. Win-Win Problem Solving (10.5 in Activities Manual/Study Guide)

Grading System Option 3: Instructor, Peer, and Self-Evaluations

Objective

To give each student as much control over his or her grade as possible while dealing with the responsibility this control demands.

Overview of Policy

To be successful and receive credit for this class, the following requirements must be met:

1. Attendance in class must be satisfactory.
2. All homework assignments must be completed and satisfactory.
3. Participation in class activities must be satisfactory to peers, self, and instructor.

   If these requirements are met satisfactorily, you will receive a C grade.
   The B-grade requirement may be met by reading two books, twelve articles, or a combination of one book and six articles.

If you wish to receive an A grade, you must complete satisfactorily the C and B requirements and, in addition, design and carry out a project concerning some aspect of interpersonal communication.

Details on Option 3 System

Attendance Requirement The student's attendance will account for 30 percent of his or her grade. Each student will receive a notice of attendance requirements at the beginning of the course. To illustrate, here is a set of regulations for an MWF class:

0 to 1 class period missed	=	A for attendance part of grade
2 class periods missed	=	B for attendance part of grade
3 class periods missed	=	C for attendance part of grade
4 class periods missed	=	D for attendance part of grade
5 or more class periods missed	=	F for attendance part of grade

Adjustments would be made for classes meeting twice (TTh) a week or once a week. Students should be reminded that attendance governs only part of the grade and that missing four class periods doesn't necessarily mean that a semester grade of D will result. It would depend on the grades in the other areas and the amount of work the student completes.

Homework Requirements There will be nine to twelve homework assignments. They will consist of journals, inventories, self-observation, and so on. There will be no letter grades on these assignments. Each assignment will be evaluated as satisfactory, unsatisfactory, or incomplete. To fulfill this requirement, the student must have all assignments handed in, completed, and satisfactory. Opportunity may be given to bring unsatisfactory homework up to a satisfactory level.

Quizzes Quizzes will be given on the first class meeting after the class has been assigned to complete the reading of a chapter in the text. These quizzes will be graded but will be counted only to help the student achieve a higher grade. In other words, you will be rewarded if you have done the assigned reading and scored well on the quiz. You may take the quiz only when it is given to the entire class—no makeups of quizzes.

Participation Requirements You are already aware that attendance is extremely important in this class. There is a considerable amount of student participation during each class meeting. There is no available way to make up the activities and exercises that involve the class. However, just being present in the classroom will not satisfy the participation requirement. It is necessary for you to take an active part because you will be evaluated by fellow classmates, instructor, and yourself. Heading the listed criteria for these evaluations will be class participation.

Instructor's Evaluation The instructor's evaluation will account for 30 percent of your grade. In arriving at that grade, your homework and classroom participation (with particular attention to improvement and attitude) will be reviewed. All class participants are expected to cooperate with the various activities and exercises in class and to be supportive of classmates. You should realize that some of the instructor's grade will come from impressions formed of your actions and reactions in the class. In other words, the instructor will form a subjective opinion of your effort in the class.

Peer Evaluation This will account for 20 percent of the final grade. Each student is required to grade all the other students in the class. This evaluation will be done with criteria that have been published and in most cases developed by the class.

In this feedback process, students should place special emphasis on improvement that has been observed and improvement that needs to be made.

To make this process manageable, we will use the following method. Twice during the term, you will be asked to give feedback to your classmates—at about the halfway point and again at the end of the semester. The second evaluation will include a grade from each member of the class. You will arrive at your final peer-evaluation grade by finding the average of all the grades you receive.

Self-Evaluation This will count for 20 percent of your final grade. At the end of the course, you will assign yourself a grade, which you must be able to justify in terms of criteria worked out before this assignment. Should there be any question about the self-grade assigned, the instructor will confer with the student so that they may reach an understanding.

B Grade Attendance, instructor's and peer evaluation, and self-evaluation must be satisfactory before a student is eligible for a C grade. If a student wants to pursue a B grade, he or she must complete the previous requirements plus the following:

Select from the book list provided two books, read them, and write reports on the forms provided and/or give an oral report to a small group of classmates. In either case, the student must demonstrate that he or she has read the book, from the information given in the report.

or

Select twelve articles from a list of articles that have been collected and placed on reserve in the library by the instructor. These articles are to be read and reported on by completing an Article Report Form that will be provided for each article. The student may also be required to give oral reports to small groups in class.

or

Do a combination reading assignment of one book and six articles. Article and book reports that are not written in acceptable form—complete sentences, correct spelling, sensible paragraphs, and so on will be returned as unsatisfactory. They may be corrected and resubmitted, provided there is enough time for the instructor to review them a second time.

A Grade If a student expects to receive an A grade, he or she must demonstrate the capacity to do superior work.

In this class, this will take the form of some kind of project concerned with interpersonal communication.

This project will earn an A grade only if it is of excellent quality and both the B and C grade requirements are met.

The A project must follow this schedule:

Within the first ten class hours, a plan must be submitted to the instructor. Remember, designing your own individual project is part of the assignment. Under no circumstances will the instructor give you a project to complete.

At the halfway mark, the instructor will meet with each student attempting an A project. It will be determined at that time if the project is of a kind that will be informative for all the class. If this is the case, it would be presented during a class period. If not, it would be submitted in written form. The specific written form will be agreed on at this time.

As soon as the projects are finished, they should be presented in class or submitted in writing. No project will be received for credit during the last two class meetings.

Some projects that have been attempted in the past follow.

Research Papers

How to Break Up and Remain Friends

Giving and Receiving Criticism Effectively

Interpersonal Communication in Personnel Management

A Study in How We Learn to Be Parents

An Investigation into the Language of Men and Women

Methods for Improving the Handling of Human Conflict.

Personal Projects

Improving my relationships with my co-workers

Becoming a better partner in my marriage

Improving the quality of communication with my fourteen-year-old daughter

Increasing my participation in class

Improving my relationship with my stepfather

Showing more positive independence around my parents

Other Projects

Do T-shirts communicate? (presented as a slide show to the class)

How conditioned are we to our sex roles? (class participation)

How do married couples want their mates to say, "I love you"?

How much does another's expectations of me influence my actions?

Establishing effective family meetings.

All of the projects were acceptable. Not all of them, however, earned their designer an A—not because of the subject matter but rather because of an insufficient amount of effort on the student's part.

SUGGESTED COURSE SYLLABUS

The following course syllabus is a sample outline that uses *Looking Out/Looking In* as the basic text. You may find a part or all of this syllabus useful in designing your own course outline. Since the lengths of semesters vary, we have arbitrarily assumed a 15-week duration for this course with classes meeting three times a week for 50-minute sessions.

Week 1

Class 1

Topic: Getting Started

The instructor explains the nature of the course and completes normal beginning-of-course housekeeping chores. Particular emphasis should be made on the classroom participation that will be expected from each student.

To reinforce the participation dimension of the course, begin at once with the exercise Name Calling, wherein each member of the group learns the names of all the others.

Exercise: Name Calling

(Find under Chapter One Notes following this section of Instructor's Manual.)

Assignment:

Obtain your own copy of *Looking Out/Looking In* and the Activities Manual/Study Guide. Begin Chapter One.

NOTE: Students should read all the material presented in each chapter, including the poetry, quotations found in the page margins, pictures and cartoons, exercises, and the regular text. All the material in each chapter is part of the message.

Class 2

Topic: Getting to Know One Another

Activity: Explain the importance of knowing one another in a communication skills class. It is important that students feel as comfortable as possible to experience less anxiety in trying out new communication behaviors.

Exercise: Introductions
(Find under Chapter One Notes following this section of Instructor's Manual.)

Assignment:
Complete your communication skills inventory (1.1 in Activities Manual/Study Guide).
Read Chapter One (quiz to verify reading—next class session).
Complete the Study Guide section of the Activities Manual/Study Guide for Chapter One.

Class 3

Quiz: Chapter 1

Topic: The Importance of Human Communication

Activity: Encourage discussion of basic human needs and how communication is necessary to obtain them. Use the student's Communication Skills Inventory to identify goals for the class.

Assignment: Expanding Your Communication Effectiveness (1.2 in Activities Manual/Study Guide)

Week 2

Class 1

Topic: Effective Communication

Exercise: Mediated Messages—Channels (1.4 in Activities Manual/Study Guide) and Your Call— Communication Basics (1.5 in Activities Manual/Study Guide).

Assignment: Read Chapter Two of text. Complete the Study Guide section of the Activities Manual/Study Guide for Chapter Two.

Class 2

Quiz: Chapter Two

Topic: The Self-Concept

Activity: Instigate discussion of the different ways in which our self-concept may have developed.

Exercise: Who Do You Think You Are? (2.1 in Activities Manual/Study Guide)

Assignment: Self-Concept Inventory (2.3 in Activities Manual/Study Guide)

Class 3

Topic: Characteristics of Your Self-Concept

Exercise: Discuss Self-Concept Inventory (2.3 in Activities Manual/Study Guide).
Ego Boosters and Busters (2.2 in Activities Manual/Study Guide)

Assignment:
Ego Boosters and Busters (2.2 in Activities Manual/Study Guide)
Reevaluating Your "Can'ts" (2.4 in Activities Manual/Study Guide)

Week 3

Class 1

Topic: Self-fulfilling Prophecies/Changing the Self-Concept

Exercises: Your self-fulfilling prophecies (2.5 in Activities Manual/Study Guide)

Assignment: Prepare Mediated Messages—Identity Management (2.7 in Activities Manual/Study Guide) for the next class.

Class 2

Topic: Managing Impressions

Exercise:
Discussion groups compare their prepared responses to Mediated Messages—Identity Management (2.7 in Activities Manual/Study Guide)
Success in Managing Impressions (2.6 in Activities Manual/Study Guide)

Assignment: Read Chapter Three for quiz. Complete the Study Guide section of the Activities Manual/Study Guide for Chapter Three.

Class 3

Quiz: Chapter Three

Topic: The Process of Perception

Activity: Discuss the process of perception; students give examples and discuss in groups how perception influences communication. Relate to concept of self and how clear messages are or are not given.

Assignment: Guarding Against Perceptual Errors (3.1 in Activities Manual/Study Guide)

Week 4

Class 1

Topic: Accuracy and Inaccuracy of Perception

Exercise: Discuss Guarding Against Perceptual Errors (3.1 in Activities Manual/Study Guide) in class. Compare and discuss in groups physiology and perception. In the same groups, discuss New Body, New Perspective (text) and compare group findings with class.

Assignment:
Examining Your Interpretations (3.2 in Activities Manual/Study Guide)
Observation and Perception (3.4 in Activities Manual/Study Guide)

Class 2

Topic: Role of Culture and Society in Perception

Activity: Discuss sex roles, occupational roles, and cultural influences in the perceptual process. Use the Perception-Checking Stimulus games in this Instructor's Manual (see Perception-Checking Stimuli in section 3 of Notes on Class and Student Activities in this Instructor's Manual) or 3.6—Perception Checking in Activities Manual/ Study Guide.

Assignment: Prepare perception-checking statements to deliver in class based on today's activity (3.5 and 3.6 in Activities Manual/Study Guide)

Class 3

Topic: Empathy

Activity:
Deliver perception-checking statements (3.5 and 3.6 in Activities Manual/Study Guide).
Discuss differences between understanding someone and agreeing with that person.

Exercise: Punctuation Practice (text, p. 101)

Assignment: Shifting Perspectives (3.3 in Activities Manual/ Study Guide)

Week 5

Class 1

Topic: Broadening Perception

Activity: Group discussions of Mediated Messages—Perception (3.7 in Activities Manual/Study Guide) and Your Call—Perception (3.8 in Activities Manual/Study Guide).

Assignment: Read Chapter Four for quiz. Complete the Study Guide section of the Activities Manual/Study Guide for Chapter Four.

Class 2

Quiz: Chapter Four

Topic: Emotions: Thinking and Feeling

Exercise: How Does It Feel? (text, pp. 137–138)
Discuss difficulty we have in expressing our emotions. Explore benefits resulting from being able to express our emotions and the variations in expression due to culture and gender.

Assignment:
The Components of Emotion (4.1 in Activities Manual/Study Guide)
Your Call—Emotions (4.7 in Activities Manual/Study Guide)

Class 3

Topic: Emotions and Thought/Talking to Yourself

Exercise:
    Talking to Yourself (p. 159)
    Discuss overcoming irrational thinking.
    How Irrational Are You? (p. 165)

Assignment:
    Find the Feelings (4.2 in Activities Manual/Study Guide)
    Self-Talk (4.4 in Activities Manual/Study Guide)

Week 6
Class 1

Topic: Expressing Feelings

Exercise: Stating Emotions Effectively (4.3 in Activities Manual/Study Guide)
    Discuss how to minimize debilitating emotions and when and how to share feelings.

Assignment: Disputing Irrational Thoughts (4.5 in Activities Manual/Study Guide)

Class 2

Topic: Disputing Irrational Thoughts

Exercise: Compare and correct student assignments to Disputing Irrational Thoughts (4.5 in Activities Manual/Study Guide)

Assignment: Read Chapter Five for quiz. Complete the Study Guide section of the Activities Manual/Study Guide for Chapter Five.

Class 3

Quiz: Chapter Five

Topic: Words and Meanings

Exercise: In groups, students discuss Your Linguistic Rules (text, p. 190).
    Discuss meanings people have for words and their emotional reaction to words.

Assignment: Complete Label the Language (5.1 in Activities Manual/Study Guide).

Week 7
Class 1

Topic: Abstraction and Language

Activity: Discuss the nature of language (a symbol system) and abstraction. Introduce and have class members work with the abstraction ladder and the assignment exercises from the last class.

Assignment: Behavioral Descriptions (5.2 in Activities Manual/Study Guide)

Class 2

Topic: Responsibility in Language

Activity: Discuss communication issues involved with the Language of Responsibility. Complete Practicing "I" Language (5.3 in Activities Manual/Study Guide).

Assignment: Prepare "I" Language (Oral Skill) (5.4 in Activities Manual/Study Guide) for next class.

Class 3

Topic: "I" Language

Activity: "I" Language (Oral Skill) (5.4 in Activities Manual/Study Guide)

Assignment: Down-to-earth Language (text, p. 185)

Week 8
Class 1

Topic: Language in action

Activity: Examining Your Language (5.6 in Activities Manual/Study Guide)

Assignment: Record at least ten examples of language that is gender- or culture-related for the next class.

Class 2

Topic: Language, Gender, and Culture

Activity: Discuss how gender and cultural variables affect language use. Discuss in groups Mediated Messages—Language (5.6 in Activities Manual/Study Guide) and Your Call—Language (5.7 in Activities Manual/Study Guide).

Assignment: Read Chapter Six for quiz. Complete the Study Guide section of the Activities Manual/Study Guide for Chapter Six.

Class 3

Quiz: Chapter Six

Topic: Nonverbal Communication

Exercise: Verbal and Nonverbal Communication (text, p. 236)
   Discuss awareness of nonverbal communication.

Assignment: Describing Nonverbal States (6.1 in Activities Manual/Study Guide)

Week 9
Class 1

Topic: Characteristics of Nonverbal Communication

Exercise: How-To's (6.2 in Activities Manual/Study Guide)

Assignment: Evaluating Ambiguity (6.3 in Activities Manual/Study Guide)

Class 2

Topic: Nonverbal Functions/Congruency

Activity: Discuss the six functions of nonverbal communication and relate them to the congruency and incongruency of verbal and nonverbal messages. Use Evaluating Ambiguity (6.3 in Activities Manual/Study Guide) to build upon the text.

Assignment: Your Call—Nonverbal (6.5 in Activities Manual/Study Guide)

Class 3

Topic:
Types of Nonverbal Communication

Exercise: Building Vocal Fluency (text, p. 252)
Distance Makes a Difference (text, p. 258)

Discuss proxemics, kinesics, paralanguage, clothing, territoriality, chronemics and environment.

Assignment: Observe nonverbal behaviors in a number of contexts. Take notes for discussion next class. Complete Mediated Messages—Nonverbal (6.4 in Activities Manual/Study Guide)

Week 10

Class 1

Topic: Catch-up and Finish-up Day

Activity: Discuss assignments from last class and finish Chapter Six.

Assignment: Read Chapter Seven for quiz. Complete the Study Guide section of the Activities Manual/Study Guide for Chapter Seven.

Class 2

Quiz: Chapter Seven

Topic: Listening versus Hearing

Exercise: Your Call—Listening (7.9 in Activities Manual/Study Guide)
Discuss types of nonlistening and why we don't listen. Discuss benefits of talking less and listening more.

Assignment: Listening Diary (7.1 in Activities Manual/Study Guide)

Class 3

Topic: Becoming a More Effective Listener

Exercise: One-Way and Two-Way Communication (Chapter Seven notes following this section in the Instructor's Manual)

Assignment: Responses to Problems (7.2 in Activities Manual/Study Guide)

Week 11

Class 1

Topic: Listening Responses

Exercise: Paraphrasing Practice (7.3 in Activities Manual/Study Guide)

Assignment: Listening for Feelings (7.4 in Activities Manual/Study Guide)
  Problem Solving Paraphrasing (7.5 in Activities Manual/Study Guide)

Class 2

Topic: Paraphrasing

Activity: Discuss paraphrasing as a helping response. Compare and contrast paraphrasing with other common styles discussed in the text.

Assignment: Complete Paraphrasing Information, 7.6 in Activities Manual/Study Guide.

Class 3

Topic: Listening Effectiveness

Exercise: Discuss types of listening and when to use each.
  Listening and Responding Styles (oral skill) (7.7 in Activities Manual/Study Guide)

Assignment: Read Chapter Eight for quiz. Complete the Study Guide section of the Activities Manual/Study Guide for Chapter Eight.

Week 12
Class 1

Quiz: Chapter Eight

Topic: Interpersonal Attraction/Building Positive Relationships. Discuss characteristics of relational communication, breadth and depth of relationships.

Exercise: Analyzing Interpersonal Attraction (text, p. 317).

Assignment: Breadth and Depth of Relationships (8.2 in Activities Manual/Study Guide)

Class 2

Topic: Relational Dialectics

Exercise: Discuss characteristics of relational dialectics.

Assignment: Discovering Dialectics (8.1 in Activities Manual/Study Guide)

Class 3

Topic: Developmental Stages in Intimate Relationships

Exercise: Responses in Relationships (8.5 in Activities Manual/Study Guide)

Assignment: Relational Stages and Self-Disclosure (8.6 in Activities Manual/Study Guide)

Week 13
Class 1

Topic: Self-Disclosure and Risk in Interpersonal Communication

Exercise: Have class discuss Johari Window and self-disclosure.

    Reasons for Nondisclosure (8.3 in Activities Manual/Study Guide)

    Degrees of Self-Disclosure (8.4 in Activities Manual/Study Guide)

    Discuss alternatives to self-disclosure.

Assignment: Read Chapter Nine for quiz. Complete the Study Guide section of the Activities Manual/Study Guide for Chapter Nine.

Class 2

Quiz: Chapter Nine

Topic: Confirming and Disconfirming Communication

Exercise: Discuss Gibb Categories

    Evaluating Communication Climates (text, p. 374) and Defensive and Supportive Language (9.2 in Activities Manual/Study Guide)

Assignment: Understanding Your Defensive Responses (9.1 in Activities Manual/Study Guide).

Class 3

Topic: Handling Defensiveness

Exercise: Discuss defensiveness and defense mechanisms and ways to cope with defensiveness. Defense Mechanism Inventory (text, p. 380 and Coping with Typical Criticism, 9.3 in Activities Manual/Study Guide)

Assignment: Prepare Coping with Criticism (9.4 in Activities Manual/Study Guide) for next class.

Week 14

Class 1

Topic: Coping with Criticism

Activity: Coping with Criticism (9.4 in Activities Manual/ Study Guide)

Assignment: Read Chapter Ten for quiz. Complete the Study Guide section of the Activities Manual/Study Guide for Chapter Ten.

Class 2

Quiz: Chapter Ten

Topic: Conflict Is Natural and Normal for All Persons

Activity: Discuss attitudes we're learning concerning conflict. Encourage personal testimony. Discuss how we behave in avoiding conflict and how these behaviors tend to drive us crazy.

Assignment: Your Conflict Styles (10.3 in Activities Manual/Study Guide)

    Understanding Conflict Styles (10.1 in Activities Manual/Study Guide)

Class 3

Topic: Building Clear Messages

Exercise: Writing Clear Messages (10.2 in Activities Manual/Study Guide)

Week 15

Class 1

Topic: Types of Conflict Resolution

Activity: Discuss win-lose, lose-lose, compromise, and win-win problem solving.

Assignment: The End vs. the Means (10.4 in Activities Manual/Study Guide)—prepare this to provide background for win-win problem solving next class.

Class 2

Topic: Effective Problem Solving

Exercise: Win-Win Problem Solving and Conflict Resolution Dyads (10.5 and 10.6 in Activities Manual/Study Guide)
   Use these to role-play the resolution of conflicts. Discuss effectiveness.

Assignment: Review for final exam.

Class 3

Topic: Conclusion of course

Activity: Give final examination and remarks.

USING INTERNET LINKS IN THE INTERPERSONAL COMMUNICATION COURSE

Making use of the Internet to enrich classroom instruction is easy. We provide a number of links below that we have found useful. They connect you to journals, publications, collections, bibliographies, teaching strategies, and other course-related materials such as audiotapes and videotapes. You will want to use some of the information yourself, but others can provide a valuable supplement to reading, lecture, discussion, and other activities in the classroom.

Chapter 1: A First Look

http://www.tamu.edu/scom/test203/audience/index.html
Communication Competence: Texas A&M Web site

http://www.wlv.ac.uk/select/resources/intercultural/
Intercultural Communication and Competence

These pages provide links to various organizations and resources that may be useful to people interested in intercultural communication and competence (ICC), especially as they affect management and employment practices in Europe and related areas. (University of Wolverhampton)

http://www.aimm.co.uk/connect/summer00/communication_competence.htm
Comm competence and business success (online newsletter for training firm)

http://www.pertinent.com/pertinfo/business/communication/

Interpersonal communication articles written by a diverse group of experts, speakers, professionals, consultants, and marketing companies.

http://www.engl.uic.edu/~sosnoski/cr/TERMS/metacommunication.htm

Metacommunication definitions and discussion

http://www.fortunecity.com/campus/computing/0/meta.htm

Metacommunication and children—definitions—and movie example

http://www.ph-erfurt.de/~neumann/eese/artic97/lenz/5_97.html

metacommunication, speech acts, pragmatics

http://www.siu.edu/offices/iii/comm.html

By the Illinois Intergenerational Initiative, a series of modules on communication with other generations, including preparation, understanding other generations, creative thinking and speaking, and metacommunication.

http://www.nur.utexas.edu/n310/n310intro.html

Syllabus for communication in health care settings (University of Texas)

http://www.pcm.nwu.edu/ipc/

Perceptions of medical encounters in Great Britain: Variations with **health** loci of control and sociodemographic factors.

http://uhavax.hartford.edu/~bugl/StuQuestComm.htm

Multiple-choice questions (some can serve as discussion questions) for nursing students.

http://www.chiroweb.com/archives/11/25/01.html

From ChiroWeb.com, "taking case histories" for doctors focuses on meta-messages, along with examples of positive and negative verbal and nonverbal feedback messages.

http://www.fhi.org/en/fp/fpother/bolivia/bolabs48.html

No. 48—Strengths and Deficiencies in the Use of Interpersonal Communication Techniques Between Health Professionals in Public Hospitals and Patients with Incomplete Abortion.

Chapter 2: Communication and Identity: The Self and Messages

http://wizard.ucr.edu/~bkaplan/soc/lib/goffimpr.html

The arts of impression management from Erving Goffman, *The Presentation of Self in Everyday Life*. New York: Doubleday, 1959, pp. 208–212.

http://www.theimageresourcecenter.com/im.htm

From the Image Center: a series of Image Training and Professional Development Programs made available via Web site.

Chapter 3: Perception: What You See Is What You Get

http://www.tamu.edu/scom/test203/audience/index.html

Perspective-taking: Texas A&M Web site

http://www.andrew.cmu.edu/user/sfussell/Perspective-Taking.html

Susan R. Fussell, Ph.D., Human-Computer Interaction Institute, Carnegie Mellon University
Perspective-Taking in Interpersonal Communication

http://www.law.pitt.edu/hibbitts/senses.htm

This page features links to papers and resources on the significance and role of the senses in human culture

Chapter 4: Emotions

http://www.cyberparent.com/talk/negotiations.htm
   Controlling emotions in negotiations

Chapter 5: Language

http://www.stetson.edu/departments/history/nongenderlang.html

Non-sexist language—some notes on gender-neutral language. Copyrighted by Purdue University, 1995, this is a good list of gender-neutral alternatives to sexist language.

http://dir.yahoo.com/Society_and_Culture/Gender/Gender_Neutral_Language/

A page with links to some of Yahoo!'s gender-neutral sites.

http://www-english.tamu.edu/pers/fac/bucholtz/lng/gala.html

The Official Discussion List of the International Gender and Language Association (IGALA)

http://www.ascusc.org/jcmc/vol2/issue3/savicki.html

A chapter on gender language style and group composition in Internet discussion groups with links to each of the references by Victor Savicki, Dawn Lingenfelter, and Merle Kelley, Department of Psychology, Western Oregon State College.

http://www.aitech.ac.jp/~iteslj/quizzes/dt/genderfree.html

A very fun list of 15 gender-related words that have the gender-free alternatives at a click.

http://www.britsoc.org.uk/about/antirace.htm

From "African-Carribbean" to "Whiteness," this alphabetized list of anti-racist language contains a bit of history and discussion of guidelines used by social scientists when referring to work based around ethnicity.

http://family.go.com/raisingkids/child/skills/features/family_1998_10/dony/dony108sc-words/

Words that hurt: What you should never say to your kids by Charles E. Schaefer, Ph.D. Book summary and link to Parents Anonymous.

http://www.bearyspecial.co.uk/words.html

A list of words that offend people with disabilities with discussion of them and links to related sites.

Chapter 6: Nonverbal Communication: Messages Without Words

http://zzyx.ucsc.edu/~archer/intro.html

This page introduces nonverbal communication, gives you a chance to try to guess the meaning of some REAL nonverbal communication, and describes a new video series on NONVERBAL COMMUNICATION available from the University of California with links to individual films and ordering information.

http://socpsych.lacollege.edu/nonverbal.html

This page is meant to be a resource for those working in the field of nonverbal communication. Researchers can use this page to connect with their colleagues, search relevant journals, find out about the latest books published in the field, and obtain information about resources for teaching and training.

http://www.lib.ohio-state.edu/gateway/bib/nonverbal.html

Nonverbal Communication—Useful Sources for Information in a Search Strategy Format

http://uts.cc.utexas.edu/~adgrad/

A link page to basics of nonverbal communication, including: NVC: What Is It? * Main Theory–NonVerbal Expectancy Violations Model * Other Components of NonVerbal Expectancy Violations Model Theory * *Importance of NVC * Consumer Research * Relation to Advertising * Related Links * references.

http://www2.pstcc.cc.tn.us/~dking/nvcom.htm

A professor's summary page on nonverbal basics.

http://hamp.hampshire.edu/~enhF94/kinesics.html

A paper with an overview of Kinesic theories and their histories.

http://users.rcn.com/zang.interport/personality.html

A very nonscientific "personality" test of color/shape preferences. Could be used to get reactions to colors and shapes.

http://www.symbols.com/

SYMBOLS.com contains more than 2,500 Western signs, arranged into 54 groups according to their graphic characteristics. In 1,600 articles their histories, uses, and meanings are thoroughly discussed. The signs range from ideograms carved in mammoth teeth by Cro-Magnon men, to hobo signs and subway graffiti.

http://www.lawfinance.com/ARTICLES/NONVERB.HTM

Bibliography: nonverbal communication and witness credibility

http://www.csupomona.edu/~tassi/gestures.htm

Paper on Gestures: Body Language and Nonverbal Communication—particularly Asian

http://members.aol.com/nonverbal2/nvcom.htm

Definitions of nonverbal communication with links to research, pictures, and sources for further study.

http://www.ling.gu.se/~biljana/gestures2.html#dead
Chinese Emotion and Gesture

Chapter 7: Listening: More than Meets the Ear

http://www.cyberparent.com/talk/listen.htm
Listening questions/answers

http://www.ebrainware.com/Zsel03-55.htm
Web-based training packages for listening
  • Video: The Six Essentials of Effective Listening (24 min.)
  • Audio: Listening for Results: How to Be an Attentive Listener (2 tapes)
  • 5 Self-Study Books
  • 10 Post-Assessments
  • User's Course Guide

http://www.trainingconsortium.com/powerpoint/quotes/listening.html
Twenty-five humorous quotes to inspire listening situations. Each topic includes clip art, animation, and slide transitions.

Chapter 8: Communication and Relational Dynamics

http://www.as.wvu.edu/~jmccrosk/61.htm
Two studies are reported which indicate that high communication apprehensives are perceived as less interpersonally attractive than low communication apprehensives by members of the opposite sex.

http://www.bath.ac.uk/~hsstjc/Relref.html
A bibliography of sources on interpersonal attraction.

http://www.unites.uqam.ca/dsexo/Revue/Vol3no1/Shaughnessy%20M.html
This paper discusses emotional intimacy and sexual intimacy, and examines the relationship between the two.

http://communication.wadsworth.com/casing/studentres/cases/case7/case7home.htm
Definition of dialectical tensions and links to case study (from Wadsworth).

http://digilander.iol.it/linguaggiodelcorpo/flirt6/
 An article on intimacy as an interpersonal process: the importance of self-disclosure, partner disclosure, and perceived partner responsiveness in interpersonal exchanges from the *Journal of Personality and Social Psychology* 1998 May; 74(5):1238–51.

http://www.llc.rpi.edu/people/stephen/courses/interper/urbib.htm
A bibliography on interpersonal communication and deception.

Chapter 9: Improving Communication Climates

http://www.cyberparent.com/talk/sorry.htm
Another approach to criticism—behavioral list of 15 ways to say "I'm sorry."

http://www.sew.org.uk/dispatch/personal_criticism.htm

Dealing with personal criticism from the Society of Expert Witnesses.

http://pertinent.com/pertinfo/business/kareCom8.html

Suggestions on handling criticism with honesty and grace by Kare Anderson with contributions from Chris McClean.

http://www.uwsp.edu/education/Wkirby/ntrprsnl/critic.htm

Part of an education course termed Interpersonal Relations Index, this site has a series of suggestions for receiving and giving criticism with links to: Receiving criticism from others, Giving criticism, Criticizing a person, Criticizing an idea, program or procedure, Grumbles and the grapevine, Hearing about a criticism indirectly, Professional criticism, and Constructive criticism.

http://www.bio.com/hr/search/f-FineArtofCriticism.html

An essay on The Fine Art of Criticism by David G. Jensen, Search Masters International.

Chapter 10: Managing Interpersonal Conflicts

http://www.colorado.edu/conflict/

Conflict Research Consortium of the University of Colorado, USA—provides a comprehensive gateway to information on more constructive approaches to difficult conflicts. Hundreds of links possible here.

http://www.crinfo.org/

The Conflict Resolution Information Source—focuses upon conflict resolution's major subfields (with links): business, legal, intergroup, international, interpersonal, and public policy.

http://www.crinfo.org/interpersonal/index.cfm

The interpersonal page of the Conflict Resolution Information Source with specific applications to: 9–12 student conflicts, divorce and custody, extended family issues, family, higher-ed student conflicts, K–8 student conflicts, other interpersonal, parent-child, parental conflicts, student conflicts, workplace, and youth (non-school) conflicts (i.e., gangs).

http://www.bizhotline.com/html/interpersonal_communication_sk.html

An audio/video program that provides training to minimize conflict and build collaboration in today's team-oriented workplace.

http://www.couplecommunication.com/

COUPLE COMMUNICATION program—Partners learn 11 interpersonal skills for effective talking, listening, conflict resolution, and anger management for marriage enrichment and more satisfying relationships. Developed at the University of Minnesota Study Center.

http://learn.lincoln.ac.nz/groupwork/fail/conflict_.htm

Addresses conflict and interpersonal communication problems in any group situations where there is the potential for negative interaction and conflict.

http://occ.awlonline.com/bookbind/pubbooks/devito_awl/chapter1/custom26/deluxe-content.html

A case study from Addison-Wesley encouraging students to apply concepts about conflict to a situation.

USING FEATURE FILMS IN THE INTERPERSONAL COMMUNICATION COURSE

"Are we going to see a movie today?" In most cases the sight of a video cassette recorder in the classroom results in this kind of question. Conditioned by the sophisticated production techniques and high entertainment value of many films and television programs, students often welcome the break in routine provided by video programming. When they learn that the "show" will be a feature film, their interest level goes up even more. Beyond entertainment, however, feature films provide a valuable supplement to the reading, lecture, discussion, and other activities more common in the classroom.

Uses of Film and Television

To Model Desirable Behaviors By providing positive models of skillful communication, instructors can capitalize on the power of the media to further their instructional goals. The empathic listening of Judd Hirsch in *Ordinary People*, the positive communication climate created by Robin Williams in *Dead Poets Society*, or the family values illustrated in *Running on Empty* help students understand how they can behave more effectively in their own lives.

To Illustrate Ineffective Communication In addition to providing positive models, film and television can provide illustrations of ineffective or counterproductive types of communication. The controlling behavior of Nurse Ratched in *One Flew Over the Cuckoo's Nest* provides a vivid portrait of the abuse of power. Valmont's manipulative strategies in *Dangerous Liaisons* offers a cautionary tale of the evils of deceit. Bull Meecham's autocratic domination of his family in *The Great Santini* can help future parents avoid the same sort of alienation he suffered from his children and wife.

To Provide Material for Description and Analysis Films are not only useful in skills-oriented parts of the interpersonal communication course; they can also provide outstanding examples when the goal is to illustrate or analyze communication behavior. Consider, for example, the subject of stages in relational development and deterioration. A good text and lecture can introduce various models of relational trajectories, but dramatic illustrations can make them real. Students who watch the rise and fall of the romance between Woody Allen and Diane Keaton in *Annie Hall* gain an understanding of relational stages that goes far beyond what they gain in a lecture that is not supported with illustrations. Likewise, the way a single incident can appear different from the perspectives of various observers and participants is illustrated dramatically in Akira Kurosawa's classic film *Rashomon*.

Advantages of Film and Television The value of film becomes clear when the medium is compared to the alternatives. Lecturing about how to communicate more effectively is important, but it is clearly a different matter from illustrating the actual behavior. Describing appropriate self-disclosure or use of "I" language, for instance, is no substitute for providing examples of how this behavior looks and sounds in common situations.

Films also can have advantages over students sharing their own personal experiences. While this sort of involvement can demonstrate the relevance of ideas introduced in a course, some topics do not lend themselves to personal examples. For example, it is unlikely that students or instructors will feel comfortable discussing their own experiences with deceptive communication, remediating embarrassment, or sexual involvement. With topics like these, films and television provide an ideal way to illustrate people realistically handling the issues without invading the privacy of students.

Role-playing appropriate behaviors has its advantages, but this sort of impromptu acting is often simplistic, artificial, and only remotely linked to how interactions occur in the "real" world beyond the classroom. Every instructor who has tried to demonstrate principles like self-disclosure or conflict management skills by staging a scene in the classroom knows that this approach can fall flat more often than it succeeds. Student actors are self-conscious, situations are often contrived, and the whole activity often lacks the spontaneity and dynamism that occur in real life.

Nothing in this argument should be taken to suggest that all films or television programming can be legitimately or productively used to support instruction. Works with unrealistic plots or dialogue, poor acting, and shabby production values are likely to be unusable. Furthermore, some programming may be too upsetting or otherwise inappropriate for classroom use. But well-chosen examples, supported with commentary by an instructor, can be a legitimate and uniquely effective means of enhancing principles introduced by more traditional means.

Film is never likely to replace more traditional methods of instruction. The clarity of a good textbook, the lectures and commentary of a talented instructor, and the contributions of motivated students are all essential ingredients in successful instruction.

But the addition of dramatizations from television and film provide a complement to these elements.

Advantages of Videotaped Films

Availability Not too many years ago, screening films for students was a time-consuming and expensive task. With the ubiquitous VCR and film rental sources, literally thousands of titles are available quickly, easily, and inexpensively.

Flexibility In addition to their availability, another benefit of videotaped examples from film and television is their flexibility. They can be edited in advance, played repeatedly for examination and analysis, and they are highly portable. As the following section illustrates, they can be used in a number of ways.

What Film to Use? How to Use It?

Films should be selected and used carefully in the interpersonal communication course to avoid trivializing the subject matter or confusing students. The text has suggestions for films at the end of each chapter. Look for thorough descriptions of the following films in the text:

Chapter 1

Ordinary People (communication as a transactional process)

When a Man Loves a Woman (communication misconceptions)

The Hairdresser's Husband (qualitatively interpersonal communication)

The African Queen (dimensions of relational communication)

The Great Santini (communication competence)

Chapter 2

Welcome to the Dollhouse (influences on the self-concept)

Il Postino (impression management)

Breaking Away (impression management)
Stand and Deliver (self-fulfilling prophecy)

Chapter 3

Being There (perceptual distortion)
Rashomon (multiple perspectives)
He Said/She Said (multiple perspectives)
The Doctor (developing empathy)

Chapter 4

I Never Sang for My Father (consequences of unexpressed feelings)

Chapter 5

Nell (the importance of language)
The Miracle Worker (the importance of language)
When Harry Met Sally (gender and language)
Children of a Lesser God (language and culture)

Chapter 6

Quest for Fire (the power and limitations of nonverbal communication)
The Birdcage (masculine and feminine nonverbal behavior)
Mrs. Doubtfire (masculine and feminine nonverbal behavior)
Tootsie (masculine and feminine nonverbal behavior)

Chapter 7

Jerry McGuire (ineffective listening and its alternatives)
Kramer vs. Kramer (ineffective listening and its alternatives)
Dead Man Walking (listening to help)
Ordinary People (listening to help)

Chapter 8

Shall We Dance? (culture and intimacy)
Diner (Gender and intimacy)
The Brothers McMullen (dialectical tensions in male/female relationships)
Betrayal (relational development and deterioration)
Liar Liar (risks and benefits of self-disclosure)
Secrets and Lies (risks and benefits of self-disclosure)

Chapter 9

Mr. Holland's Opus (confirming and disconfirming behavior)
Tin Men (positive and negative spirals)

When Harry Met Sally (positive and negative spirals)
The Waterdance (relational climates)

Chapter 10

On Golden Pond (letting go of aggression)
The Joy Luck Club (culture and conflict)
The War of the Roses (portrait of lose-lose conflict)

The following table also offers many suggestions for titles. In every case, it is important for the instructor to view a film in advance of a class screening to become familiar with the material and determine how it can best be used to further instructional goals. Once a film has been identified as having instructional value, it can be used in one of several ways:

In class Segments or complete films may be shown in class to illustrate points about a single topic (e.g., defense-arousing communication, self-disclosure) or to preview and/or review the entire course or major units.

In the college media center Most campuses have a media center where students can view film segments or entire films, and, if desired, complete workbook assignments.

As homework Class members can all view the same film on their own time, or they may choose a variety of titles from a pre-approved list in order to complete an analytical assignment.

Available to Adopters of *Looking Out, Looking In,* Tenth Edition

An updated film guide, *Communication in Film: Teaching Communication Courses Using Feature Films,* prepared by Russ Proctor, describes how a wide array of movies can be used to illustrate how concepts from *Looking Out, Looking In* appear in realistic situations. This guide takes advantage of students' inherent interest in the medium of film, showing them how movies can be both entertaining and educational.

An additional tool is Microsoft Cinemania '97. This CD-ROM software for Macintosh and Windows operating systems is comp'97; you can easily locate movies that will best illustrate the interpersonal concepts you want to teach. It is available free to adopters of *Looking Out, Looking In* and available to students at a significantly reduced price.

WIDELY AVAILABLE FILMS AND TOPICS ILLUSTRATED

Title	Comm. Climate	Conflict	Emo-tions	Family	Gender	Inter-cult'l	Lan-guage	Lis-tening	Non-Verbal	Percep-tion	Rela-tional Control	Rela-tional Stages	Self-Concept	Self-Dis-closure
About Last Night (R)	X	X									X	X		X
Accidental Tourist, The (PG)			X											X
African Queen, The (NR)	X	X			X						X	X		
All About Eve (NR)		X									X			X
Annie Hall (PG)	X	X											X	
Avalon (PG)	X		X	X			X							
Beaches (PG-13)	X	X												
Being There (PG)			X				X	X	X				X	
Betrayal [1983] (R)	X	X	X						X		X	X		X
Big (PG)					X		X		X	X				
Black Like Me (NR)						X				X				
Breakfast Club, The (R)	X	X	X			X				X			X	X
Breaking Away (PG)		X		X		X					X	X	X	X
Brother/Another Planet (PG)					X	X		X	X					
Children of a Lesser God (R)		X	X			X	X	X	X	X	X	X	X	
Color Purple, The (PG-13)				X									X	
Dad (R)	X			X				X					X	
Dangerous Liaisons (R)			X								X			X
Dead Poets Society (PG)	X	X											X	
Diary of a Mad Housewife (NR)			X		X									X
Diner (R)	X				X							X	X	
Do the Right Thing (R)	X	X	X			X	X	X		X				
Dominick and Eugene (PG-13)		X		X					X				X	X
Driving Miss Daisy (PG)		X				X							X	
El Norte (R)						X								
Fabulous Baker Boys, The (R)	X	X		X										X
Five Easy Pieces (R)				X									X	X
Four Seasons (PG)	X	X	X								X	X		
General, The (NR)									X					
Gods Must Be Crazy, The (NR)						X								
Good Morning Vietnam (R)							X							
Great Santini, The (PG)	X	X	X	X							X			
Gregory's Girl (NR)					X								X	
Her Life as a Man (NR)					X									
I Never Sang/My Father (PG)				X										
King Kong ['33, '76] (NR, PG)									X					
Kramer vs. Kramer (PG)		X		X	X									
Lost in America (R)	X	X												
My Fair Lady (NR)							X							
*M*A*S*H* (PG)	X		X											
Marty (NR)													X	
Mask (PG-13)				X									X	X
Mr. Mom (PG)				X	X					X				
My Life as a Dog (NR)				X						X				
Nothing in Common (PG)				X										
On Golden Pond (PG)				X				X					X	
One Flew/Cuckoo's Nest (R)	X	X									X		X	
Ordinary People (R)	X	X	X	X					X	X	X		X	X

Title	Comm. Climate	Conflict	Emotions	Family	Gender	Inter- cult'l	Lan- guage	Lis- tening	Non- Verbal	Percep- tion	Rela- tional Control	Rela- tional Stages	Self- Concept	Self- Dis- closure
Parenthood (PG-13)		X		X										
Passage to India, A (PG)			X			X								
Pump Up the Volume (R)	X	X	X	X			X	X			X	X	X	X
Quest for Fire (R)							X		X					
Rain Man (R)	X		X	X						X				
Rashomon (NR)										X				
Running on Empty (PG-13)	X	X		X										
. . . Say Anything (PG-13)	X	X	X	X	X			X			X	X	X	X
Sex, Lies, and Videotape (R)			X					X						X
Shirley Valentine (R)	X	X						X				X	X	
Stand by Me (R)	X		X											
Swept Away (R)		X									X			
Taming of the Shrew (NR)		X			X						X			
Terms of Endearment (PG)		X		X							X			
Tex (PG)				X									X	
Tin Men (R)		X												
Tootsie (PG)				X	X		X		X	X				
Trading Places (R)						X	X			X				
Twelve Angry Men (NR)	X	X	X						X	X				
Unbearable Lightness . . . (R)			X											
Vice Versa (PG)				X						X				
War of the Roses (R)	X	X									X			
When Harry Met Sally (R)												X		X
Who's Afraid/Virg Woolf (NR)	X	X	X								X			X

"Teaching Interpersonal Communication with Feature Films" by Ronald B. Adler and Russell F. Proctor reprinted from *Communication Education 40* (1991): 396–397. Used by permission of the Speech Communication Association.

The videos in the University of California series are available from:

> The Univ. of California Extension Center for Media
> 2000 Center Street, Fourth Floor
> Berkeley, California U.S.A. 94704
> PHONE (510) 642-0460; FAX (510) 643-9271
> EMAIL cmil@uclink.berkeley.edu
> Supplemental information WEB site: http://nonverbal.ucsc.edu

"PERSONAL SPACE: Exploring Human Proxemics"

This new work examines the power of personal space in our daily lives—including the importance of space in public settings, powerful cultural differences in the use of space, how space is often governed by rigid rules (e.g., for table seating, restroom spacing, etc.), the link between personal space and rank in organizations, reactions to experimental "invasions" of a person's space, and the architectural differences between "favorite" and "failed" buildings. (Now with new Instructor's Guide.)

"THE HUMAN VOICE: Exploring Vocal Paralanguage"

This video is about language and vocal "paralanguage," i.e., what is revealed about a person from the nuances of his or her voice and speech. The video explores the important clues embedded in our "vocal paralanguage." Each time we speak, we may reveal what our first language was, how much education we have had, where we grew up, and a long list of other items, e.g., our identity, age, emotions, charisma, dysfluencies, sarcasm, lifestyle, etc. "THE HUMAN VOICE" also examines "standard" and nonstandard speech patterns, preferences and prejudices for various accents, how people can try to change their own accents, the universal nature of "parentese" (how adults speak to children), the legal "theft" involved in commercial imitations of "celebrity" voices, and important differences between human voices and computer-generated voices. (Instructor's Guide)

"THE HUMAN FACE: Emotions, Identities and Masks"

This video explores the kinds of information available in our faces, and in the dynamic facial expressions we use every time we interact with other people. Topics include the differences between genuine emotions and pretend emotions; the ways our faces are "identity documents"; differences between friendly smiles and unfriendly smiles; how police officers use facial details to locate suspects; what pupil size reveals about a person's drug use; facial decorations (piercings, tattoos, and scarification) and the motives of those who adopt them; how facial clues allow those closest to us to "know" our feelings; attractiveness and what "plastic surgeons" try to change. (Instructor's Guide)

"THE HUMAN BODY: Appearance, Shape and Self-Image"

This video explores our preferences and feelings about our own bodies. Topics include bulimia and anorexia; cosmetic surgery; interviews with "super-models" about the effects such models have on the self-images of young women; tattoos and body decoration; the prejudice and effects of "weightism," etc. The video also presents powerful evidence about cultural differences in beauty standards, e.g., the viewer meets people from cultures where larger women are regarded as more beautiful, where women planning to marry go on special diets to become as heavy as possible, etc. In extremely powerful interviews, the video examines the onset, destructiveness, and treatment of eating disorders. (Instructor's Guide)

"A WORLD OF DIFFERENCES: Understanding Cross-Cultural Communication"

This video is about the power and nuances of cross-cultural communication. Topics include "culture shock," misunderstandings and embarrassment, translation problems, emotions, and appropriate etiquette. The viewer learns about when, what, and how to eat in other cultures; whether greetings should include handshakes, hugs, or kisses; how to use space and touch in specific cultures; why one never offers food or touches someone with the left hand in Islamic cultures; etc. This video is designed to sensitize viewers to the "cultural baggage" we ALL carry with us and—most important—how to prevent this baggage from causing serious cross-cultural misunderstanding. This video vividly teaches the power of culture, and the importance (and excitement) of understanding the nature and richness of cultural differences. (Instructor's Guide)

"A WORLD OF GESTURES: Culture and Nonverbal Communication"

This video is a visual "tour" of the remarkable variation in the hand gestures used in different cultures. People from many different cultures show the viewer an extraordinary range of hand gestures—friendly gestures, obscene gestures, gestures for intelligence and stupidity, gestures about love or sexual orientation, gestures from Culture A that mean the opposite in Culture B, famous gestures, secret gestures, problems when a visitor uses the wrong gesture, etc. The video also shows the development of gestures in children, the increasing fluency with age, and the danger of cross-cultural misunderstandings. This video is humorous, outrageous, and unforgettable—"A WORLD OF GESTURES" leaves viewers inspired by the remarkable human diversity found on our planet. (Instructor's Guide)

"THE INTERPERSONAL PERCEPTION TASK (IPT)" & "IPT-15"

These two video "self-tests" enable viewers to see how accurately they can "decode" nonverbal cues to correctly interpret something about the person or people shown in each IPT scene. The viewer is asked to guess which of two women is the mother of the accompanying child; which of two people won their basketball game; which of two autobiographical statements is true and which is a lie; which of two co-workers is the boss; whether a man and a woman are strangers, siblings, or lovers; etc. Each IPT question has an objectively correct answer, e.g., one of the women really IS the mother; one of the two people DID win the basketball game, etc. The IPT has 30 questions for viewers; the IPT-15 has 15 questions. (Instructor's Guide)

PART TWO

NOTES ON CLASS AND STUDENT ACTIVITIES

CHAPTER 1

A FIRST LOOK

OBJECTIVES

After studying the material in Chapter One of *Looking Out/Looking In,* you should understand:

1. The types of needs that communication can satisfy.
2. The elements and characteristics of the transactional communication model.
3. The principles and misconceptions of communication
4. The differences between impersonal and interpersonal communication.
5. The content and relational aspects of messages.
6. The concept of metacommunication.
7. The characteristics of effective communicators.

You should be able to:

1. Identify the needs you attempt to satisfy by your interpersonal communication and the degree to which you satisfy those needs.
2. Use the transactional model to
   a. diagnose barriers to effective communication in your life.
   b. suggest remedies to overcome those barriers.
3. Identify the degree to which your communication is impersonal and interpersonal.
4. Improve your effectiveness as a communicator by using models to
   a. broaden your repertoire of behaviors and your skill at performing them.
   b. identify the most appropriate communication behaviors in a variety of important situations.
5. Discover how satisfied you are with the way you communicate in various situations.
6. Identify the content and relational aspects of
   a. messages you deliver to others.
   b. messages that are sent to you.

NOTES ON CLASS AND STUDENT ACTIVITIES
A. Name Calling

1. Assemble your group, including instructor, so that everyone can see each other; a circle works well.
2. The first person (ask for a volunteer) begins by giving his or her name to the whole group, speaking loudly enough to be heard clearly by everyone. ("My name is Sheila.") Instructors may want to repeat what they've heard to check whether the speaker has been heard correctly. If you're not sure of a name, ask to have it repeated.

3. The group member seated on the first speaker's left will then give his or her own name followed by the first speakers. ("My name is Gordon, and this is Sheila.")
4. Now the person to the left of the second speaker gives his or her name, followed by the second and first speaker's names. ("My name is Wayne, this is Gordon, and that's Sheila.") This procedure is followed around the whole group so that the last person names everyone in the class. It sounds as if it will be impossible for the last few people, but when you try it, you'll be surprised at how many names arc remembered.
5. Things to watch for:
    a. If you forget a name, don't worry; that person will help you after you've had a little time to think.
    b. If you don't catch the speaker's name, ask to have it repeated.
    c. You may want the person who begins the activity to end it also. After that, anyone who wants to should try to "name them all."
    d. Above all, keep the atmosphere informal. As you know, personal comments and humor have a way of lessening pressure.

Objectives

1. To learn the names of all the group members, thus forming a foundation for future interaction.
2. To achieve immediate participation from every class member.
3. To demonstrate that making mistakes is an acceptable, normal part of learning.
4. To provide an activity that calls for a minimal contribution with relatively little threat.

NOTE: WE STRONGLY RECOMMEND THAT THIS BE THE FIRST CLASS ACTIVITY! Over many semesters, it has proved to be one of the activities most often reported by the students as being of extreme value.

Variations

Use first names only, or work with both first and last. Both approaches have their advantages. Try both methods to see which works best for you.

Have each person attach a descriptive word to his or her name, for example, Gardening (or Digger) Dan, Patient Cindy, and so on. The variety of names is good for several laughs, thus making the exercise an even better icebreaker.

Discussion Questions

1. Was remembering all the names as difficult as you expected?
    The answer is usually no, and you can make the point that what was true here will likely hold true for other activities, both in and out of class. Taking risks isn't always as dangerous as it seems.

2. What will you do if you can't remember someone's name the next time you see him or her?
    This is a good time to talk about a common problem. Is it better to pretend you remember a person's name, or come right out and tell the person you forgot? Just how valuable is "tact" in social situations?

3. How did you feel as your turn approached? How did you feel after you were done?
    This question invites the students to reveal the feelings of anxiety they had and to discover that their fears in social situations are not unique but are rather like their classmates'.

4. Which name(s) do you think you'll remember easily? Why?
    This question invites discussion on what factors make names or people stand out in our memories. It is the differences that make individuals unique. This question leads into the next activity very naturally.

B. Introductions

1. Form dyads (groups of two). If possible, pair up with someone you've not known previously. The instructor or facilitator should use himself or herself to even out the dyads if necessary. In any event, someone should introduce the instructor.
2. Each member of a dyad will interview the other. Try to allow about 20 minutes for this activity.
    a. You should find three unique things to tell the group about the person you're introducing. These may be actions, characteristics, or experiences that set your partner apart from other people. (For example, the fact that your partner graduated from Lincoln High School probably isn't as important as the fact that he or she is thinking about getting married, quitting school, or planning an interesting career.) Remember that most people feel uncomfortable talking about themselves, so you'll have to probe to get those unique aspects from your partner.
    b. Use the name of the person you're introducing instead of the pronoun he or she. This will help everyone learn names.
3. Back in the large group, students introduce their partners to the class until everyone has been introduced.

Objective
To assist the students further in becoming acquainted by having them learn some personal characteristics of their classmates.

Discussion Questions (in addition to those found in the text)

1. Did you feel scared or threatened during any of the steps in this exercise? When?
    This question may encourage group members to discover something about beginning acquaintances.
2. How successful were you in finding out unique things about your partner? Why?
    Students may shed some light on the difficulty we seem to have in getting most persons to talk about themselves. The group may also discover the prevalence of clichés in our conversation.
3. This experience was different from the usual way you get to know someone. What parts of it did you like? Were there parts that you didn't like? Why?
4. Now that you know more about each other, have your feelings changed about any of the individuals? How? Have your feelings changed in regard to the group? How?

C. Autograph Party
Objective
This exercise in getting to know others in the group is outstanding as an icebreaker.

Purpose
To help you become acquainted with others in the group.

Instructions
Your task is to find someone who fits each of the descriptions below, and get his or her signature on this sheet. Try to find a different person for each description.

Find someone who

is an only child _____

skipped breakfast today _____

drives an imported car _____

was born east (west) of the Mississippi _____

isn't getting enough sleep _____

plays a musical instrument _____

is a parent _____

is left-handed _____

is taller than you _____

has an unusual hobby _____

is married _____

goes to church regularly _____

knows someone you know _____

has schedule problems _____

writes poetry _____

has traveled overseas _____

has read a book you've read _____

is in love _____

speaks a language besides English _____

knows some information helpful to you _____

is self-employed _____

D. A Model Muddle (Text, p. 12)

Objectives

1. To apply the transactional communication model to communication challenges.
2. To formulate steps to address these challenges.

Discussion Questions

1. In which elements of the transactional model are you likely to experience difficulties?
2. How do the experiences of others in your group compare to yours?

E. How Personal Are Your Relationships? (Text, p. 22)

Objectives

1. To enable the student to classify communication relationships along the impersonal-interpersonal spectrum.
2. To evaluate the relationship according to the characteristics of interpersonal communication.

Discussion Questions

1. What are the unique qualities of your relationships?
2. How irreplaceable are your relationships?
3. How much interdependence characterizes your different relationships?
4. Compare the amounts of self-disclosure present in your relationships along the impersonal-interpersonal spectrum.
5. Distinguish the rewards (extrinsic and intrinsic) in your different relationships.

F. Measuring Your Relationships (Text, p. 28 and 1.3 in Activities Manual/Study Guide)

Objectives

1. To identify relational messages.
2. To compare the relational messages of affinity, respect, and control sent in an important interpersonal relationship.

Discussion Questions

1. How do the needs for relational messages of affection, respect, and control vary in relationships?
2. What bad outcomes can occur as a result of these relational messages? What good outcomes?

G. Check Your Competence (1.2 in Activities Manual/Study Guide)

Objectives

1. To develop awareness of a personal range of communication behaviors with people important to the student.
2. To evaluate the effectiveness of the current range of behaviors.
3. To propose effective communication behaviors that might widen the range of personal communication behaviors.

Discussion Questions

1.   How did your partner(s) see you in terms of commitment to the relationship? Were you surprised at his or her comments?
2.   Did your partner(s) see you as committed to the messages you send? In what ways do people communicate commitment to their messages?
3.   How did your partner(s) evaluate your desire for mutual benefit and your desire for interaction? How accurate were the ratings?
4.   Relate the range of behaviors your partner(s) observed to your own evaluation of your skill at performing them. Comment specifically on how a communicator then chooses appropriate behaviors.
5.   How accurate were your partner's(s') ratings? Is there any reason why they might be inaccurate?
6.   What behaviors that you don't engage in currently would you like to develop? Why?

CHAPTER 2

COMMUNICATION AND IDENTITY:
THE SELF AND MESSAGES

OBJECTIVES

After studying the material in Chapter Two of *Looking Out/Looking In*, you should understand:

1. How the self-concept is defined.
2. How the self-concept develops.
3. Two characteristics of the self-concept.
4. Four reasons why the self-concept is subjective.
5. Differences between public and private selves.
6. The role of self-fulfilling prophecies in shaping the self-concept and in influencing communication.
7. Four requirements for changing the self-concept.
8. The ethics of impression management.

You should be able to:

1. Develop a self-concept that enhances your communication by
   a. identifying the key elements of your self-concept.
   b. identifying the people who have had the greatest influence on your self-concept.
   c. describing the ways in which your self-concept may be inaccurate, and suggesting ways of improving its accuracy.
   d. identifying the differences between your public and private selves.
   e. recognizing and giving proper credit to your personal strengths.
2. Describe the ways in which you influence the self-concept of others.
3. Avoid destructive self-fulfilling prophecies that affect your communication and create positive self-fulfilling prophecies that can improve your communication.
4. Manage impressions to meet social, personal, and relational goals.

NOTES ON CLASS AND STUDENT ACTIVITIES
A. Take Away (Text, p. 47)
Objective
To demonstrate that the concept of self is perhaps our most fundamental possession.

Discussion Questions

1. What types of descriptors seem most fundamental to your self-concept?
2. What descriptors do you see as the most vulnerable to change?
3. Do you think others would describe you as you have described yourself?

B. Ego Boosters and Busters (Text, p. 49 and 2.2 in Activities Manual/Study Guide)

Objectives

1. To enable the student to see how his or her self-concept developed.
2. To enable the student to understand how his or her communication affects the self-concept of others.

Discussion Questions

1. What sorts of things were "busters"? Why did they affect your self-concept negatively? What sorts of things were "boosters"?
2. Are there any differences of opinions among class members about what indicates a booster or buster? Why might that occur? Are there any universal boosters and busters?
3. Is it possible to always send booster messages and avoid sending intentional and unintentional busters? If not, how can one deal with this state of affairs?

C. Recognizing Your Strengths (Text, p. 59)

Objectives

1. To illustrate the disproportionate emphasis we place on negative parts of the self-concept.
2. To demonstrate the value of feeling positive about oneself.
3. To build class cohesiveness and morale.
4. To further develop the acquaintance of group members.

D. Reevaluating Your "Can'ts" (Text, p. 69 and 2.4 in Activities Manual/Study Guide)

Objective

To demonstrate how an obsolete self-concept becomes a self-fulfilling prophecy that keeps the student from growing.

NOTE: This is one of the most effective exercises in the book, for it clearly demonstrates many ways in which students can change and develop their communication habits.

E. Your Personal Coat of Arms

Objectives

1. To help the group members search out some of the positive aspects of their lives.
2. To further acquaint the class members with each other.

NOTE: If the instructor wishes, he or she may assign this as an out-of-class activity. All students may be supplied with an enlargement of the shield outline provided in the Activities Manual/Study Guide and allowed to use pictures from magazines, snapshots, or their artistic talents to complete their own "coats of arms."

Our groups seem to like to have their coats of arms displayed without names in the classroom for a few days so that they can see all of them. They like to try to guess the owners.

Discussion Questions

1. When you have seen the coats of arms of your whole group, do you find any similarities?
2. In what ways are the coats of arms most alike? What could be an explanation?
3. In what ways are the coats of arms most different? Explain.

There are no set answers to these questions, but they usually promote good discussion, and the search for explanations leads students to the areas of their lives that they share with most others and also those in which they differ.

Purpose

To help you identify the important parts of yourself and to become better acquainted with other group members.

Instructions

1. Create a personal coat of arms that represents important information about you, such as
    a. people who are important to you.
    b. locations that are significant to you.
    c. activities with which you are associated.
    d. personal traits that characterize you.
    e. your ambitions.
    f. physical features that identify you.

    g.   talents and skills you have.

    h.   anything else you think is an important part of you.

2.   Remember that you needn't be a professional artist to complete this activity. This is a getting-acquainted activity, not a contest.

3.   In addition to pencil or pen, you might use other materials to construct your coat of arms: photos, crayons, felt-tip pens, rub-on letters, paint, and newspaper or magazine clippings.

4.   After completing your coat of arms, explain it to other class members.

F. Interpersonal Interviews

If you haven't done Introductions (B in this manual) in Chapter One, a good, nonthreatening way to help all class members begin to talk to one another and in front of the class is to conduct interpersonal interviews.

    Pair class members and ask them to exchange information about themselves (biographical, interests, values, family, school, work, etc.). Allow them about 15–20 minutes to interview one another, and ask them to take brief notes about the other person.

    Stop the interviews and allow about 2–3 minutes for all persons to organize the information they have about their partners so that they can introduce their partners to the class.

    Sitting in a circle so that everyone can see everyone else, ask class members to introduce their partners. After the introduction, other class members may ask questions of their partners or the partners may clarify or correct any information given about them to the class.

Variations

Do shorter interviews on a number of days, using one topic at a time (e.g., only biographical information one day, only interests another, and only future goals another). Or, after the interviews have occurred, ask students to analyze how they have presented their self-concept to the partner (different from the way they present to others?) and how they would change the way they interacted if they could. Another idea is to have class members go around the circle after the interviews, using one positive adjective to describe each of the persons introduced.

G. Your Many Identities (Text, p. 74 and Success in Managing Impressions, 2.6 in Activities Manual/Study Guide)

Objectives

1.   To recognize how manner, appearance, and setting affect identity management.

2.   To illustrate the appropriateness of different presenting selves.

H. Self-Monitoring Inventory (Text, p. 77)

Objectives

1.   To recognize your level of self-monitoring.

2.   To consider the appropriate level of self-monitoring in different situations.

Discussion Questions

1.   What are the advantages of high self-monitoring? The disadvantages?

2.   How can we balance paying attention to our own behavior with focusing on that of others?

CHAPTER 3

PERCEPTION:
WHAT YOU SEE IS WHAT YOU GET

OBJECTIVES

After studying the material in Chapter Three of *Looking Out/Looking In*, you should understand:

1. How the processes of selection, organization and interpretation operate in the perception process.
2. The physiological and cultural factors, social roles, gender roles, occupational roles, and self-concept variables that influence the perceptual process.
3. Five factors that influence the accuracy and inaccuracy of our perceptions.
4. Requirements for developing empathy to improve the accuracy of perceptions.

You should be able to:

1. Identify
   a. the physiological factors which cause your perceptual differences.
   b. the cultural, social, and occupational factors which cause your perceptual differences.
   c. perceptual errors which contribute to your opinions of others.
2. Engage in perception-checking by
   a. using appropriate nonverbal behaviors (eyes, voice).
   b. describing clearly and accurately the behavior you observed.
   c. posing at least two possible interpretations of the behavior you described.
   d. requesting feedback from your partner about the accuracy or inaccuracy of your observations and interpretations.
3. Communicate empathy by
   a. using appropriate nonverbal behaviors (eyes, proximity, touch, voice).
   b. describing the correct or understandable elements of your position and/or the position of your partner.
   c. describing the incorrect or difficult elements of your position and/or the position of your partner.
   d. describing at least two different ways these elements might affect your relationship.

NOTES ON CLASS AND STUDENT ACTIVITIES
A. Your Perceptual Filters (Text, p. 98)
Objectives

1. To recognize the perceptual, physical, role, interaction, psychological, and membership constructs that help us categorize others.
2. To consider the validity of our constructs.

Discussion Questions

1. How do constructs limit our perceptions of others?
2. How do constructs help us relationally?

B. Punctuation Practice (Text, p. 101)
Objective
To appreciate the importance of punctuation in our perceptual organization.

Discussion Question
How can you use the concept of punctuation to appreciate the perception of others?

C. New Body, New Perspective (Text, p. 105)
Objective
To enable students to understand how perception can be changed by different physiological conditions.

Discussion Questions

1. How did the situation you chose differ when you changed the physiological "symptoms"?
2. Is it difficult to understand how someone else would "see" in each of those conditions? Why?
3. Did any of the people of your group foresee differences of opinion, problems, or conflicts when under any of the different conditions?

D. Role Reversal (Text, p. 114)
Objective
To give the student firsthand experience with an orientation different from his or her own.

NOTE: This can be an outstanding assignment, well worth the time and effort necessary to make it work.

An effective warm-up is to have the class members name a person, group, or philosophical position they do not understand at all—which should provide each student with at least one target for the assignment.

An alternate approach is to stage debates in which students are required to defend positions opposed to their own. You might even want students actually to assume the role they're playing, that is, have conservatives pretend they're radicals, children play parents, and so on.

In many cases, you'll need to become the director to help students get into their roles. You may need to goad them into acting out contrasting positions, play alter ego, or just plain put words into their mouths until they get the idea.

E. Perception-Checking Stimuli

Objectives

To enable students to take on the perceptions of others.

To provide situations in which perceptions can be aired, discussed, and "perception checked." Here are two activities designed for group interaction.

1. The Gender Game. Divide the class into men and women. Each group is to come up with 5–10 questions they have always wanted to ask the opposite gender but, for some reason or another, never have. They are to rank their questions in importance because the class may not get to all the questions. Two simple rules govern the limits here: (1) you may not ask a question of the opposite gender that you are unwilling to answer yourself, and (2) you should avoid questions that are insulting (i.e., specific sexual behaviors that might embarrass some class members) or that tend to group all members of a gender together (e.g., "Why do women always go to the bathroom in pairs?").

    Groups meet face to face after about 20 minutes allotted to question-generation, and the instructor acts as moderator as one "side" and then another asks one question at a time; each time the opposite side can "put the question back to them." The instructor should encourage all members of the class to answer the question put to the group, but no one should be pressured if he or she feels uncomfortable.

2. The Intercultural Game. Using the same format as The Gender Game, this activity makes good use of any diverse population your institution may have. If your class has members of many different cultures, you can divide them that way. Or, make use of foreign language classes or English as a Second Language (ESL) classes, and coordinate your activity with another instructor. In addition to providing a forum for perception checking, you can further interdisciplinary relationships at the same time.

NOTE: Both of these activities can be used as the stimulus for the oral perception-checking skill in the Activities Manual/Study Guide. Ask students to keep track of perceptions they have during the course of the activity and prepare 2–5 perception-checking statements to be delivered to specific individuals during the next class. (Examples: "Shelley, when you said that men didn't take enough responsibility for birth control in relationships, I didn't know if you meant that men should bring up the subject of birth control first or if you thought that men should just take it upon themselves more to be the ones that actually use protection. Did you mean either of those two things or something else?" Or "Jose, when you said most white people in the U.S. made no effort to understand you, I wondered if you were referring to just your language, or if you meant more than that—like trying to understand what you think and feel. What did you mean?")

F. Perception-Checking Practice (Text, p. 121 and 3.5 and 3.6 in Activities Manual/Study Guide)

Objective

To apply perception checking to a variety of situations.

Discussion Questions

What aspects of perception checking are most/least useful? How can you use perception checking most effectively in your life?

G. Pillow Talk (Text, p. 129 and Shifting Perspectives 3.3 in Activities Manual/Study Guide)

Objective
To provide students with a systematic tool for exploring the perceptions of those who differ from them on important issues.

NOTE:

1. The pillow method is a culmination of the entire chapter. The measure of a student's success in understanding perceptual variability is the ability to move through the steps on a personal problem.
2. Working through the pillow becomes more difficult with the immediacy of the issue. You will most likely want to work through several cases in class. You may need to suggest to students some possible reasons for position 2, in which the "opponent" is right.
3. We urge you not to become discouraged when students say they "can't" understand a position different from their own. Although this kind of understanding is difficult, the reward of increased empathy is well worth the effort.

H. Empathy Skills

Objective
To give students practice in demonstrating their abilities to build common ground and express empathy.

Name _____ Class day/time _____ Date _____

Goal
This assignment will allow you to demonstrate your ability to build common ground and empathy.

Instructions

1. Choose an interpersonal issue with a person who is important to you. This person may be a friend, family member, fellow student or worker, instructor, or any other person who matters to you. This person must be available to you for feedback during the time you are completing this assignment.
2. Compose a draft paper, describing the issue from the other's point of view. Write your description in the first person as if you were the other person. (You may choose to meet with the other person before writing your description to understand his or her perspective better.)
3. Show your completed draft to the other person to verify its accuracy. Based on the comments you receive, revise your description.
4. Show your revised description to your partner. If you have represented his or her thoughts and feelings accurately, have this person verify its correctness by signing the paper. If your description is still not accurate, keep revising it until the other person is willing to sign it.

NOTE: As you write your description, remember that you are not required to agree with the other person's position—only to understand it.

5. Add a written summary to your paper describing the following dimensions of the issue:
   a. There are understandable reasons for the behavior of both parties in the issue.
   b. Both parties have engaged in at least some erroneous thinking and behavior with regard to this issue.
   c. In at least one way the issue may be seen as less important than the parties have perceived it to be.

CHAPTER 4

EMOTIONS

OBJECTIVES

After studying the material in Chapter Four of *Looking Out/Looking In*, you should understand:

1. The four components of emotions.
2. Reasons why emotions are not expressed.
3. The characteristics of facilitative and debilitative emotions.
4. The relationship between activating events, thoughts, and emotions.
5. Seven fallacies that result in unnecessary, debilitative emotions.
6. Four steps in the rational-emotive approach to coping with debilitative feelings.

You should be able to:

1. Identify the components of the emotions you experience.
2. Recognize the emotions you experience and the circumstances and consequences surrounding them.
3. Distinguish true feeling statements from counterfeit expressions of emotions.
4. Distinguish between debilitative and facilitative emotions and label the emotions.
5. Express facilitative emotions you experience clearly and appropriately by using the guidelines for sharing feelings.
6. Minimize your difficult/debilitative emotions.

NOTES ON CLASS AND STUDENT ACTIVITIES
A. How Does It Feel? (Text, pp. 137–138)

Objective
To provide a vehicle with which the student may learn more about his or her proprioceptive senses.

NOTE:

1. This exercise can be altered and tailored to almost any situation. Perhaps you would like to add areas of the body that aren't mentioned in this narrative. You should feel free to do this. Perhaps you'll want to shorten it.
2. We have found that this exercise gives the group something to talk about that they have experienced in common as individuals. It seems to promote openness.
3. Some groups like to repeat this experience. If you find this to be the case with your group, suggest that one student take the role of tour guide.
4. Discussion of the suggested questions is quite important if the group is to have other reactions with which to compare their individual reactions.

B. Recognizing Your Emotions (Text, p. 143)

Objective

To further the student's awareness of his or her feelings and how these feelings register themselves physically in the body.

NOTE:

1. We find that when we provide a duplicate form for the diary/journal, the students tend to take the assignment a bit more seriously. Design a form to fit your situation.
2. Another way of adding importance to the assignment is to collect the diaries and take a number of the better entries and publish them for the whole group. It goes without saying that this is done without disclosing the individuals' names.
3. You'll find that this diary technique is used on many occasions in the text. Our experience is that this is one of the best ways to promote out-of-class effort.

C. Feelings and Phrases (Text, p. 156 and 4.3 in Activities Manual/Study Guide)

Objective

To help students develop ways of expressing feelings clearly.

NOTE: In a group activity, have members evaluate the effectiveness of different forms of expressing emotions (or of not expressing the feelings). Encourage group members to comment on the clarity of each expression and emotion.

Discussion Questions

1. How does the expression of feelings vary from situation to situation? from receiver to receiver?
2. What are some reasons for/for not expressing true feelings in each situation with each receiver?

D. Talking to Yourself (Text, p. 159)

Objective

To help students better understand how their thoughts can shape their feelings.

E. How Irrational Are You? (Text, p. 165)

Objective

To help students to identify debilitative feelings and check their biases. Do biases involve irrational thinking based on common fallacies?

F. Rational Thinking (Text, p. 168)

Objective

To assist students in replacing irrational thinking with rational thinking. This exercise affords students a chance to practice the procedure before a monitor.

NOTE: The instructor should probably go through the exercise with two others as a demonstration. The instructor should take the part of the "second party" (monitor).

CHAPTER 5

LANGUAGE: BARRIER AND BRIDGE

OBJECTIVES

After studying the material in Chapter Five of *Looking Out/Looking In*, you should understand:

1. The symbolic nature of language.
2. That language is rule-governed.
3. That meanings are in people, not words.
4. The various types of troublesome language described in this chapter.
5. That language describes events at various levels of abstraction.
6. The problems that occur when overly abstract language is used.
7. How behavioral descriptions clarify thinking and communicating.
8. The manner in which a speaker's language can reflect responsibility.
9. The ways that sexist and racist language shape the attitudes of both speaker and person described.
10. How language and culture are related.

You should be able to:

1. Avoid using troublesome language by identifying the problematic terms you use, and compose alternatives.
2. Label inferences contained in your statements and separate them from the facts in your language.
3. Identify overly abstract statements you and others make and propose less abstract alternatives.
4. Identify ways in which your language and the language of others you know reflect degrees of responsibility.
5. Increase the clarity of your language by using
   a. behavioral descriptions.
   b. lower-level abstractions.
6. Identify the gender variables of language.
7. Identify the culture variables of language.

NOTES ON CLASS AND STUDENT ACTIVITIES
A. Your Linguistic Rules (Text, p. 190)
Objective
To give students awareness of their own and others' linguistic rules.

NOTE: Coordinated Management of Meaning Theory is initially a difficult concept for students. Use Table 5-1 from the text to develop more confidence and encourage individual application of the concept.

B. Down-to-Earth Language (Text, p. 185)

Objective
To give students practice using lower abstractions.

NOTE: This exercise can be a good precursor to coping with criticism in Chapter Nine, as it may enable students to criticize themselves specifically and constructively before having to cope with the criticism of others later.

C. Practicing "I" Language (Text, p. 203 and 5.3 and 5.4 in Activities Manual/Study Guide)

Objective
To give students practice speaking descriptively rather than evaluatively.

NOTE: This exercise can be very difficult for students who are not used to describing behavior. It is best to give them many examples before they actually do this exercise (e.g., change "You're not telling me the truth!" to "I heard from Jane that you went out with the boys last night and you just told me you stayed home and watched a movie").

D. Conjugating Irregular Verbs (Text, p. 198)

Objective
To give the student some practice with using emotive words. To become sensitive to the practice we often have of using words that we think describe something or somebody but really announce to the receiver our attitude about it.

NOTE: This particular exercise seems to be one that the students like. It is, therefore, quite easy to get them to come up with their own "I am _____" and then pass it on to the next person in line for the "You are _____" and to a third person for the "He is _____" responses.

When you use this as a group exercise, it is important not to leave it as just a game; the discussion should be pursued to the point where students can identify instances in which they have unconsciously done the same.

CHAPTER 6

NONVERBAL COMMUNICATION: MESSAGES WITHOUT WORDS

OBJECTIVES

After studying the material in Chapter Six of *Looking Out/Looking In*, you should understand:

1. The importance of nonverbal communication.
2. The six characteristics of nonverbal communication.
3. The seven functions of nonverbal communication.
4. The differences between verbal and nonverbal communication.
5. The twelve types of nonverbal communication described in this chapter.

You should be able to:

1. Identify and describe
   a. your nonverbal behavior in a particular situation.
   b. examples of nonverbal behavior that repeats, substitutes for, complements, accents, regulates, or contradicts a verbal message.
   c. nonverbal behaviors of a variety of people in the same context.
   d. the emotions expressed in selected examples of your own nonverbal behavior.
2. Describe another's nonverbal behavior and use perception-checking statements to verify its meaning.
3. Describe the differences between verbal and nonverbal communication.
4. Explain why deception cues are not easy to detect.

NOTES ON CLASS AND STUDENT ACTIVITIES

A. Verbal and Nonverbal Communication (Text, p. 224)

Objective

To help students experience several dimensions of nonverbal communication.

NOTE: This is a good exercise to use before reading the material that follows. In this way, the students' experiences with the exercises aren't influenced by what they "think" are correct behaviors. Reactions to this activity usually lead directly to the text information.

B. Reading "Body Language" (Text, p. 239)

Objectives

1. To increase the participant's skill in observing nonverbal behavior.

2. To become more aware of some of the dangers inherent in interpreting nonverbal behavior.

NOTE: It is suggested that this exercise be done in pairs, but it can be done in larger groups.

C. The Eyes Have It (Text, p. 249)

Objective
To investigate the role eye contact plays in social influence.

NOTE: The instructor should be careful not to generalize one student's experience to all situations. The context and other participants involved will certainly affect the outcome no matter how much eye contact is (is not) used.

D. Building Vocal Fluency (Text, p. 252)

Objective
To help participants realize how much the words of a message are aided by the accompanying qualities of the voice; how much the meaning of a message can depend on the paralanguage: the tone of the voice, the pace, the punctuation (spacing of words), the emphasis, and so on.

NOTE: There are many variations of this particular activity. The partner doing the speaking can be given a list of things he or she is to attempt by means of paralanguage, with the listener responding as to what he or she is receiving. A single, short sentence can be used several times, putting the accent or emphasis on a different word each time.

E. The Rules of Touch (Text, p. 255)

Objective
To develop an awareness of appropriate touch and the ability to describe it within various relationships.

NOTE: This exercise can trigger strong feelings from students about their own instances of both appropriate and inappropriate touch. Guide students to use the language skills (e.g., "I" language) from Chapter Five to voice their pleasure or displeasure to the person touching.

F. Distance Makes a Difference (Text, p. 258)

Objective
To let each student experience the difference distance can make to him or her when relating to another person.

NOTE: Often the room is not large enough to give the partners enough room so that they are not distracted by those lined up beside them. If this is the case, do the exercise in several groups so that there is at least an arm's length separating everyone from one another.

CHAPTER 7

LISTENING: MORE THAN MEETS THE EAR

OBJECTIVES

After studying the material in Chapter Seven of *Looking Out/Looking In*, you should understand:

1. Seven types of nonlistening.
2. The reasons why people listen poorly in most circumstances.
3. The characteristics of informational listening as they are used to gather information.
4. Seven styles of listening to help others with problems, and the strengths and drawbacks of each.

You should be able to:

1. Identify your ineffective listening behavior, including
   a. the circumstances in which you listen ineffectively.
   b. the nonlistening styles you use in each set of circumstances.
   c. the reasons why you listen ineffectively in each set of circumstances.
   d. the consequences of your nonlistening behaviors.
2. Paraphrase another person by
   a. using appropriate nonverbal attending behaviors.
   b. fluently and concisely paraphrasing the speaker's thoughts.
   c. fluently and concisely paraphrasing the speaker's feelings.
   d. making open-ended requests for the speaker to verify the accuracy of your paraphrasing statements.
3. Demonstrate your ability to use the following response styles to help others with their problems:
   a. advising
   b. judging
   c. analyzing
   d. questioning
   e. supporting
   f. prompting
   g. paraphrasing

NOTES ON CLASS AND STUDENT ACTIVITIES
A. Listening Breakdowns (Text, p. 271)

Objective
To overcome common listening myths.

NOTE: If students have a difficult time coming up with examples of how they failed at listening, let them start with examples of how *others* have failed in listening to them. Then guide the students back into self-awareness.

B. Speaking and Listening with a "Talking Stick" (Text, p. 284)

Objective

To focus the student's attention on the benefits of talking less and listening more.

NOTE:

1. Encourage students to talk about anything of interest to them. What happened to them this morning may seem as important as serious world events.
2. After the exercise, a valuable discussion can come from students discussing times they have not felt listened to, and in turn, not listened themselves.

C. Counterfeit Questions (Text, p. 287)

Objective

To illustrate the negative effects of counterfeit questions in listening situations.

NOTE: Extend this activity to include other situations in which the five types of counterfeit questions cause problems in relationships.

D. Paraphrasing Practice (Text, p. 290)

Objective

To give the student practice in paraphrasing.

NOTE: Discussion questions are indicated in the text.

E. What Would You Do? (Text, p. 292)

Objectives

1. To show students their typical style of responding to another person's problem.
2. To demonstrate the frequent ineffectiveness of the typical response styles.

NOTE: To vary the exercise, assign one or two students each of the typical response styles, having them react to another student who "plays" the problems listed.

F. What Would You Do? (Text, p. 292)

Objectives

1. To show students their typical style of responding to another's problem.
2. To demonstrate the frequent ineffectiveness of the typical response styles.

NOTE: In a variation of the exercise, assign one or two students each of the typical response styles, having them react to another student who role-plays the problems listed.

F. One-Way and Two-Way Communication

Objective

To demonstrate the advantages of checking back with the sender of a message.

NOTE:

1. You can alert the observers (mentioned in step 3) to watch for certain behaviors: level of frustration, perceived confidence, and mistaken assumptions or misinterpretations. These observations will be helpful in the post-exercise discussion.
2. In the post-exercise discussion, make sure the students recognize all the characteristics of one-way and two-way communication.

ONE-WAY

Low sender frustration, High receiver frustration

Low accuracy

Short time necessary

TWO-WAY

High sender frustration, Low receiver frustration

High accuracy

Long time necessary

Instructions

1. Copy the following chart onto a chalkboard so that everyone can see it.

ONE-WAY			TWO-WAY	
TIME			TIME	
NUMBER CORRECT			**NUMBER CORRECT**	
ESTIMATE	ACTUAL		ESTIMATE	ACTUAL
		5		
		4		
		3		
		2		
		1		
		0		

2. Select one member of the group to act as a sender. The sender's job will be to describe two simple drawings to the rest of the group.
3. Select two observers, one to note the sender's behavior in the exercise, and the other to note the behavior of the group members.
4. Supply the group members with sheets of unlined 8½ × 11-inch paper.
5. Make sure everyone hears and understands the following directions: "In a minute, the sender will describe a simple set of figures that the group members should draw as accurately as possible. The group members should ask no questions or respond in any way to the sender's directions. The idea is to create a one-way communication situation."

6. The sender now stands or sits so that he or she can be heard but not seen by the group. The instructor then gives the sender a copy of the first drawing found here. (Actually, any simple drawing will work in this exercise. In a variation, the sender creates his or her own drawing and describes it to the group. Remember, however, that the drawing should be quite simple. This exercise is hard enough this way!)

7. The sender should describe this drawing to the group as quickly and as accurately as possible. The instructor should make sure that the group members don't communicate with each other during this step. All should understand that a glance at another's drawing furnishes an additional source of information, thus destroying a one-way communication situation.

8. After the sender has finished, note the time that his or her description took and place it on the chart. Next, find out how many group members think they've drawn all five figures exactly, how many think they got four, three, and so on. Place the numbers in the appropriate spaces on the chart.

9. Now the sender should move so that he or she can see and be seen by the group. The instructor will give the sender the drawing he or she is to describe. This time, however, the group members should ask necessary questions to make sure they understand the drawing being described. This should be two-way communication. The only limitation on communication here is that the sender must use words only—no gestures—to describe the drawing to the group.

10. Remember, the goal is to have all group members reproduce the drawing perfectly, so everyone should feel free to ask plenty of questions.

11. Repeat step 8.

12. Now show the drawings one at a time to the group members so they can see how accurate their reactions are. The instructor should then record the accuracy of the group's drawings. For a figure to be correct, its size should be correct proportionately, and it should be positioned in the correct relationship to the preceding and following figures.

13. Now note the data the exercise has produced on your chart. After looking it over, what assumptions might you make about one-way and two-way communication? Which takes longer? Which is more accurate?

14. Which is more frustrating for the sender? For the receiver?

15. What parallels does this exercise have in your everyday life? Does the exercise tell you anything about the way you listen?

16. Consider the efficiency of one-way and two-way communication. Remember, efficiency takes into account time, cost, and so on. Are there situations in society where one-way communication is used? Consider the military, police and fire departments, and so on. What precaution is taken to ensure effective communicating situations where time is so important?

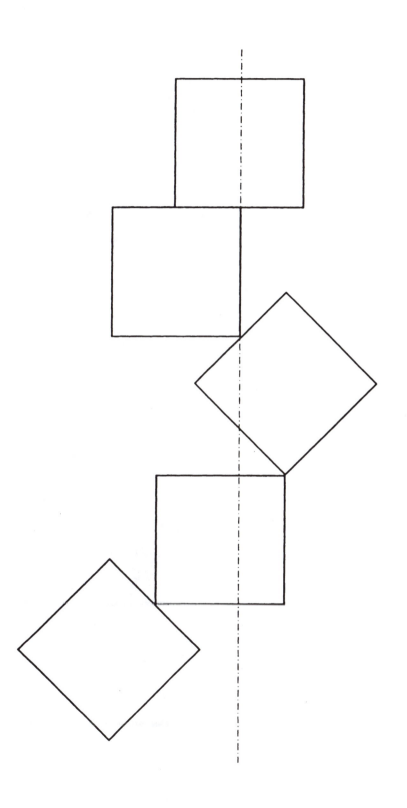

CHAPTER 8

COMMUNICATION AND RELATIONAL DYNAMICS

OBJECTIVES

After reading the material in Chapter Eight of *Looking Out/Looking In*, you should understand:

1. The four dimensions of intimacy.
2. Five variables affecting interpersonal attraction.
3. The ten stages of interpersonal relationships.
4. How self-disclosure is defined.
5. How the Johari Window represents the relationship between self-disclosure and self-awareness and how it can describe self-disclosure in a dyadic relationship.
6. How the four types of self-disclosure affect breadth and depth in a relationship.
7. Seven guidelines for self-disclosure.
8. The alternatives to self-disclosure.

You should be able to:

1. Identify
   a. three reasons why we form relationships.
   b. three dialectical tensions at work in relationships.
   c. seven strategies for managing dialectical tensions.
   d. reasons why you self-disclose or fail to disclose.
   e. stages of development in interpersonal relationships.
2. Describe
   a. the breadth and depth of relationships that are important to you.
   b. the levels of self-disclosure you engage in and how they affect your relationships.
   c. behaviors reflecting stages in your relationships and your satisfaction with the relationships.
   d. the alternatives you have to self-disclosure and the ethics of evasion.

NOTES ON CLASS AND STUDENT ACTIVITIES
A. Analyzing Interpersonal Attraction (Text, p. 317)
Objective
To help students identify the attraction variables that lead them to be attracted to certain people.

Questions

1. To what extent are your strong, positive personal relationships based on the listed attraction variables?

2. Do you believe that knowing these attraction variables can influence the relationships you would like to make stronger?
3. To what extent do you "fit" the attraction variables for those people that you wish you were attractive to?

B. Your IQ (Intimacy Quotient) (Text, p. 323)

Objective

To help students determine the levels of intimacy in their important relationships.

NOTE: Reinforce for students the many different types of intimacy (many think only of physical intimacy at first).

C. Your Dialectical Tensions (Text, p. 336 and 8.1 in Activities Manual/Study Guide)

Objective

To increase students' knowledge of the tensions at work in relationships.

NOTE: Have students make a column for each of the strategies for dealing with dialectical tensions. Record how frequently each is used and in which types of situations.

D. Your Relational Stage (Text, p. 331 and 8.6 in Activities Manual/Study Guide)

Objective

To increase the student's awareness of stages of relational development.

NOTE:

1. Some students have a tendency to describe romantic relationships of even a short duration as "bonded." Encourage them to see the value of behaviors at each stage in building the relationship over time. Remind them that one behavior does not make the stage, but rather a pattern and consistency of types of behavior.
2. Another problem some students have with relational stages is that they think "the higher the better." Help them to see that mutual understanding of and satisfaction with the stage is a far better guide.

E. Building a Johari Window (Text, p. 344)

Objective

To examine the level of self-disclosure in an ongoing relationship.

Discussion Questions

1. How do you notice reciprocity of self-disclosure at work in your relationship?
2. What level of self-disclosure is appropriate in this relationship versus others?

F. Examining Your Self-Disclosure (Text, p. 341)

Objective

To increase students' awareness of the levels of self-disclosure they use with a significant other.

NOTE: Question 4 in the exercise provides a good basis for class and/or small-group discussion after the three-day journal period that is done individually.

G. Appropriate Self-Disclosure (Text, p. 350 and 8.5 in Activities Manual/Study Guide)

Objective

To examine the potential risks and benefits of self-disclosure.

NOTE: Have students compare the risks and benefits of disclosing in various situations. They can often reinforce for one another the guidelines for appropriate self-disclosure with their "war stories."

CHAPTER 9

IMPROVING COMMUNICATION CLIMATES

OBJECTIVES

After studying the material in Chapter Nine of *Looking Out/Looking In*, you should understand:

1. How confirming and disconfirming messages create positive and negative communication climates.
2. The relationship between a communicator's self-concept and his or her defensive reaction to a message.
3. How defense mechanisms operate when a communicator perceives attacking messages.
4. How and why Gibb's defensive and supportive behaviors can minimize or increase defensive responses to your message.
5. How seeking more information from a critic and agreeing with the criticism can minimize a communicator's defensive responses.

You should be able to:

1. Use feedback from a significant other to list the kinds of confirming and disconfirming messages you presently send.
2. Identify your unproductive defensive responses to perceived verbal attacks by listing
   a. the defense mechanisms you commonly use.
   b. the circumstances in which you use them.
   c. the parts of your presenting self-image you are attempting to defend.
   d. the consequences of your defensive behavior.
3. Send confirming messages by using Gibb's supportive behaviors:
   a. description
   b. problem-orientation
   c. empathy
   d. spontaneity
   e. equality
   f. provisionalism
4. Respond to the criticism of others nondefensively by
   a. seeking additional information from your critic.
   b. agreeing with your critic.

NOTES ON CLASS AND STUDENT ACTIVITIES
A. Evaluating Communication Climates (Text, p. 374)
Objective
To identify the communication climate in important relationships and to describe the confirming and disconfirming behaviors that help define this climate.

NOTE: One way to help the discussion along in this exercise is to allow some students to describe the negative behaviors, disconfirming ones, that their partners use (it is easier to criticize others) and again to describe the positive, confirming behaviors that their partners use (they don't have to brag about themselves in this instance). As this discussion progresses, lead the discussion into the spiral effect of behaviors in relationships (Gibb), and the effects of the students' own behaviors become more apparent.

B. Defense Mechanism Inventory (Text, p. 380 and 9.1 in the Activities Manual/Study Guide)

Objective
To encourage the student to reflect on the patterns of defensive behavior he or she may have and to encourage the student to create a plan for more satisfying behaviors.

NOTE: The Understanding Your Defensive Responses in the Activities Manual/Study Guide and Defense Mechanism Inventory are similar exercises. We believe they are both needed to help the student recognize his or her own defensive behaviors. It is better if some time elapses between the assignment of these exercises.

C. Defensiveness Feedback (Text, p. 385)

Objective
To provide the student with more information about the patterns of his or her defensive behaviors.

NOTE: The instructor may wish to use the statements in the concluding remarks (question 6) as the topics for discussion.

D. Coping with Criticism (Text, p. 396 and 9.3 and 9.4 in the Activities Manual/Study Guide)

Objective
To practice responding nondefensively to criticism.

NOTE: Picking some students who are "good sports" to role-play some of these situations in front of the class is a good illustration to class members of "real" people responding in this manner. Encourage students to role-play situations that are real to them so that the practice is especially meaningful.

CHAPTER 10

MANAGING INTERPERSONAL CONFLICTS

OBJECTIVES

After studying the material in Chapter Ten of *Looking Out/Looking In,* you should understand:

1. That conflict is natural and inevitable.
2. Five personal styles of conflict:
   a. nonassertive
   b. direct aggression
   c. passive aggression
   d. indirect communication
   e. assertion
3. The characteristics of four types of conflict resolution:
   a. win-lose
   b. lose-lose
   c. compromise
   d. win-win

You should be able to:

1. Describe your personal conflict style by
   a. identifying the conflict style(s) you most commonly use.
   b. evaluating the appropriateness of the style(s).
   c. when necessary, choosing more productive alternatives.
2. Make clear, assertive statements that include
   a. behavior.
   b. your interpretation(s).
   c. feelings.
   d. consequences.
   e. your intentions.
3. Use the win-win problem-solving method by
   a. identifying your unmet needs.
   b. choosing the best time and place to resolve the conflict.
   c. describing your problem and unmet needs clearly and assertively.
   d. considering your partner's point of view.
   e. negotiating a win-win solution whenever possible.
   f. following up on the solution.

NOTES ON CLASS AND STUDENT ACTIVITIES

A. Your Conflict Style (Text, p. 413 and 10.3 in Activities Manual/Study Guide)

Objective

To discover some of the ways we deal with conflict in our lives.

NOTE: If your group is willing, this exercise can be more meaningful if the contents of the completed charts are discussed in small groups.

Perhaps it might help to stress that we can change nothing until we discover something we wish to change. In this context, this activity can be of great importance to the group members. However, care should be taken not to suggest that everyone needs to make changes. This decision needs to be made by the individual.

B. Behaviors and Interpretations (Text, p. 417)

Objectives

1. To encourage both the description of interpretations and the consideration of alternate interpretations.
2. To apply description and interpretation to the clear message format.

C. Name the Feelings (Text, p. 419)

Objective

To recognize the feelings the students would be likely to have in the listed circumstances and to evaluate the effect on the message based on expressing the feeling or not expressing the feeling.

NOTE: An interesting adaptation of this exercise is to have students come up with messages in which strong feelings existed but wouldn't, couldn't, or shouldn't be expressed. Compare and contrast these statements with the ones in the text. Sometimes class members will argue at this point that many more feelings should, could, or would be expressed if others only knew how to express them.

D. Putting Your Message Together (Text, p. 423 and 10.2 in Activities Manual/Study Guide)

Objectives

1. To enable the student to practice expressing a satisfactory message.
2. To enable the student to gain confidence in communicating.
3. To enable the student to get feedback form his or her classmates.

Discussion Questions

1. What were some of the characteristics of satisfactory messages?
2. Were the messages difficult to clarify and express? Why or why not?
3. What were some useful bits of feedback you received?

NOTE: The instructor might wish to write these suggestions on the chalkboard or make photocopies that can be given to each student in the class.

E. Understanding Conflict Styles (Text, p. 426 and 10.1 in Activities Manual/Study Guide)

Objectives

1. To illustrate how conflict styles differ.
2. To apply the concept of conflict style to conflict management.

F. Your Conflict Rituals (Text, p. 428)

Objective

To describe positive and negative conflict rituals.

NOTE: Because conflict rituals are unacknowledged patterns, they are often hard to recognize. Some students need help recognizing the role their behaviors play in the ritual (rather than just blaming the other person for the conflict).

G. Win-Win Solutions and You (Text, p. 445 and 10.4, 10.5 and 10.6 in Activities Manual/Study Guide)

Objective

To apply win-win problem-solving to real situations in which the students are involved.

Discussion Questions

1. Were there difficulties in getting the other people involved in your conflict to try win-win problem-solving?
2. Which of the win-win problem-solving steps seemed the easiest? The most difficult?
3. What kinds of brainstorming ideas were generated? Can you think of more ideas now that you are away form the other people? Can the class think of ideas not generated already?
4. What degree of satisfaction do you have with your first attempt at this method? How could you change that degree of satisfaction?
5. What adaptations may need to be made in different situations to make conflict resolution work for you?

H. Play to Win

(This simulation exercise is not found in the text or the Activities Manual/Study Guide.)

Objective

To demonstrate through a simulation exercise the behaviors different people exhibit when they are in a situation they perceive as conflict or competition or win-lose.

1. Copy the following chart onto the chalkboard.

HOW TO SCORE POINTS

WHEN VOTE IS	GROUP'S SCORE
X X X X	Each group gets +50 pts.
X X X Y	Groups voting X get –100 pts.
	Groups voting Y get +300 pts.

WHEN VOTE IS	GROUP'S SCORE
X X Y Y	Groups voting X get –200 pts.
	Groups voting Y get +200 pts.
X Y Y Y	Groups voting X get –300 pts.
	Groups voting Y get +100 pts.
Y Y Y Y	Each group gets –50 pts.

How to Score

Each of the four groups will cast either an X or Y vote in each round. When the vote is tabulated, one of the preceding five combinations will result, and each group will score accordingly. (At this point, there's apt to be some confusion and questions such as "What are we voting on?" Don't get bogged down here. Everyone will understand the process as you move along.)

2.   Divide your class into four equal groups.
3.   Each group should now move to a corner of the room so that the members can talk together without interruption. There should be no communication—verbal or nonverbal—among groups except when instructions permit.
4.   The group's first task is to decide on how it will make decisions: unanimous agreement, majority vote, decision of the leader, consensus, and so on.
5.   Place this scoreboard where it can be easily seen.

ROUND	VOTE	GROUP I	GROUP II	GROUP III	GROUP IV
1					
2					
(N) 3					
4					
(N) 5	(2X)				
6					
(N) 7					
(N) 8					
9 (10X)					

The object of the game is for each group to score the greatest number of positive points possible.

6.   Notice that there will be nine rounds of voting. In round 5 the scores will be doubled, and in round 9 they'll be multiplied by 10. The (N) that appears before rounds 3, 5, 7, and 8 means that the groups will be allowed to negotiate before voting in those rounds.
7.   Take three minutes for each group to discuss how it will vote in round 1.
8.   After the three minutes, the instructor will collect a ballot from each group. Tally the votes and score for round 1 on the scoreboard.
9.   Repeat the same procedure for the remaining rounds. Before each N round, one negotiator from each team should come to the center of the room, and if they desire, negotiate the next vote or votes.
10.   During negotiations, only negotiators can speak—group members must remain quiet so that they may hear negotiations. There will be time to discuss the vote in the groups after negotiations are completed.

11. After all rounds are completed, discuss the following questions:
    a. Who won the game?
    b. If two groups with the same goal finished with a tie score, did they both win? Did both lose?
    c. In this game, can there be more than one winner? Why?
    d. Did the groups cooperate during the game, helping the others reach their goals, or did they compete by trying to "beat" everyone?
    e. Did the simulation provide opportunities for the students to behave either cooperatively or competitively, or did the students add these as they went along?
    f. What did the students' behavior in this exercise tell them about how they handle conflict in their lives?

NOTE: This game usually illustrates some common ways people act when going after something they want. Most groups assume that to reach the goal they've chosen, they must keep others from reaching theirs, when, in fact, the surest way to succeed is to work together so all groups can score well. As one woman said when shown how all the groups could have reached their goal by cooperating, "But there can't be winners unless there are losers!"

PART THREE

TEST BANK

CHAPTER 1

A FIRST LOOK

1. According to Chapter One the ability to speak and listen effectively ranks higher than the degree earned in helping college graduates find jobs.

   Answer: T   **Type: T**   **Page: 7**   **Recall**

2. Adventurer W. Carl Jackson, who sailed across the Atlantic Ocean alone, said he found life without people had no meaning.

   Answer: T   **Type: T**   **Page: 3**   **Recall**

3. Chapter One cites a professor who claims that informal interpersonal relationships are the most dynamic sources of power in organizations today.

   Answer: T   **Type: T**   **Page: 7**   **Recall**

4. Chapter One claims we can describe characteristics that distinguish competent communicators from less competent ones.

   Answer: T   **Type: T**   **Pages: 32–36**   **Recall**

5. In a story at the beginning of Chapter One, King Frederick II of Germany's experiment was inhumane because he wouldn't let nurses bathe or wash the children.

   Answer: F   **Type: T**   **Page: 3**   **Recall**

6. The opposite of interpersonal communication is mass communication.

   Answer: F   **Type: T**   **Page: 17**   **Knowledge**

7. We learn who we are through communicating.

   Answer: T   **Type: T**   **Page: 6**   **Knowledge**

8. The major difference between impersonal communication and interpersonal communication is the number of people involved.

   Answer: F   **Type: T**   **Pages: 16–17**   **Analysis**

9. You can fill even your instrumental goals through communication.

   Answer: T   **Type: T**   **Page: 7**   **Knowledge**

10. One element of the transactional communication model in the text is "needs."

    Answer: F   **Type: T**   **Page: 8–9**   **Comprehension**

11. Communication competence is a trait that people either possess or lack.

    Answer: F   **Type: T**   **Page: 31**   **Knowledge**

12. Just as judges instruct juries to disregard some statements made in court, we can reverse or erase the effects of communication interactions in everyday life.

    Answer: F   **Type: T**   **Page: 14**   **Comprehension**

13. There is no such thing as the "same" message: words and behavior are different each time they are spoken or performed.

    Answer: T   **Type: T**   **Page: 14**   **Knowledge**

14. It is impossible to repeat the same communication event.

    Answer: T   **Type: T**   **Page: 14**   **Knowledge**

15. The transactional model of communication suggests that communicators usually send and receive messages simultaneously.

    Answer: T   **Type: T**   **Page: 11**   **Knowledge**

16. The transactional model represents communication as static—more like a gallery of still photographs than a motion picture film.

    Answer: F   **Type: T**   **Page: 11**   **Knowledge**

17. The presence or absence of communication can affect both physical and psychological health.

    Answer: T   **Type: T**   **Page: 4**   **Comprehension**

18. Socially isolated people are much more likely to die prematurely than those with strong social ties.

    Answer: T   **Type: T**   **Page: 4**   **Knowledge**

19. Socially isolated people compensate effectively for lack of communication so that their longevity rates are about the same as those of people with strong social ties.

    Answer: F   **Type: T**   **Page: 5**   **Knowledge**

20. According to your text, impersonal communication is dehumanizing and should be avoided.

    Answer: F   **Type: T**   **Page: 20**   **Comprehension**

21. According to your text, effective communicators are able to establish warm relationships with everyone they encounter.

    Answer: F   **Type: T**   **Page: 20**   **Analysis**

22. Communicators who rely on standardized rules to guide their interactions are usually ineffective communicators.

    Answer: T   **Type: T**   **Page: 17**   **Analysis**

23. Your text argues that it is important to react in unique ways to every person we meet and respond to each as a unique individual.

    Answer: F   **Type: T**   **Page: 17**   **Synthesis**

24. As the term is used in your text, communication consists only of messages a sender deliberately conveys.

    Answer: F   **Type: T**   **Page: 13**   **Comprehension**

25. It's impossible to stop communicating.

    Answer: T   **Type: T**   **Page: 14**   **Knowledge**

26. Impersonal communication follows standardized rules for behavior learned from parents, teachers, and other people with whom we interact.

    Answer: T   **Type: T**   **Page: 17**   **Comprehension**

27. Of the communication models described in your text, the linear model most accurately describes the interpersonal communication process.

    Answer: F   **Type: T**   **Pages: 8–12**   **Application**

28. We disclose more to people in interpersonal relationships than in impersonal ones.

    Answer: T   **Type: T**   **Page: 18**   **Knowledge**

29. The best way to study the process of communication is to break it into a series of discrete acts.

    Answer: F   **Type: T**   **Page: 16**   **Analysis**

30. All sexual encounters qualify as a form of interpersonal communication, as the term is used in your text.

    Answer: F   **Type: T**   **Pages: 16–20**   **Synthesis**

31. As the text points out, your goal should be to become a perfect communicator.

    Answer: F   **Type: T**   **Page: 33**   **Comprehension**

32. All you need to develop good communication skills is common sense.

    Answer: F   **Type: T**   **Page: 34**   **Analysis**

33. According to your text, awareness of new ways of communicating is usually sufficient to enable people to communicate more effectively.

    Answer: F   **Type: T**   **Pages: 34**   **Analysis**

34. All two-person interactions qualify as interpersonal communication.

   Answer: F   **Type: T**   **Page: 16**   **Knowledge**

35. Communication is so important that its quantity and quality can affect physical health.

   Answer: T   **Type: T**   **Page: 4**   **Synthesis**

36. When people communicate, they are often both senders and receivers of messages at the same time.

   Answer: T   **Type: T**   **Page: 11**   **Knowledge**

37. According to your text, the axiom "the more communication the better" is true.

   Answer: F   **Type: T**   **Page: 15**   **Knowledge**

38. Your text promises that if you communicate skillfully enough, you should be able to solve every problem you encounter.

   Answer: F   **Type: T**   **Page: 16**   **Knowledge**

39. In impersonal communication we treat others as individuals.

   Answer: F   **Type: T**   **Page: 16**   **Knowledge**

40. Fortunately, just knowing about a communication skill makes us able to put it into practice.

   Answer: F   **Type: T**   **Page: 34**   **Comprehension**

41. The absence of communication can affect physical health in extremely negative ways.

   Answer: T   **Type: T**   **Page: 4**   **Knowledge**

42. Almost all verbal messages have a content dimension as well as convey relational information.

   Answer: T   **Type: T**   **Page: 24**   **Comprehension**

43. Your text argues that the physical setting in which communication takes place is not useful as a basis for categorizing whether the interaction is interpersonal or impersonal.

   Answer: T   **Type: T**   **Page: 20**   **Knowledge**

44. In symmetrical relationships, the partners seek an equal amount of control.

   Answer: T   **Type: T**   **Page: 27**   **Knowledge**

45. The person who exercises the greatest amount of conversational control doesn't always make the decisions in interpersonal relationships.

   Answer: T   **Type: T**   **Page: 26**   **Comprehension**

46. Whenever we discuss our mutual relationship with the other person, we are meta-communicating.

    Answer: T   **Type: T**   **Page: 28**   **Synthesis**

47. In complementary relationships, the distribution of power is unequal.

    Answer: T   **Type: T**   **Page: 27**   **Knowledge**

48. According to Chapter One, interpersonal relationships are associations in which the parties meet each other's social needs to a greater or lesser degree.

    Answer: T   **Type: T**   **Pages: 6, 17**   **Knowledge**

49. Relational dimensions of messages make statements about how the parties feel toward one another.

    Answer: T   **Type: T**   **Page: 26**   **Knowledge**

50. A competent communicator strives for symmetrical relationships in all interpersonal encounters.

    Answer: F   **Type: T**   **Pages: 27,31**   **Synthesis**

51. Relational messages are frequently nonverbal.

    Answer: T   **Type: T**   **Pages: 24–26**   **Comprehension**

52. Metacommunication is a destructive substitute for real communication.

    Answer: F   **Type: T**   **Page: 28**   **Comprehension**

53. In symmetrical relationships the parties agree to take turns making decisions.

    Answer: F   **Type: T**   **Page: 27**   **Knowledge**

54. Parallel relationships are characterized by an equal sharing of power in each situation.

    Answer: F   **Type: T**   **Page: 27**   **Knowledge**

55. Lovers who argue constantly cease to have an interpersonal relationship.

    Answer: F   **Type: T**   **Pages: 17, 26**   **Analysis**

56. Affinity is defined as the degree to which two or more people like or appreciate one another.

    Answer: T   **Type: T**   **Page: 26**   **Knowledge**

57. There are two types of relational control: decision control and conversational control.

    Answer: T   **Type: T**   **Page: 26**   **Knowledge**

58. In relationships that are characterized by symmetry, the partners are both trying to dominate the other.

    Answer: F   **Type: T**   **Page: 27**   **Knowledge**

59. In complementary relationships one partner exercises control and the other goes along.

   Answer: T   **Type: T**   **Page: 27**   **Knowledge**

60. Complementary relationships are the most satisfying type of relationship.

   Answer: F   **Type: T**   **Page: 27**   **Analysis**

61. One story in Chapter One describes how the children in Frederick II of Germany's experiment

   a. became great communicators.
   b. were loved because of their smiles and laughter.
   c. died from lack of human communication.
   d. found only sadness in their homes because of poor communication.
   e. had parents who were effective communicators.

   Answer: c   **Type: M**   **Page: 3**   **Recall**

62. In a story in Chapter One, Emperor Frederick II of Germany conducted an experiment with children to find out

   a. which language they would speak.
   b. how they could survive on their own.
   c. how parents can teach communication.
   d. which side of their brains was used more often.
   e. if they could talk before they learned to walk.

   Answer: a   **Type: M**   **Page: 3**   **Recall**

63. When the famous "Wild Boy of Aveyron" was discovered, he

   a. lacked any identity as a human being.
   b. spoke an unintelligible language.
   c. had amazing social skills.
   d. related well with animals in the zoo.
   e. could use sign language only.

   Answer: a   **Type: M**   **Page: 5**   **Recall**

64. "The Electronic Block Party" in Chapter One describes how

   a. men spend time on the Internet and neglect their marriages.
   b. neighbors connected themselves by e-mail.
   c. teens organized a street party electronically.
   d. divorce rates have gone up since the Internet has been around.
   e. romantic relationships bloom after exchanging e-mail messages.

   Answer: b   **Type: M**   **Page: 21**   **Recall**

65. The relational dimension of the problem between Macon and Muriel in the "Accidental Tourist" Communication Transcript involved

    a. sex.
    b. money.
    c. time together.
    d. television.
    e. commitment.

    Answer: e   **Type: M**   **Page: 29**   **Recall**

66. In the "Accidental Tourist" Communication Transcript in Chapter One, Macon

    a. takes Muriel to Paris to get married.
    b. fights with Muriel about her addiction to soap operas.
    c. works out a problem involving beer drinking and TV watching.
    d. has to take a trip to find out he has an interpersonal relationship.
    e. wants to talk about Alexander's math skill.

    Answer: e   **Type: M**   **Page: 29**   **Recall**

67. In Chapter One Deborah Tannen claims that

    a. electronic mail can transform the quality of relationships.
    b. the typical American man's language that avoids "wasting time" with small talk works well in business dealings with most Japanese.
    c. American tourists are better at bargaining because of their direct, no-nonsense language.
    d. women are more likely than men to "take back" what they say with words.
    e. all of the above are claimed by Tannen.

    Answer: a   **Type: M**   **Page: 20**   **Recall**

68. In the Looking at Diversity reading in Chapter One, Daria Muse says that a big part of communicating well is

    a. speaking more than one language.
    b. staying true to your own communication style.
    c. understanding communication models.
    d. adjusting.
    e. having experiences in more than one culture.

    Answer: d   **Type: M**   **Page: 37**   **Recall**

69. Psychologist Abraham Maslow suggests that the most basic human needs

    a. are invented by other psychologists.
    b. must be satisfied before we concern ourselves with other ones.
    c. are proof that animals ascended from lower animal forms.
    d. prove the existence of a superior being.
    e. are generated by others in interpersonal interaction.

    Answer: b   **Type: M**   **Page: 7**   **Knowledge**

70. All of the following elements are included in the communication model introduced in Chapter One except

    a. feedback.
    b. environment.
    c. channel.
    d. control.
    e. noise.

    Answer: d   **Type: M**   **Pages: 8–9**   **Knowledge**

71. All of the following are involved in learning to perform effective communication skills effectively except

    a. awareness.
    b. prowess.
    c. awkwardness.
    d. skillfulness.
    e. integration.

    Answer: b   **Type: M**   **Page: 34**   **Knowledge**

72. The environments that communicators occupy are

    a. fields of experience that help them understand others' behavior.
    b. gaps that make common understanding impossible.
    c. the places where they stand or sit when they communicate.
    d. the attitudes they have about nature.
    e. the space that they require to communicate effectively.

    Answer: a   **Type: M**   **Page: 9**   **Knowledge**

73. "Decoding" is the process whereby

    a. we put our thoughts into words.
    b. we make sense out of the messages sent by others.
    c. we engage others in conversation.
    d. we choose the appropriate way to send messages.
    e. we create new ways of teaching reading and communication to children.

    Answer: b   **Type: M**   **Page: 8**   **Knowledge**

74. When Jeb decides that his grandson didn't mean to insult him by using slang, Jeb has

    a. encoded.
    b. integrated.
    c. related.
    d. decoded.
    e. metacommunicated.

    Answer: d   **Type: M**   **Page: 8**   **Analysis**

75. Almost all messages have

    a. a content dimension.
    b. a relational dimension.
    c. both content and relational dimensions.
    d. no dimensions unless the communicators intend them to.

    Answer: c   **Type: M**   **Page: 24**   **Comprehension**

76. The three types of noise that can block communication are

    a. loud, moderate, and soft.
    b. mass communicational, personal, and transactional.
    c. external, physiological, and psychological.
    d. sociological, psychological, and communicational.
    e. linear, interactional, and transactional.

    Answer: c   **Type: M**   **Pages: 8–9**   **Knowledge**

77. Skillful, integrated communicators are characterized by

    a. a conscious focus on communicating effectively.
    b. a greater degree of sociability.
    c. communicating competently without needing to think constantly about how to behave.
    d. exposure to a wide range of communication styles.
    e. others helping them out.

    Answer: c   **Type: M**   **Page: 34**   **Comprehension**

78. Research has shown that competent communicators achieve effectiveness by

    a. using the same types of behavior in a wide variety of situations.
    b. developing large vocabularies.
    c. apologizing when they offend others.
    d. giving lots of feedback.
    e. adjusting their behaviors to the person and situation.

    Answer: e   **Type: M**   **Pages: 31–36**   **Synthesis**

79. According to your text, feedback is

    a. vastly overrated as a communication tool.
    b. both verbal and nonverbal.
    c. not present in impersonal communication.
    d. only possible when communicators speak the same language.
    e. all of the above.

    Answer: b   **Type: M**   **Page: 10**   **Analysis**

80. When you carefully plan the words you use to avoid offending someone, you are

    a. decoding.
    b. encoding.
    c. self-actualizing.
    d. communicating impersonally.
    e. all of the above.

    Answer: b   **Type: M**   **Page: 8**   **Comprehension**

81. A family arguing about whether to spend the weekend together or apart might be trying to satisfy what social need?

    a. companionship
    b. affection
    c. control
    d. all of the above
    e. none of the above

    Answer: d   **Type: M**   **Page: 6**   **Application**

82. You want to let a close friend know how much she/he means to you in a way that is sincere and doesn't embarrass either of you. Following the advice on communication competence in your text, you would

    a. follow the approach that you saw another friend use successfully, assuming it would work for you.
    b. avoid sending any message until you were sure it would be well received.
    c. try to follow exactly the approach you used successfully with others in the past.
    d. react in the way that first occurred to you.
    e. consider a variety of alternatives, choosing the one that you think will be most successful under these circumstances.

    Answer: e   **Type: M**   **Page: 33**   **Evaluation**

83. Maslow's hierarchy of needs is important to the study of interpersonal communication because

    a. we all have needs.
    b. we can't understand our needs without communication.
    c. communication can help us meet each of the needs.
    d. communication was Maslow's greatest need.
    e. the need for communication is the sixth "hidden" need.

    Answer: c   **Type: M**   **Page: 8**   **Comprehension**

84. Noise in the communication process is

    a. more than one communicator talking at a time.
    b. the nonverbal behaviors that accompany communication.
    c. the process of maintaining direct eye contact or not.
    d. the process of translating thoughts into words.
    e. any force that interferes with effective communication.

    Answer: e   **Type: M**   **Page: 8**   **Knowledge**

85. Which of the following is most clearly an example of interpersonal communication?

    a. Gaudet buys a sweater from the clerk.
    b. Rich invites the team to a party.
    c. Royce asks Jane about her sick child.
    d. Trent pleads for the class to vote.

    Answer: c   **Type: M**   **Pages: 16–18**   **Analysis**

86. In order for communication to take place, the sender and receiver need to be

    a. experiencing identical environments.
    b. alone together.
    c. looking at each other so that eye contact can be made.
    d. in the absence of all "noise."
    e. sending and receiving any type of message.

    Answer: e   **Type: M**   **Page: 11**   **Analysis**

87. Some of the social needs we strive to fulfill by communicating are

    a. encoding and decoding.
    b. control and affection.
    c. empathy and sympathy.
    d. talking and listening.
    e. communicating both verbally and nonverbally.

    Answer: b   **Type: M**   **Page: 6**   **Comprehension**

88. Some of the characteristics that make relationships more interpersonal than impersonal are

    a. higher levels of self-disclosure and intimacy.
    b. intrinsic rewards and proximity.
    c. scarcity, disclosure and intimacy.
    d. uniqueness, irreplaceability, and interdependence.

    Answer: d   **Type: M**   **Pages: 17–18**   **Comprehension**

89. Integrated communicators express themselves in skillful ways because

    a. their communication is a self-conscious act.
    b. they have had more experience.
    c. they have internalized effective behavior.
    d. skills are basic to communication.
    e. others help them out.

    Answer: c   **Type: M**   **Page: 34**   **Comprehension**

90. Effective communicators have been found to

    a. have a consistent set of five behaviors they can call up at will.
    b. have a wide range of behaviors from which to choose.
    c. exhibit behaviors that are predictable by their partners.
    d. exhibit unique behaviors more often than less effective communicators.
    e. frequently rehearse about 20 behaviors until they get them right for any interaction.

    Answer: b   **Type: M**   **Page: 32**   **Comprehension**

91. When you pay attention to your behavior in relationships, you are

    a. unlikely to pay attention to others.
    b. too uptight.
    c. probably ego-driven.
    d. self-monitoring.
    e. intrinsic.

    Answer: d   **Type: M**   **Page: 35**   **Knowledge**

92. Identity and communication are related in that we

    a. gain an idea of who we are from the way others communicate with us.
    b. are drawn to communicators who test and challenge our identity.
    c. find others' identities become our own through communication.
    d. control communication with our identity.

    Answer: a   **Type: M**   **Page: 5**   **Comprehension**

93. Which is an example of "noise" as the term is defined in your text?

    a. a jet flying low overhead while you're trying to talk
    b. a headache that interferes with your listening
    c. feelings of anger directed toward a partner
    d. preoccupation with another topic during a lecture
    e. all of the above

    Answer: e   **Type: M**   **Pages: 8–9**   **Application**

94. Which is an example of "noise" as the term is defined in your text?

    a. a jet flying low in the desert
    b. a headache on a TV commercial
    c. feeling happy
    d. preoccupation with another topic during a lecture

    Answer: d   **Type: M**   **Page: 8–9**   **Application**

95. Decoding is the same as

    a. a self-fulfilling prophecy.
    b. an irrational belief.
    c. interpreting.
    d. encoding.
    e. communication environment.

    Answer: c   **Type: M**   **Page: 8**   **Comprehension**

96. Two friends communicating would most likely be

    a. taking turns sending and receiving messages.
    b. primarily sending messages.
    c. primarily receiving messages.
    d. sending and receiving messages at the same time.
    e. neither sending nor receiving messages.

    Answer: d   **Type: M**   **Page: 11**   **Application**

97. Feedback is

    a. the discernible response of a receiver to a sender's message.
    b. a smile you give to the joke teller.
    c. the R.S.V.P. you give when you receive an invitation.
    d. the frown on your boss's face when you say you need time off.
    e. all of the above may be examples of feedback.

    Answer: e   **Type: M**   **Page: 10**   **Analysis**

98. Feedback is

    a. the discernible response of a receiver to a sender's message.
    b. encoding your message.
    c. writing an invitation to a party.
    d. telling your boss you need time off.

    Answer: a   **Type: M**   **Page: 10**   **Analysis**

99. When you call three of your friends in one night to avoid studying, you are communicating to fulfill the social need of

    a. escape.
    b. control.
    c. affection.
    d. companionship.
    e. pleasure.

    Answer: a   **Type: M**   **Page: 6**   **Application**

100. Which of the following is an example of feedback?

 a. silence from a partner
 b. words spoken by a partner
 c. eye contact from a partner
 d. all of the above
 e. none of the above

Answer: d **Type: M** **Page: 10** **Application**

101. Which of the following is a channel for communication?

 a. touching
 b. writing
 c. gesturing
 d. talking
 e. all of the above

Answer: e **Type: M** **Pages: 8** **Comprehension**

102. Which of the following is a channel for communication?

 a. escape
 b. control
 c. inclusion
 d. esteem
 e. touch

Answer: e **Type: M** **Page: 8** **Comprehension**

103. Maslow's hierarchy of human needs lists self-actualization as the highest need. What need is the most fundamental, or the lowest, in Maslow's hierarchy?

 a. safety
 b. psychological
 c. social
 d. esteem
 e. physical

Answer: e **Type: M** **Page: 7** **Comprehension**

104. Interpersonal relationships

 a. develop unique qualities.
 b. are mostly alike.
 c. follow the same basic rules about how control is distributed between communicators.
 d. have more relational talk than content talk.
 e. are none of the above.

Answer: a **Type: M** **Page: 17** **Comprehension**

105. Relational dimensions of a message

    a. deal with one or more social needs.
    b. make statements about how the parties feel toward one another.
    c. are usually expressed nonverbally.
    d. all of the above
    e. none of the above

    Answer: d   **Type: M**   **Page: 24**   **Comprehension**

106. Relational dimensions of messages

    a. must deal with individual problems and needs.
    b. must make statements about facts and thoughts.
    c. are usually expressed verbally.
    d. all of the above
    e. none of the above

    Answer: e   **Type: M**   **Page: 24**   **Comprehension**

107. When you are unsure of the relational dimension of a message, it is best to

    a. go with the verbal interpretation.
    b. go with the nonverbal interpretation.
    c. metacommunicate.
    d. listen for all the possible messages.
    e. go back to the content dimension of the message for meaning.

    Answer: c   **Type: M**   **Page: 28**   **Comprehension**

108. Your roommate says, "It's your turn to take out the trash" in a demanding tone of voice. If you want to find out the relational dimension of the message, you should

    a. remind your roommate nicely that you took it out last night.
    b. point out the tone of voice and ask if your roommate is upset with you.
    c. negotiate other ways of dealing with the trash problem.
    d. ask your roommate's friends to explain the real problem.
    e. point out how defensive your roommate sounds.

    Answer: b   **Type: M**   **Page: 28**   **Application**

109. According to Chapter One, the two dimensions of most messages are

    a. content and relational.
    b. verbal and contextual.
    c. semantic and syntactic.
    d. defensive and supportive.
    e. controlling and affecting.

    Answer: a   **Type: M**   **Page: 24**   **Knowledge**

110. In any relationship, the power to determine what will happen in the relationship is a type of relational control called

    a. decision control.
    b. conversational control.
    c. distributional control.
    d. powerful control.
    e. context control.

    Answer: a   **Type: M**   **Page: 26**   **Knowledge**

111. The type of relationship where both parties struggle to exercise control is a _____ relationship.

    a. symmetrical
    b. doomed
    c. parallel
    d. complementary
    e. none of the above

    Answer: a   **Type: M**   **Page: 31**   **Knowledge**

112. Talking the most, interrupting the other person, and changing the topic most often are all common indicators of

    a. conversational control.
    b. decision control.
    c. powerful control.
    d. context control.
    e. distributional control.

    Answer: a   **Type: M**   **Page: 30**   **Knowledge**

113. Relational dimensions of messages

    a. deal with one or more social needs.
    b. make statements about how the parties feel toward one another.
    c. are usually expressed nonverbally.
    d. all of the above
    e. none of the above

    Answer: d   **Type: M**   **Page: 24**   **Comprehension**

114. Relational dimensions of messages

    a. deal with individual problems and needs.
    b. make statements about facts and thoughts.
    c. are usually expressed verbally.
    d. are usually expressed nonverbally.
    e. tell us the content of the message.

    Answer: d   **Type: M**   **Page: 24**   **Comprehension**

115. Parallel relationships are characterized by

    a. a balance of power.
    b. equal power in each instance.
    c. one party assuming the "one-up" position.
    d. one party assuming the "one-down" position.
    e. conversational control.

Answer: a   **Type: M**   **Page: 27**   **Comprehension**

116. Whenever we discuss a relationship with others, we are

    a. arguing.
    b. improving our relationship.
    c. self-disclosing.
    d. metacommunicating.
    e. receiving double messages.

Answer: d   **Type: M**   **Page: 28**   **Knowledge**

117. The degree to which the partners in an interpersonal relationship like or appreciate one another is called

    a. appreciation.
    b. self-respect.
    c. the communication of honesty.
    d. affinity.
    e. the like-love phenomenon.

Answer: d   **Type: M**   **Page: 26**   **Knowledge**

118. The ability to construct a variety of different frameworks for viewing an issue is termed

    a. feedback framework.
    b. cognitive complexity.
    c. communication competence.
    d. metacommunicating
    e. integration.

Answer: b   **Type: M**   **Page: 35**   **Knowledge**

119. Which of the following is true about Computer Mediated Communication (CMC) as it relates to interpersonal communication?

    a. CMC can enhance the quantity and quality of interpersonal communication.
    b. CMC distances us from one another.
    c. CMC replaces interpersonal communication.
    d. CMC is an inferior form of communication to interpersonal communication.

Answer: a   **Type: M**   **Page: 19**   **Comprehension**

INSTRUCTIONS for questions 120–124: Match each of the statements below with the element of the communication model it illustrates most clearly.

    a. receiver
    b. environment
    c. behavior
    d. message
    e. psychological noise

120. An unintentional action that is observed

    Answer: c   **Type: Matching**   **Page: 8**   **Application**

121. Alex listens to a speech.

    Answer: a   **Type: Matching**   **Page: 8**   **Application**

122. Your friend's religion is different from yours, but you went to the same high school and college.

    Answer: b   **Type: Matching**   **Page: 9**   **Evaluation**

123. You are worried about how you'll get home today while your boss is giving the quarterly report.

    Answer: e   **Type: Matching**   **Page: 9**   **Application**

124. Alec tells Chan directly: "Your snoring bothers me."

    Answer: d   **Type: Matching**   **Page: 8**   **Application**

INSTRUCTIONS for questions 125–129: Match each of the statements below with the element of the communication model it illustrates most clearly.

    a. feedback
    b. external noise
    c. decoding
    d. channel
    e. sender

125. Chris is silent when you ask him to fix your car.

    Answer: a   **Type: Matching**   **Page: 10**   **Application**

126. Deciding what Dana meant by that scowl

    Answer: c   **Type: Matching**   **Page: 8**   **Application**

127. Ellen is the person who takes flowers for the office to the boss in the hospital.

    Answer: e   **Type: Matching**   **Page: 8**   **Evaluation**

128. Your classmate repeatedly clicks his pen during the lecture.

    Answer: b   **Type: Matching**   **Page: 9**   **Application**

129.   You write your friend a note instead of calling her.

      Answer: d   **Type: Matching**   **Page: 8**   **Application**

INSTRUCTIONS for questions 130–134: Match the descriptions of relationships below with the terms they best describe.

    a. complementary
    b. one-down
    c. one-up
    d. parallel
    e. symmetrical

130.   Type of relationship in which one party exercises control and the other is willing to go along

      Answer: a   **Type: Matching**   **Page: 27**   **Knowledge**

131.   Type of relationship in which all decisions are made jointly

      Answer: e   **Type: Matching**   **Page: 27**   **Knowledge**

132.   The partner in a relationship who is the controller

      Answer: c   **Type: Matching**   **Page: 27**   **Knowledge**

133.   The partner in a relationship who is the one being controlled

      Answer: b   **Type: Matching**   **Page: 27**   **Knowledge**

134.   Type of relationship in which there is a balance of power

      Answer: d   **Type: Matching**   **Page: 27**   **Knowledge**

135.   Describe an interpersonal communication incident from your experience, identifying at least five elements of the transactional model of communication shown in *Looking Out/ Looking In.*

      Answer   **Type: E**   **Pages: 8–12**   **Synthesis**

136.   Using the characteristics of "Communication Competence: What makes an effective communicator?" in Chapter One, evaluate your communication competence in the context of one interpersonal relationship in which you are involved. Discuss the range of behaviors in which you engage, your ability to choose the most appropriate behavior, your skill in performing certain behaviors, and your commitment to the relationship. Be sure to discuss this relationally, involving the behaviors of the other person, and how you adapt or fail to adapt to them.

      Answer   **Type: E**   **Pages: 30–36**   **Synthesis**

137.   Using your own experiences as examples, explain the difference between interpersonal communication and impersonal communication.

      Answer   **Type: E**   **Pages: 16–18**   **Application**

138. Describe how you have filled each of the social needs listed in Chapter One through interpersonal communication.

    Answer   **Type: E**   **Page: 6**   **Application**

139. Explain the concept of feedback. First, define it according to its role in the transactional model of communication in Chapter One. Next, give interpersonal examples of both effective and ineffective uses of feedback from your own experiences.

    Answer   **Type: E**   **Page: 10**   **Evaluation**

140. Define the three types of relational messages presented in Chapter One and illustrate each of them with examples from your life.

    Answer   **Type: E**   **Page: 26**   **Application**

141. Describe an interpersonal relationship that you are in that involves at least some degree of Computer Mediated Communication (CMC). List the limitations of CMC in maintaining this relationship. Lastly, describe the ways in which CMC enhances the quantity and/or quality of this relationship.

    Answer   **Type: E**   **Page: 19**   **Application**

CHAPTER 2

COMMUNICATION AND IDENTITY: THE SELF AND MESSAGES

1. "Cipher in the Snow" in Chapter Two is a story about the death of a young boy.

   Answer: T   **Type: T**   **Pages: 54–55**   **Recall**

2. In an impression management study described in Chapter Two, subjects expressed facial disgust when eating very salty sandwiches only when another person was present.

   Answer: T   **Type: T**   **Page: 79**   **Recall**

3. The influence of significant others becomes less powerful as we grow older.

   Answer: T   **Type: T**   **Page: 51**   **Comprehension**

4. The self-concept is extremely resistant to change.

   Answer: T   **Type: T**   **Page: 59**   **Comprehension**

5. While the self may change radically, the self-concept tends to remain static.

   Answer: T   **Type: T**   **Page: 59**   **Comprehension**

6. Once formed, a self-concept rarely, if ever, changes.

   Answer: F   **Type: T**   **Page: 59**   **Comprehension**

7. In many cases a self-concept is based on data which may have been true at one time, but are now obsolete.

   Answer: T   **Type: T**   **Page: 56**   **Knowledge**

8. The influence of significant others becomes less powerful as people grow older.

   Answer: T   **Type: T**   **Page: 52**   **Knowledge**

9. The self-concept is extremely subjective, being almost totally a product of interaction with others.

   Answer: T   **Type: T**   **Page: 53**   **Comprehension**

10. You are unlikely to reveal all of the perceived self to another person.

    Answer: T   **Type: T**   **Page: 72**   **Knowledge**

11. People with high self-concepts can handle every conflict productively.
    Answer: F   **Type: T**   **Page: 58**   **Comprehension**

12. People who think highly of themselves are likely to think highly of others too.
    Answer: T   **Type: T**   **Page: 58**   **Knowledge**

13. Our concept of self is shaped by the culture in which we have been reared.
    Answer: T   **Type: T**   **Page: 61**   **Synthesis**

14. The self-concept is a relatively stable set of perceptions you hold of yourself.
    Answer: T   **Type: T**   **Page: 46**   **Knowledge**

15. The self-concept is a constantly changing set of perceptions that others have of you.
    Answer: F   **Type: T**   **Page: 46**   **Knowledge**

16. Both verbal and nonverbal messages contribute to a developing self-concept.
    Answer: T   **Type: T**   **Page: 50**   **Synthesis**

17. Behaviors like tone of voice and touch can contribute to the development of the self-concept, even before the age of one.
    Answer: T   **Type: T**   **Page: 50**   **Knowledge**

18. People who don't like themselves are likely to believe that others don't like them either.
    Answer: T   **Type: T**   **Page: 58**   **Knowledge**

19. The tendency to cling to an outmoded self-perception holds only when the new image would be less favorable than the old one.
    Answer: F   **Type: T**   **Page: 56**   **Comprehension**

20. All inaccurate self-concepts are overly negative.
    Answer: F   **Type: T**   **Page: 56**   **Knowledge**

21. It is possible to have a more favorable image of yourself than the objective facts or the opinions of others warrant.
    Answer: T   **Type: T**   **Page: 56**   **Knowledge**

22. The person you believe yourself to be in moments of honesty is called the presenting self.
    Answer: F   **Type: T**   **Page: 72**   **Knowledge**

23. The face you try to show to others is called the perceived self.
    Answer: F   **Type: T**   **Page: 72**   **Knowledge**

24. The text advises that we shouldn't acknowledge our strengths because we will develop overly positive, distorted self-concepts.

    Answer: F   **Type: T**   **Page: 68**   **Comprehension**

25. Most Western cultures have what is called a collective identity.

    Answer: F   **Type: T**   **Page: 61**   **Knowledge**

26. The self-concept begins to develop sometime between the ages of two and four years.

    Answer: F   **Type: T**   **Page: 49**   **Knowledge**

27. Fortunately, unintentional messages do not affect the self-concept.

    Answer: F   **Type: T**   **Page: 52**   **Comprehension**

28. Nonverbal behaviors play a big role in managing impressions.

    Answer: T   **Type: T**   **Page: 82**   **Knowledge**

29. The process of impression management can result in dishonest behavior.

    Answer: T   **Type: T**   **Page: 86**   **Knowledge**

30. Most researchers agree that we are born with a self-concept.

    Answer: F   **Type: T**   **Page: 49**   **Knowledge**

31. According to your text, the self-concept influences much of our communication behavior.

    Answer: T   **Type: T**   **Page: 67**   **Knowledge**

32. According to your text, the self-concept is shaped by communication.

    Answer: T   **Type: T**   **Pages: 48–52**   **Knowledge**

33. According to your text, the self-concept is influenced by significant others from both the past and present.

    Answer: T   **Type: T**   **Page: 56**   **Comprehension**

34. Luckily, communication from others does not affect our self-concept.

    Answer: F   **Type: T**   **Pages: 50–52**   **Comprehension**

35. You shouldn't listen to the "boosters" and "busters" others give you since your self-concept is only your view of yourself.

    Answer: F   **Type: T**   **Page: 49**   **Comprehension**

36. All communication behavior is aimed at making impressions.

    Answer: F   **Type: T**   **Page: 75**   **Comprehension**

37. In the U.S. Census Bureau example in Chapter Two, clerks

    a. punched more cards if they weren't told an expected number.
    b. developed self-concept problems from too much exposure to numbers.
    c. began to see themselves just as "numbers" in the U.S.
    d. refused to calculate the census if given too many cards.
    e. made self-concept development cards for others.

    Answer: a   **Type: M**   **Page: 67**   **Recall**

38. In the example of schoolchildren taken from the book *Pygmalion in the Classroom*

    a. the less intelligent children performed better than expected.
    b. the more intelligent children performed better than expected.
    c. the children teachers predicted would do better, did so.
    d. all the children performed the same because they had similar self-concepts.
    e. teachers improved their self-concepts by working with good children.

    Answer: c   **Type: M**   **Page: 66**   **Recall**

39. In Chapter Two, "Will the Real Me Please Stand Up?" concerned

    a. a woman whose self-concept was so low that she couldn't stand up to give a speech.
    b. a woman torn between the different aspects of her self-concept.
    c. two women whose self-concepts were amazingly similar.
    d. a woman who struggled to stand again after a serious accident that affected her self-concept.
    e. all women trying to stand up to prejudice against their sex that inevitably affects self-concepts.

    Answer: b   **Type: M**   **Pages: 80–81**   **Recall**

40. "Will the Real Me Please Stand Up?" dealt with

    a. a woman who overcame a physical handicap.
    b. a girl who hung around photo galleries having her picture taken.
    c. a person who was trying to overcome society's demands and become herself.
    d. the foolishness of television situation comedies.
    e. the need for assertiveness when meeting strangers.

    Answer: c   **Type: M**   **Page: 80–81**   **Recall**

41. According to the author, the boy in "Cipher in the Snow" died

    a. when he was unable to communicate how cold he was.
    b. after being late for the school bus one winter morning.
    c. after his parents repeatedly beat him.
    d. because he believed he was a "nothing."
    e. of a brain tumor.

    Answer: d   **Type: M**   **Pages: 54–55**   **Recall**

42. Which of the following is definitely not an example of a self-fulfilling prophecy?

   a. A child fails a test after hearing her teacher tell her mother that she is an underachiever.
   b. A student who previously complained of stage fright loses his place during a class speech and can't go on.
   c. A husband reluctantly agrees, with reservations, to his wife's request that they spend the holiday visiting Disneyland. He has a terrible time.
   d. Both b and c above qualify as examples of self-fulfilling prophecies.
   e. All of the above qualify as examples of self-fulfilling prophecies.

   Answer: e   **Type: M**   **Pages: 64–66**   **Analysis**

43. All of the following are methods you could use to make your self-concept more realistic except :

   a. Share your perception of yourself with a friend.
   b. Try to engage in more accurate self-talk.
   c. Make an effort to recognize more "ego buster" messages.
   d. Pay less attention to your past and more attention to your present behavior.

   Answer: c   **Type: M**   **Page: 69**   **Analysis**

44. All of the following are true of the self-concept except that

   a. it is objective.
   b. it is changing.
   c. it is, in part, a product of interaction with others.
   d. it is, in part, a product of our early childhood experience.
   e. it can be changed.

   Answer: a   **Type: M**   **Page: 53**   **Comprehension**

45. The term "self-concept" refers to

   a. the sum of one's physiological, social, and psychological attributes as perceived by an impartial observer.
   b. the way an individual believes others perceive her/him.
   c. the total of an individual's beliefs about his/her physical characteristics, intelligence, aptitudes, and social skills.
   d. the sum of one's psychological, social, and physical attributes as perceived by a significant other.
   e. none of the above.

   Answer: c   **Type: M**   **Page: 46**   **Comprehension**

46. A "significant other" is best defined as

   a. a powerful adult.
   b. a person who has affected one's self-concept.
   c. a totally supportive person.
   d. an extremely negative influence.
   e. all of the above.

   Answer: b   **Type: M**   **Page: 51**   **Comprehension**

47. According to your text, "ego-boosters and busters" are

    a. examples of how people ruin their self-concepts by taking drugs.
    b. people or words that influence the self-concept positively or negatively.
    c. the two essential elements of self-concept development.
    d. ways to predict how children will become good or bad readers.
    e. intentionally vague labels we give to mask true self-concepts.

    Answer: b   **Type: M**   **Page: 49**   **Knowledge**

48. The higher levels of anxiety about speaking out in countries such as China, Korea, and Japan indicate that

    a. shyness is a problem in some cultures.
    b. reticence is valued in these cultures.
    c. assertiveness has not been taught correctly.
    d. the individualistic identity is better than the collective one.
    e. children are not taught public speaking in these countries.

    Answer: b   **Type: M**   **Page: 61**   **Comprehension**

49. People who are high self-monitors

    a. are much more aware of their impression management behavior than others.
    b. express what they are feeling without paying much attention to the impression their behavior creates.
    c. are usually bad actors.
    d. are not usually good "people readers."
    e. are easier to "read" than low self-monitors.

    Answer: a   **Type: M**   **Page: 78**   **Comprehension**

50. The relatively stable set of perceptions you hold of yourself is called your

    a. self-concept.
    b. interpersonal self.
    c. perceptual bias.
    d. self-feedback.
    e. self-orientation.

    Answer: a   **Type: M**   **Page: 46**   **Knowledge**

51. A self-fulfilling prophecy is

    a. an accurate prediction about another's behavior, based on background knowledge.
    b. a prediction about one's own behavior, based on past experience.
    c. a prediction which affects the outcome of one's own or another's behavior.
    d. a mistaken prediction which fails to occur.
    e. none of the above.

    Answer: c   **Type: M**   **Page: 64**   **Comprehension**

52. In individualistic cultures, a view of self would involve all of the following except

    a. self-sufficiency.
    b. high value on tradition.
    c. high value on equality.
    d. high value on change.
    e. personal credit or blame.

    Answer: b   **Type: M**   **Page: 61**   **Comprehension**

53. A self-fulfilling prophecy is, in part,

    a. a way to discover how to act in the future.
    b. a test one can take to gauge one's self-concept.
    c. a way to discover the "real you."
    d. a prediction which affects behavior.
    e. a process to help you feel more satisfied with relationships.

    Answer: d   **Type: M**   **Page: 64**   **Comprehension**

54. Someone who is a "significant other" is

    a. "socially" conscious.
    b. a person whose opinion we especially value.
    c. always a supportive person.
    d. a person with significant goals.

    Answer: b   **Type: M**   **Page: 51**   **Knowledge**

55. A person whose opinions of you matter deeply is called a(n)

    a. all-knowing adult.
    b. superior.
    c. nonverbal influence.
    d. significant other.
    e. dyad.

    Answer: d   **Type: M**   **Page: 51**   **Comprehension**

56. The self-concept

    a. causes all of our communication behavior.
    b. prevents low self-esteem.
    c. is partially shaped by significant others from our past.
    d. is the way significant others will view us in the future.

    Answer: c   **Type: M**   **Page: 46**   **Synthesis**

57. If you want to change your self-concept, you should

    a. have realistic expectations and perceptions.
    b. ask others to send you only positive messages.
    c. take yourself less seriously.
    d. It is not possible to change the self-concept.

    Answer: a   **Type: M**   **Pages: 68–70**   **Comprehension**

58. People who have low self-esteem

    a. are likely to approve of others.
    b. perform well when being watched.
    c. work harder for critical people.
    d. expect to be rejected by others.
    e. had traumatic childhoods.

    Answer: d   **Type: M**   **Page: 58**   **Comprehension**

59. People who have high self-esteem

    a. expect to be accepted by others.
    b. have less of a need to work hard for people who demand high standards.
    c. are unable to defend themselves against negative comments.
    d. don't perform well when being watched.

    Answer: a   **Type: M**   **Page: 58**   **Comprehension**

60. The process of judging ourselves by how we think others evaluate or judge us is called

    a. the "sell-out" self.
    b. self-matching.
    c. reflected appraisal.
    d. totality viewing.
    e. the feedback self.

    Answer: c   **Type: M**   **Page: 50**   **Knowledge**

61. The kind of person you believe yourself to be is called the

    a. perceived self.
    b. desired self.
    c. presenting self.
    d. myth of self.
    e. transient self.

    Answer: a   **Type: M**   **Page: 72**   **Knowledge**

62. The tendency to look for people who confirm our view of self is termed

    a. the confirmation hypothesis.
    b. the self-fulfilling prophecy.
    c. self-verification.
    d. tunnel vision.
    e. the "head-nod" phenomenon.

    Answer: c   **Type: M**   **Page: 56**   **Knowledge**

63. The most significant part of one person's self-concept is

   a. social roles.
   b. appearance.
   c. health.
   d. accomplishments.
   e. dependent on the individual.

   Answer: e   **Type: M**   **Pages: 46–48**   **Analysis**

64. During childhood, the self-concept is affected by what type(s) of behavior of others?

   a. verbal
   b. nonverbal
   c. verbal and nonverbal
   d. only positive behavior
   e. only negative behavior

   Answer: c   **Type: M**   **Pages: 50–52**   **Application**

65. "Reference groups" are

   a. people whose self-concepts we have influenced.
   b. individuals whose self-esteem has been diminished.
   c. groups against which a person compares him/herself.
   d. groups formed to improve shaky self-esteem.
   e. people who hang around the library.

   Answer: c   **Type: M**   **Page: 52**   **Knowledge**

66. According to your text, the word "can't" often serves to

   a. let others share control in the relationship.
   b. help us accept our limitations.
   c. create a self-fulfilling prophecy.
   d. express equality through our humanity.

   Answer: c   **Type: M**   **Page: 69**   **Analysis**

67. Jane did better than Barbara on the math test. Jane can't do math as well as Barbara
   normally, but her teacher kept telling her how smart she was, and how her hard work
   would help her do better on the test. The fact that Jane did do better because of her
   own expectations is an example of

   a. distorted feedback.
   b. a good math teacher.
   c. clear message format.
   d. defensiveness.
   e. a self-fulfilling prophecy.

   Answer: e   **Type: M**   **Page: 64**   **Application**

68. When trying to change one's self-concept, it is important to remember all of the following except that

   a.   one should set realistic goals.
   b.   one should have a real desire to change.
   c.   one should expect rapid change.
   d.   one should possess the skills to change.
   e.   all of the above

   Answer: c   **Type: M**   **Pages: 68–70**   **Comprehension**

69. Which of the following would definitely not contribute to the formation of a self-concept?

   a.   promotion to a more responsible job
   b.   a conversational partner who blames you for fights
   c.   having one's birthday or anniversary forgotten
   d.   having one's child win a scholarship
   e.   All of the above might contribute.

   Answer: e   **Type: M**   **Pages: 50–52**   **Application**

70. Negative self-fulfilling prophecies you impose upon yourself are a form of

   a.   psychological noise.
   b.   inclusion need.
   c.   reflected appraisal.
   d.   the presenting self.
   e.   none of the above.

   Answer: a   **Type: M**   **Pages: 9, 65**   **Synthesis**

71. If you want to feel more self-confident when meeting new people, your text advised you to

   a.   subscribe to the myth of perfection.
   b.   compare yourself to reference groups above you.
   c.   quit thinking you can change.
   d.   disregard obsolete or inaccurate feedback.

   Answer: d   **Type: M**   **Page: 56**   **Analysis**

72. All of the following are examples of social comparison except

   a.   being graded for a test on a class curve.
   b.   judging your attractiveness while working out at Nautilus Gym.
   c.   reflecting on how you've changed in the last year.
   d.   being offered a job after competitive interviews.
   e.   All of the above are examples of social comparison.

   Answer: c   **Type: M**   **Page: 52**   **Application**

73. Nonverbal messages we receive from significant others about our competence are always a kind of

    a. self-fulfilling prophecy.
    b. feedback.
    c. positive influence.
    d. defensiveness.
    e. competitive symmetry

    Answer: b   **Type: M**   **Pages: 10, 51**   **Synthesis**

74. A self-fulfilling prophecy is

    a. a way to discover how to act in the future.
    b. a test one can take to analyze one's self-concept.
    c. a way to discover the "real you."
    d. an expectation that affects behavior.
    e. a psychological form of extrasensory perception

    Answer: d   **Type: M**   **Page: 64**   **Comprehension**

75. The tendency to seek and attend to information that conforms to an existing self-concept has been labeled

    a. reflected appraisal.
    b. significance posturing.
    c. the stability hypothesis.
    d. cognitive conservatism.
    e. the weak spine phenomenon.

    Answer: d   **Type: M**   **Page: 59**   **Knowledge**

76. The tendency to look for people who confirm our existing self-concept is termed

    a. behavioral conservatism.
    b. self-verification.
    c. cognitive monitoring.
    d. self-fulfillment.
    e. relational prophecy.

    Answer: b   **Type: M**   **Page: 56**   **Knowledge**

77. The communication strategies people use to influence how others view them is the process of

    a. ego-video.
    b. reflected appraisal.
    c. manipulation.
    d. social ethics.
    e. identity management.

    Answer: e   **Type: M**   **Page: 72**   **Knowledge**

78. People try to shape the opinion others have of them in order to

    a. get feedback.
    b. manipulate cognitive complexity.
    c. get affiliation or respect.
    d. establish effective listening patterns.

    Answer: c   Type: M   Pages: 79–82   Comprehension

INSTRUCTIONS for questions 79–83: Match each description below with the most accurate term.

    a. reflected appraisal
    b. significant other
    c. self-fulfilling prophecy
    d. presenting self
    e. perceived self

79. The private self you honestly believe you are

    Answer: e   Type: Matching   Page: 72   Knowledge

80. A prediction that affects behavior

    Answer: c   Type: Matching   Page: 64   Knowledge

81. A person whose opinion we especially value

    Answer: b   Type: Matching   Page: 51   Knowledge

82. Process of judging ourselves by the evaluations of others

    Answer: a   Type: Matching   Page: 50   Knowledge

83. The "face" you show to others

    Answer: d   Type: Matching   Page: 73   Knowledge

84. Pick the three most important communication-related "can'ts" (using the exercise on page 69 in your text or exercise 2.4 in your activities manual). Next, explain whether each item is really a "can't," a "won't," or a "don't know how." Next, describe how that item affects your relationship with the person in question. Finally, explain how happy or unhappy you are with each item and what, if anything, you could do to change it.

    Answer   Type: E   Page: 73   Evaluation

85. Barry Stevens's piece in the text entitled "Will the Real Me Please Stand Up?" talks about a split between the basic spirit and that which is learned through experience—the social self. From your own background, explain the nature of this split, the struggle between different aspects of the self, and talk about its effect on your self-concept.

    Answer   Type: E   Pages: 80–81   Synthesis

86. Explain two recent changes that took place in your self-concept. Indicate how communication influenced the change.

   Answer   **Type: E**   **Pages: 68–70**   **Analysis**

87. Describe two people for whom you are a significant other. Describe your communication behavior with each of them, giving examples of how (a) you deliver "booster" and "buster" messages to each of them; (b) you create self-fulfilling prophecies that work for and against each of them; and (c) they allow your communication with them to affect their behavior.

   Answer   **Type: E**   **Pages: 49–67**   **Synthesis**

88. Describe a recent self-fulfilling prophecy which you have imposed upon yourself that affects your communication. In what cases have you imposed it? What have the results been? How realistic was the prophecy? Does answering these questions change how you"ll talk to yourself in the future? How? Next, describe a self-fulfilling prophecy you have imposed upon another person. How did you communicate it (i.e., what messages did you send, and what channels did you use)? What effect did your prophecy have upon your partner? Does answering this question affect how you"ll communicate with the other person in the future? How?

   Answer   **Type: E**   **Pages: 64–67**   **Evaluation**

89. We have certain expectations which are products of our prejudices. How do you think these expectations have affected certain groups of people (e.g., blacks, Chicanos, women, college students, the elderly)? Select two groups of people you think have been affected by prejudice, and explain how reflected appraisal influences identity.

   Answer   **Type: E**   **Pages: 50–52**   **Evaluation**

90. Explain how you managed impressions with others in a recent important event in your life. Cite the reasons why you managed impressions and then evaluate the way you presented yourself.

   Answer   **Type: E**   **Pages: 82–84**   **Analysis**

91. Describe how you have managed your manner, appearance, and setting to create desired impressions in two different specific instances.

   Answer   **Type: E**   **Pages: 82–84**   **Application**

CHAPTER 3

PERCEPTION:
WHAT YOU SEE IS WHAT YOU GET

1. In the "Trying on Old Age" story in the perception chapter, college students role-played older versions of themselves.

    Answer: T   **Type: T**   **Page: 108**   **Recall**

2. The "Pillow Education" method described in Chapter Three was originally used by marriage counselors to help couples understand each other more clearly.

    Answer: F   **Type: T**   **Page: 125**   **Recall**

3. In the "Operation Empathy" police experiment described in this chapter, the police committed petty crimes to experience what a criminal's life was like.

    Answer: F   **Type: T**   **Page: 112**   **Recall**

4. The text argues that an ailment may have a strong impact on how you relate to others.

    Answer: T   **Type: T**   **Page: 104**   **Knowledge**

5. Total empathy is impossible to achieve.

    Answer: T   **Type: T**   **Page: 122**   **Knowledge**

6. Practicing empathy tends to make people more tolerant of others.

    Answer: T   **Type: T**   **Page: 122**   **Comprehension**

7. It's hardest to empathize with people who are radically different from us.

    Answer: T   **Type: T**   **Page: 122**   **Comprehension**

8. In order to understand another's thinking on an issue empathically, you must accept it as being valid or true.

    Answer: F   **Type: T**   **Page: 122**   **Comprehension**

9. It is necessary to feel sympathy in order to truly empathize with another person.

    Answer: F   **Type: T**   **Page: 123**   **Knowledge**

10. Identical foods can actually taste different to various individuals.

    Answer: T   **Type: T**   **Page: 103**   **Knowledge**

11. Sensory data can be different to different people.

    Answer: T   **Type: T**   **Page: 103**   **Knowledge**

12. Periodic changes (hormonal, emotional) in men and women are all in their minds, but they try to blame them on physical factors.

    Answer: F   **Type: T**   **Page: 104**   **Comprehension**

13. We can change our emotional cycles by refusing to let biology interfere with our lives.

    Answer: F   **Type: T**   **Page: 104**   **Comprehension**

14. Since older people have a greater number of experiences from which to draw, their perceptions are more accurate than those of younger people.

    Answer: F   **Type: T**   **Page: 104**   **Comprehension**

15. We are influenced more by subtle stimuli rather than obvious ones.

    Answer: F   **Type: T**   **Page: 96**   **Knowledge**

16. In our perceptions, we cling more strongly to first impressions, even when they are wrong.

    Answer: T   **Type: T**   **Page: 118**   **Knowledge**

17. In our perceptions, we tend to assume that others are similar to us.

    Answer: T   **Type: T**   **Page: 119**   **Knowledge**

18. Your text points out that people with high self-esteem are quicker to assume the worst possible motives on the part of others.

    Answer: F   **Type: T**   **Page: 115**   **Knowledge**

19. In perceiving others, we usually blame their problems on their personal qualities rather than on factors outside them.

    Answer: T   **Type: T**   **Page: 117**   **Knowledge**

20. Since we are the ones who experience reality, we have a complete idea of what that reality is.

    Answer: F   **Type: T**   **Page: 102**   **Comprehension**

21. Luckily, we've been gifted with our senses, which usually make us aware of all that is going on around us.

    Answer: F   **Type: T**   **Page: 103**   **Comprehension**

22. It's simply impossible to be aware of everything, no matter how attentive we may be.

    Answer: T   **Type: T**   **Page: 95**   **Analysis**

23. Since stimuli that are intense often attract our attention, we're more likely to remember extremely talkative people than those who are quiet.

Answer: T   **Type: T**   **Page: 96**   **Knowledge**

24. Most of the time, people to whom we're repetitiously exposed become noticeable.

Answer: T   **Type: T**   **Page: 96**   **Comprehension**

25. Unchanging people or things become less noticeable, and thus occupy less of our attention than those that change.

Answer: T   **Type: T**   **Page: 96**   **Comprehension**

26. Selection is an objective process.

Answer: F   **Type: T**   **Page: 96**   **Comprehension**

27. No two people perceive a given set of sense data identically.

Answer: T   **Type: T**   **Page: 103**   **Comprehension**

28. The sensory data we receive are the same for all of us; perceptual differences occur only after we begin to process those data.

Answer: F   **Type: T**   **Page: 103**   **Comprehension**

29. After using the "Pillow Method" you should typically conclude that the issue being considered is not important enough to worry about.

Answer: F   **Type: T**   **Page: 128**   **Comprehension**

30. Effective interpersonal communication between two persons would tend to narrow their perceptual differences.

Answer: T   **Type: T**   **Pages: 122–123**   **Analysis**

31. The times you disagree with someone most strongly may be the times when you can't "see" the other side of the issue.

Answer: T   **Type: T**   **Page: 100**   **Analysis**

32. People's occupations have little bearing on their perception of the world.

Answer: F   **Type: T**   **Page: 111**   **Knowledge**

33. Only women are affected by changes in mood.

Answer: F   **Type: T**   **Page: 104**   **Comprehension**

34. The self-serving bias illustrates our tendency to judge others more charitably than ourselves.

Answer: F   **Type: T**   **Page: 117**   **Knowledge**

35.   An individual's idea of reality is incomplete.

   Answer: T   **Type: T**   **Page: 94**   **Synthesis**

36.   True empathy involves agreeing with the other person's point of view.

   Answer: F   **Type: T**   **Page: 122**   **Comprehension**

37.   Your text claims that there is nothing wrong with the generalizations we make, using our organization constructs, as long as they are accurate.

   Answer: T   **Type: T**   **Page: 98**   **Knowledge**

38.   Punctuation is the process of organizing a series of events to determine causes and effects.

   Answer: T   **Type: T**   **Page: 100**   **Knowledge**

39.   According to your text, each of us experiences a different reality.

   Answer: T   **Type: T**   **Page: 94**   **Knowledge**

40.   Silence is valued over talk in most Asian cultures.

   Answer: T   **Type: T**   **Page: 107**   **Knowledge**

41.   The three phases of perception—selection, organization, and interpretation—can occur in differing sequences.

   Answer: T   **Type: T**   **Page: 102**   **Knowledge**

42.   Whites are more likely than blacks to use eye contact as a measure of how closely the other person is listening.

   Answer: T   **Type: T**   **Page: 108**   **Knowledge**

43.   According to your text, unhappy spouses are more likely than happy ones to make negative interpretations of their mates' behavior.

   Answer: T   **Type: T**   **Page: 102**   **Knowledge**

44.   In Philip Zimbardo's mock prison experiment described in Chapter Three, the ten subjects who became "prisoners"

   a.   took over the prison.
   b.   actually began acting and thinking like prisoners.
   c.   were able to remain apart from their "roles."
   d.   became emotionally stronger as they experienced prison.
   e.   became empathetic for prisoners and formed a rights group.

   Answer: b   **Type: M**   **Page: 113**   **Recall**

45. According to a story about smelling another person's breath in the Middle East, anthropologist Edward Hall points out that when American diplomats put on their best manners and don't breathe in people's faces, the Arabs think this communicates

    a. good manners.
    b. shame.
    c. power.
    d. honesty.
    e. manipulation.

    Answer: b   **Type: M**   **Page: 107**   **Recall**

46. The "Looking at Diversity" reading in the perception chapter focuses on

    a. a Cambodian who works in a U.S. fast-food restaurant.
    b. a man with attention deficit disorder.
    c. a mystic who studies perception.
    d. a man who had a sex-change operation.
    e. a former hang glider who is now a wheelchair user.

    Answer: b   **Type: M**   **Page: 106**   **Recall**

47. In a perception reading in Chapter Three, a police officer temporarily assumed the role of a derelict and

    a. was shot by another officer.
    b. was recognized by a fellow officer.
    c. was beaten up by a street gang.
    d. panicked and identified himself to other officers.
    e. prevented a robbery while in disguise.

    Answer: d   **Type: M**   **Page: 112**   **Recall**

48. All of the following are perceptual errors described in Chapter Three except:

    a. We are influenced by what is most obvious.
    b. We tend to assume others are different from us.
    c. We tend to favor negative impressions over positive ones.
    d. We often judge ourselves more charitably than others.
    e. All of the above were perceptual errors described in Chapter Three.

    Answer: b   **Type: M**   **Pages: 116–119**   **Recall**

49. The Perception-Checking Communication Transcript in Chapter Three focuses on using the Pillow Method to understand the perceptions of a couple who are

    a. moving into a new apartment.
    b. planning a wedding.
    c. traveling across the country with friends.
    d. dating cross-racially.
    e. joining different religions.

    Answer: b   **Type: M**   **Page: 127**   **Recall**

50. Studies of the effects of geography on perception revealed that people living in the southern latitudes of the U.S. have all of the following traits except that

   a.   they are more socially isolated.
   b.   they are less tolerant of ambiguity.
   c.   they are lower in self-esteem.
   d.   they are more likely to touch others.
   e.   they are more likely to verbalize their thoughts and feelings.

   Answer: c   **Type: M**   **Page: 108**   **Recall**

51. All of the following would be included in a good definition of empathy except:

   a.   It helps rid communication of an indifferent quality.
   b.   It minimizes threat to self-concept.
   c.   It includes nonverbal behavior.
   d.   It is likely to reduce defensiveness.
   e.   It involves agreeing with the other's position.

   Answer: e   **Type: M**   **Page: 122**   **Synthesis**

52. A perception check includes

   a.   a description of the behavior you have noticed.
   b.   two possible interpretations of the behavior.
   c.   a request for clarification about how to interpret the behavior correctly.
   d.   all of the above
   e.   none of the above

   Answer: d   **Type: M**   **Page: 120**   **Knowledge**

53. What's missing from this perception check? "When you didn't do the grocery shopping today like you usually do, I figured you weren't feeling good or were mad at me."

   a.   It doesn't describe behavior.
   b.   It has only one interpretation.
   c.   It doesn't request clarification.
   d.   It is too specific.
   e.   Nothing is missing from this perception check.

   Answer: c   **Type: M**   **Page: 120**   **Application**

54. What's missing from this perception check? "I figure you're either upset with me or worried about your test. Is it something like that?"

   a.   It doesn't describe behavior.
   b.   It has only one interpretation.
   c.   It doesn't request clarification.
   d.   It is too wordy.
   e.   Nothing is missing from this perception check.

   Answer: a   **Type: M**   **Page: 120**   **Application**

55. What's missing from this perception check? "When I saw you having lunch with Emily, I figured you liked her more than me. What's going on?"

    a. It doesn't describe behavior.
    b. It has only one interpretation.
    c. It doesn't request clarification.
    d. It is too wordy.
    e. Nothing is missing from this perception check.

    Answer: b   **Type: M**   **Page: 120**   **Application**

56. What's missing from this perception check? "When you bought that pink shirt, I figured you did it just to please me or really liked how you looked in it. Why did you buy it?"

    a. It doesn't describe behavior.
    b. It has only one interpretation.
    c. It doesn't request clarification.
    d. It is too wordy.
    e. Nothing is missing from this perception check.

    Answer: e   **Type: M**   **Page: 120**   **Application**

57. How could you improve this perception-checking statement? "When you gave me an F on my essay, I figured you hated me. Right?"

    a. Describe behavior.
    b. Give another interpretation.
    c. Request clarification.
    d. Say less.
    e. It is great as a perception-checking statement just the way it is.

    Answer: b   **Type: M**   **Page: 120**   **Analysis**

58. Communicating to a friend how sorry you are about the breakup of his or her romance is an example of

    a. sympathy.
    b. role-taking.
    c. perception-checking.
    d. assumption.

    Answer: a   **Type: M**   **Page: 123**   **Application**

59. All of the following are physiological factors shaping perception except:

    a. the senses.
    b. age and health.
    c. fatigue.
    d. ethnicity.
    e. hunger.

    Answer: d   **Type: M**   **Pages: 103–104**   **Knowledge**

60. The recognition of a "figure" as standing out from a "ground" of other stimuli takes place during what phase of the perception process?

    a. ideation
    b. stimulation
    c. verification
    d. organization
    e. sensation

    Answer: d   **Type: M**   **Page: 97**   **Knowledge**

61. All of the following perceptual factors influence the way we interpret behavior except:

    a. relational satisfaction
    b. assumptions about human behavior
    c. androgynous style
    d. past experience
    e. expectations

    Answer: c   **Type: M**   **Pages: 101–102**   **Comprehension**

62. All of the following are terms to describe the ability to put ourselves into another person's shoes (to view an experience from his or her perspective) except:

    a. sympathy.
    b. empathy.
    c. role-taking.
    d. perspective-taking.

    Answer: a   **Type: M**   **Page: 122**   **Analysis**

63. Talk is viewed as desirable and useful for both task and social purposes in

    a. Western culture.
    b. Asian culture.
    c. upper- and middle-class groups.
    d. older people.
    e. all of the above.

    Answer: a   **Type: M**   **Page: 107**   **Knowledge**

64. Which of the following statements is not true?

    a. People agree about what smells good or bad.
    b. People's sensitivity to temperature varies significantly.
    c. Odors that please some people repel others.
    d. Men have mood cycles of ups and downs.
    e. All of the above are true.

    Answer: a   **Type: M**   **Pages: 103–104**   **Analysis**

65. We notice some stimuli over others in our environment because they are

    a. mild.
    b. singular.
    c. contrasting or changing.
    d. related to modular communication.

    Answer: c   **Type: M**   **Page: 96**   **Knowledge**

66. The three stages in the perception process are

    a. initial, intermediate, final.
    b. assumption, experience, expectation.
    c. physical, psychological, experimental.
    d. selection, organization, interpretation.
    e. response, action, interaction.

    Answer: d   **Type: M**   **Pages: 95–102**   **Comprehension**

67. Our own perceptions can sometimes be distorted due to

    a. defending our own positions.
    b. situational constraints.
    c. acknowledging the fact that people are different.
    d. the needs and biases of others.

    Answer: a   **Type: M**   **Page: 117**   **Synthesis**

68. In order to understand another person's perception of a problem, it is necessary to

    a. assume that person's social role.
    b. spend time in that person's culture or subculture.
    c. experience that person's physiological differences.
    d. all of the above
    e. none of the above

    Answer: e   **Type: M**   **Page: 122**   **Synthesis**

69. Empathy is related to perception in that

    a. the more perceptive you are, the less empathetic you need be.
    b. the more perceptive you are, the easier it is to forget to be empathetic.
    c. empathy is facilitated by trying to perceive things from the other person's point of view.
    d. empathy and perception are both a result of self-fulfilling prophecies.

    Answer: c   **Type: M**   **Page: 122**   **Analysis**

70. Which of the following is the best example of a cultural perceptual difference?

    a. Women are expected by some to act "dizzy"; men aren't.
    b. Instructors and students often disagree about examinations.
    c. Your boyfriend or girlfriend is mechanically oriented; you don't know much about machines.
    d. In the U.S., direct eye contact between men and women is considered assertive; in Latin America it is perceived as provocative.
    e. Not all Americans agree about the acceptability of abortion.

    Answer: d   **Type: M**   **Page: 105**   **Comprehension**

71. All of the following are causes of inaccurate perception except

    a. We cling to first impressions.
    b. We're influenced by what is most obvious.
    c. We assume others are similar to us.
    d. We rate ourselves more negatively than others see us.
    e. We judge ourselves more charitably than others.

    Answer: d   **Type: M**   **Pages: 116–119**   **Comprehension**

72. When you can't find any reasons to accept the behavior of another person, it can be helpful to

    a. use perception checking.
    b. examine your own self-concept.
    c. use a different communication channel.
    d. use the Pillow Method.
    e. reduce the level of feedback.

    Answer: d   **Type: M**   **Page: 125**   **Evaluation**

73. Being able to pick out your sister's statements from a babble of voices at a party illustrates the organizational principle of

    a. figure-ground organization.
    b. alternative patterning.
    c. perceptual freezing.
    d. selection of empathetic other.
    e. attention to the irritating.

    Answer: a   **Type: M**   **Page: 97**   **Application**

74. Classifying people according to age, sex, and physical attractiveness, rather than education or occupation, illustrates the cognitive framework called

    a. figure-ground organization.
    b. perceptual schema.
    c. perceptual freezing.
    d. selection.
    e. selective attention.

    Answer: b   **Type: M**   **Page: 94**   **Application**

75. Five-year-old Johnny picks out his friend Matt because he is also five and likes Legos. Johnny never even realizes that Matt's skin is a different color from his own or that his family goes to a different church. This illustrates the organizing framework called

    a. organizational clusters.
    b. perceptual schema.
    c. perceptual freezing.
    d. evolutional selection.
    e. trivial attention.

    Answer: b   **Type: M**   **Page: 97**   **Application**

76. Two people organize a series of events in different ways; the man says that he goes out drinking with the guys because she always fusses at him when he gets home; she says she fusses at him when he gets home because he always goes out drinking after work. This process of organizing events in different ways is called

    a. selection.
    b. interpretation.
    c. omission.
    d. punctuation.
    e. blocking.

    Answer: d   **Type: M**   **Page: 100**   **Comprehension**

77. Perception checking focuses on what part of the perception process?

    a. selection
    b. organization
    c. interpretation
    d. all of the above
    e. none of the above

    Answer: d   **Type: M**   **Pages: 95–102, 120**   **Synthesis**

78. Shannon says that she works out in the evenings instead of the afternoons because Roger is always late coming home from work. Roger says he doesn't bother to rush home from work because Shannon is always working out. This process of organizing the series of events in different ways is called

    a. punctuation.
    b. interpretation.
    c. perceptuation.
    d. conjugation.
    e. intrepidation.

    Answer: a   **Type: M**   **Page: 100**   **Application**

79. The term that refers to men and women possessing a mixture of traits that have previously been considered exclusively masculine or feminine is

   a.   chauvinistic.
   b.   adaptable.
   c.   rhetorically sensitive.
   d.   androgynous.
   e.   amalgamous.

   Answer: d   **Type: M**   **Page: 110**   **Knowledge**

80. What's missing from this perception check? "I'm not sure you bought me that present as a genuine thank you, or if you were hoping I'd be less angry about what you said last night. I'd like to know what your reason was."

   a.   It doesn't describe behavior.
   b.   It has only one interpretation.
   c.   It doesn't request clarification.
   d.   It is too wordy.
   e.   Nothing is missing from this perception check.

   Answer: e   **Type: M**   **Page: 120**   **Application**

81. Using the skill of perception checking will help prevent

   a.   negative self-fulfilling prophecies.
   b.   physiological noise.
   c.   inaccurate decoding of messages.
   d.   excessive feedback.
   e.   none of the above.

   Answer: c   **Type: M**   **Page: 120**   **Synthesis**

82. Exaggerated beliefs associated with a perceptual categorizing system are

   a.   role constructs.
   b.   self-judgments.
   c.   white lies.
   d.   subcultural translations.
   e.   stereotypes.

   Answer: e   **Type: M**   **Page: 99**   **Knowledge**

INSTRUCTIONS for questions 83–87: Match each of the descriptions below with the term it best describes.

   a.   punctuation
   b.   interpretation
   c.   empathy
   d.   attribution
   e.   androgynous behavior

83. You communicate your understanding of a friend's housing problem to that friend.

   Answer: c   **Type: Matching**   **Page: 122**   **Application**

84. You exhibit both sensitivity and strength when faced with a difficult decision.

    Answer: e   **Type: Matching**   **Page: 110**   Application

85. You say you're late because your partner is never ready on time; your partner says she takes her time getting ready because you're always late.

    Answer: a   **Type: Matching**   **Page: 100**   Application

86. You think all children are hyperactive.

    Answer: d   **Type: Matching**   **Page: 98**   Application

87. You figure your friend's smile means she's happy.

    Answer: b   **Type: Matching**   **Page: 101**   Application

INSTRUCTIONS for questions 88–92: Match each of the descriptions below with the term it best describes.

    a. self-serving bias
    b. organization
    c. sympathy
    d. narrative
    e. selection

88. You hear the laugh of your boss in a crowded, noisy room.

    Answer: b   **Type: Matching**   **Page: 97**   Application

89. You notice car advertisements more when you need a new car.

    Answer: e   **Type: Matching**   **Page: 96**   Application

90. You show you're sorry that your friend was robbed.

    Answer: c   **Type: Matching**   **Page: 123**   Application

91. You claim your roommates are lazy when they don't clean up, but when you fail to clean up, it's because of your many commitments.

    Answer: a   **Type: Matching**   **Page: 117**   Application

92. Your interaction with your co-workers creates a shared perspective of your boss.

    Answer: d   **Type: Matching**   **Page: 115**   Application

INSTRUCTIONS for questions 93–100: Match each of the perceptual schema examples below with constructs that describe it.

    a. appearance
    b. social roles
    c. interaction style
    d. psychological trait
    e. membership

93. Jeri thinks Alicia is a typical lawyer.

| **Answer: b** | **Type: Matching** | **Page: 97** | **Application** |

94. Bertha did not want to associate with the girl wearing a ring in her nose.

| **Answer: a** | **Type: Matching** | **Page: 97** | **Application** |

95. "Hi, Janina's mother," the new play group member said.

| **Answer: b** | **Type: Matching** | **Page: 97** | **Application** |

96. Darin decided LuAnn was insecure when he heard her ask for help twice.

| **Answer: d** | **Type: Matching** | **Page: 97** | **Application** |

97. "Chad's the organizer in our group," Linda said.

| **Answer: c** | **Type: Matching** | **Page: 97** | **Application** |

98. "That's just what a Democrat would say," Mario thought.

| **Answer: e** | **Type: Matching** | **Page: 97** | **Application** |

99. The bartender decided to ask the woman for identification to prove she was 21.

| **Answer: a** | **Type: Matching** | **Page: 97** | **Application** |

100. Alexandria thought John was friendly from the first time they met.

| **Answer: c** | **Type: Matching** | **Page: 97** | **Application** |

101. Explain the differences between understanding someone and agreeing with him/her. Use a specific interpersonal example from your own life.

| **Answer** | **Type: E** | **Pages: 122–123** | **Analysis** |

102. Identify a situation from your recent experience in which you disagree with another person due to differing physiological environments. Show how these different environments led to the disagreement.

| **Answer** | **Type: E** | **Pages: 103–104** | **Synthesis** |

103. Describe the four perceptual accuracies/inaccuracies identified by researchers in Chapter Three. What role has each played/not played in the formation of your perceptions of three people important to you?

     Answer   **Type: E**   **Pages: 116–119**   **Application**

104. Apply the Pillow Method to an interpersonal issue which has recently affected you. Describe your thoughts and feelings at each position on the pillow.

     Answer   **Type: E**   **Pages: 125–128**   **Synthesis**

105. Describe two people with whom you live, work, or study. For each person, (a) record at least five of your perceptions of the person, and (b) describe the perceptual influence factors listed on pages 103–115 in your text that contribute to each of your perceptions.

     Answer   **Type: E**   **Pages: 103–115**   **Application**

(Note: The following essay questions work best as "take-home" exams because of the time necessary to effectively complete them.)

106. Imagine yourself a member of the opposite sex. Describe all the events of a particular day from the vantage point of your "new" sex. What clothes would you want to wear? How would you greet your friends? How would you eat? How would you play? How would your perceptions of the world change? Be very specific and use concrete examples as well as vocabulary items from this chapter.

     Answer   **Type: E**   **Page: 110**   **Evaluation**

107. Describe a subculture to which you belong. Give examples and explain several misunderstandings you have had with members of another subculture. What do these misunderstandings indicate about the way in which you view the world? Use terms and theory from the text.

     Answer   **Type: E**   **Pages: 105–108**   **Evaluation**

CHAPTER 4

EMOTIONS

1. Our society encourages the direct expression of most emotions.

    Answer: F   **Type: T**   **Page: 147**   **Recall**

2. Chapter Four stated that it is impossible to offer a list of guidelines about when and how to express emotions.

    Answer: F   **Type: T**   **Pages: 149–154**   **Recall**

3. The Communication Transcript in the emotions chapter dealt with emotional support groups that deliver therapy to students.

    Answer: F   **Type: T**   **Page: 169**   **Recall**

4. Emotions are often revealed by nonverbal behavior.

    Answer: T   **Type: T**   **Page: 138**   **Knowledge**

5. Men are more likely than women are to reveal their strengths and positive emotions.

    Answer: T   **Type: T**   **Page: 147**   **Comprehension**

6. Research indicates that we are usually better at recognizing the emotions of members of our same gender than we are of the opposite gender.

    Answer: T   **Type: T**   **Page: 147**   **Comprehension**

7. When a person has strong emotions, many bodily changes occur.

    Answer: T   **Type: T**   **Page: 136**   **Knowledge**

8. Chapter Four argued that the complete and open expression of emotions is one key to positive relationships.

    Answer: F   **Type: T**   **Page: 154**   **Comprehension**

9. According to the text, irrational beliefs are usually an indication of pathological mental states.

    Answer: F   **Type: T**   **Page: 160**   **Synthesis**

10. By thinking rationally, you will be able to eliminate debilitative emotions from your life.

    Answer: F   **Type: T**   **Page: 165**   **Knowledge**

11. When sharing your feelings, it's not necessary to accept responsibility for them because so often others cause them.

    Answer: F   **Type: T**   **Page: 154**   **Knowledge**

12. Proprioceptive messages, while important to biologists, offer no clues to understanding emotions in everyday life.

    Answer: F   **Type: T**   **Page: 136**   **Knowledge**

13. Fortunately for people who want to hide their emotions, all the physical changes that accompany emotions are internal.

    Answer: F   **Type: T**   **Page: 136**   **Knowledge**

14. Some people fail to communicate their emotions clearly because they understate or downplay them.

    Answer: T   **Type: T**   **Page: 153**   **Knowledge**

15. Some people chronically overstate the strength of their emotions.

    Answer: T   **Type: T**   **Page: 143**   **Knowledge**

16. Since collectivist cultures pay more attention to nonverbal behaviors, they are better at expressing both positive and negative emotions.

    Answer: F   **Type: T**   **Page: 146**   **Knowledge**

17. The physiological changes that accompany many strong emotions are similar.

    Answer: T   **Type: T**   **Page: 136**   **Comprehension**

18. The event that generates facilitative self-talk for one person might stimulate debilitative thinking for someone else.

    Answer: T   **Type: T**   **Page: 156**   **Comprehension**

19. Emotional states are connected to physical behavior.

    Answer: T   **Type: T**   **Page: 136**   **Comprehension**

20. While there is a link between physical behavior and emotional states, mental behavior plays no role in determining how we feel.

    Answer: F   **Type: T**   **Page: 139**   **Comprehension**

21. The approach to handling emotions described in your text involves talking yourself out of feeling unnecessarily bad.

    Answer: T   **Type: T**   **Page: 167**   **Knowledge**

22. The chapter on emotions argues that we can stop others from doing things that make us feel bad.

    Answer: F   **Type: T**   **Page: 157**   **Analysis**

23. It is important to express all your emotions to all the important people in your life as soon as you experience those emotions.

    Answer: F   **Type: T**   **Page: 154**   **Knowledge**

24. Your text advises that when you feel a certain way, you should act on that feeling.

    Answer: F   **Type: T**   **Page: 154**   **Knowledge**

25. All emotions are caused by self-talk.

    Answer: F   **Type: T**   **Page: 157**   **Comprehension**

26. People will respect and like you more if you go out of your way to please them.

    Answer: F   **Type: T**   **Page: 160**   **Comprehension**

27. One of the primary reasons we don't express emotions is that we don't recognize when they occur.

    Answer: T   **Type: T**   **Page: 139**   **Knowledge**

28. The text explains that you should always share your positive feelings (love, affection, etc.).

    Answer: F   **Type: T**   **Page: 154**   **Knowledge**

29. By avoiding the fallacy of approval, you will become unconcerned about what other people think of you.

    Answer: F   **Type: T**   **Page: 160**   **Knowledge**

30. Anger can be either a facilitative or debilitative emotion.

    Answer: T   **Type: T**   **Page: 156**   **Comprehension**

31. One way to reduce your anxiety about communicating is to stop talking to yourself.

    Answer: F   **Type: T**   **Page: 157**   **Analysis**

32. Most of our feelings are a direct result of the beliefs we hold.

    Answer: T   **Type: T**   **Page: 157**   **Knowledge**

33. In the emotions chapter, psychologist Philip Zimbardo describes himself as a perspiring professor who discovers that

    a. his lectures are boring.
    b. his room is hot.
    c. the students have played a trick on him.
    d. his nervousness is out of control.
    e. he is in the wrong classroom.

    Answer: b   **Type: M**   **Page: 139**   **Recall**

34. A study of married couples revealed that the partners shared all of the following except:

    a. complementary feelings.
    b. positive feelings about absent third parties.
    c. face-saving feelings.
    d. hostility.
    e. negative feelings about absent third parties.

    Answer: d   **Type: M**   **Page: 147**   **Recall**

35. The "Looking at Diversity" reading in the emotions chapter focuses on

    a. differences between the ways Zuni and Anglo cultures deal with emotional expression.
    b. Native American emotions rituals.
    c. Latin American substitutes for emotion verbalizations.
    d. similarities in emotional expression across cultures.
    e. All of the above were mentioned by the reading.

    Answer: a   **Type: M**   **Pages: 144–145**   **Recall**

36. Social scientists generally agree that there are four components to the phenomena we label as "feelings." They are

    a. physiological changes, nonverbal reactions, cognitive interpretations, and verbal expression.
    b. physical changes, mental recognition, nonverbal reactions, and verbal description.
    c. sensing, organizing, interpreting, and encoding.
    d. verbal and nonverbal manifestations, physical depression, and catharsis.
    e. stimulus, proprioception, emotional contagion and response.

    Answer: a   **Type: M**   **Pages: 136–140**   **Comprehension**

37. Most feelings we experience are a direct result of

    a. activating events.
    b. beliefs we hold.
    c. other people"s actions.
    d. self-fulfilling prophecies.
    e. none of the above.

    Answer: b   **Type: M**   **Page: 157**   **Comprehension**

38. Proprioceptive stimuli refer to

    a. deep-seated fears of emotional breakdown.
    b. messages sent from the brain to the proprioceptor.
    c. sensations that are activated by movement of internal tissues.
    d. messages communicated by people who perceive danger prior to its happening.
    e. thoughts that trigger emotions.

    Answer: c   **Type: M**   **Page: 136**   **Knowledge**

39. Your text tells you that you should

    a. express all your emotions to your friends.
    b. try to recognize your emotions.
    c. be glad you have debilitative emotions.
    d. express only positive emotions.
    e. stop being so emotional.

    Answer: b   **Type: M**   **Page: 151**   **Comprehension**

40. Your book categorizes emotions in all of the following ways except

    a. primary and mixed.
    b. intense and mild.
    c. facilitative and debilitative.
    d. internal and external.

    Answer: d   **Type: M**   **Pages: 142–143, 156**   **Synthesis**

41. According to Chapter Four, one reason people don't express feelings is

    a. they aren't aware of having them.
    b. it's a waste of time.
    c. interpretations are easier to understand.
    d. they are rarely asked to do so.
    e. many people rarely have feelings.

    Answer: a   **Type: M**   **Page: 151**   **Comprehension**

42. Robert Plutchik's "emotion wheel" illustrates

    a. proprioceptive stimuli.
    b. rational emotive therapy.
    c. primary and mixed emotions.
    d. cognitive interpretations.
    e. facilitative and debilitative emotions.

    Answer: c   **Type: M**   **Page: 142**   **Comprehension**

43. Research by Ekman described in this chapter found that when volunteers were coached to move their facial muscles in ways so that they appeared afraid, angry, disgusted, amused, sad, etc., others responded

    a. as if they themselves were having these feelings.
    b. by showing the opposite feeling.
    c. by showing more intense feelings than the volunteers.
    d. with no emotion at all.
    e. with pity for the volunteers.

    Answer: a   **Type: M**   **Page: 138**   **Comprehension**

44. Many of our debilitative feelings come from

    a. the way others treat us.
    b. an overly flexible self-concept.
    c. the anxiety we experience when positive expectations are placed on us.
    d. accepting irrational beliefs which lead to illogical conclusions.
    e. experiencing activating events.

    Answer: d   **Type: M**   **Page: 160**   **Knowledge**

45. Which of the following is true of debilitative feelings?

    a. They often last a long time.
    b. They keep you from functioning effectively.
    c. They are intense.
    d. They are a product of your beliefs.
    e. All of the above are true of debilitative feelings.

    Answer: e   **Type: M**   **Pages: 156–157**   **Comprehension**

46. People who subscribe to the fallacy of perfection believe

    a. everyone is perfect except them.
    b. there's no point in striving for perfection since it is unattainable.
    c. a worthwhile communicator should be able to handle any situation with confidence and skill.
    d. perfection requires much practice.
    e. only professors are perfect.

    Answer: c   **Type: M**   **Page: 160**   **Knowledge**

47. Which of the following is an example of falling for the fallacy of causation?

    a. "People at parties make me nervous."
    b. "If I ask her/him for a date the answer will probably be no."
    c. "I'm no good at anything!"
    d. "Everybody is against me."
    e. "I should be a better person."

    Answer: a   **Type: M**   **Page: 163**   **Application**

48. Which of the following does the text offer as a guideline for expressing emotions?

    a. The sooner a feeling is shared, the better.
    b. Try to avoid sharing negative feelings whenever possible.
    c. Share mixed feelings when appropriate.
    d. Let others know that they have caused you to feel a certain way.
    e. Try to avoid getting too emotional.

    Answer: c   **Type: M**   **Page: 153**   **Application**

49. Which of the following is the best statement to describe a feeling clearly?

    a. "I get embarrassed when you tease me about the shape of my nose."
    b. "I get a little confused when you tease me about being Polish."
    c. "You're driving me crazy with that teasing."
    d. "I get angry when you tease me."
    e. "Stop teasing me or I'll leave you."

    Answer: a   **Type: M**   **Pages: 149–154**   **Application**

50. All of the following are parts of the procedure for dealing with debilitative feelings except:

    a. Pay attention to your self-talk.
    b. Become more aware of your emotional reactions.
    c. Dispute irrational beliefs.
    d. Identify the activating event.
    e. Analyze your motives.

    Answer: e   **Type: M**   **Pages: 165–167**   **Comprehension**

51. "Men are so egotistical; I'm never getting involved with a man again" is an example of subscribing to the fallacy of

    a. overgeneralization.
    b. perfection.
    c. shoulds.
    d. causation.
    e. helplessness.

    Answer: a   **Type: M**   **Page: 162**   **Application**

52. Stan felt angry when Sue, a woman he'd gone out with twice, went out with Steve. Stan's anger is a direct result of

    a. Sue going out with Steve.
    b. Steve betraying Stan.
    c. Stan believing Sue should go out only with him.
    d. Stan's childishness.
    e. Sue's and Steve's thoughtlessness.

    Answer: c   **Type: M**   **Page: 157**   **Analysis**

53. John felt discouraged when he got a "C" on his speech. John's discouragement was a direct result of

    a. giving an average speech.
    b. his parents' expectations.
    c. an unfair teacher.
    d. John's friend getting a "B" for the same speech.
    e. John thinking he should get an "A."

    Answer: e   **Type: M**   **Page: 157**   **Analysis**

54. "My roommate ought to be more understanding." This quote is an example of the fallacy of

    a. shoulds.
    b. causation.
    c. approval.
    d. perfection.
    e. helplessness.

    Answer: a   **Type: M**   **Page: 161**   **Application**

55. Which of the following is the best advice for sharing feelings?

    a. Accept responsibility for your own feelings.
    b. Express your feelings as soon as they occur.
    c. Recognize that feeling and acting out the feeling are the same.
    d. Express only primary feelings.
    e. Tell yourself you shouldn't feel bad.

    Answer: a   **Type: M**   **Page: 154**   **Evaluation**

56. According to your text, women are more likely than men to express all of the following emotions except

    a. vulnerability.
    b. loneliness.
    c. strength.
    d. fear.
    e. sadness.

    Answer: c   **Type: M**   **Page: 147**   **Comprehension**

57. When you believe that a worthwhile communicator should be able to handle every situation with complete confidence and skill, you are falling for the fallacy of

    a. perfection.
    b. causation.
    c. approval.
    d. shoulds.
    e. overgeneralization.

    Answer: a   **Type: M**   **Page: 160**   **Knowledge**

58. When you think it is not just desirable but vital to get the acceptance of virtually every person, you are falling for the fallacy of

    a. perfection.
    b. causation.
    c. approval.
    d. shoulds.
    e. overgeneralization.

    Answer: c   **Type: M**   **Page: 160**   **Knowledge**

59. When you believe that others cause your emotions rather than your own self-talk, you are falling for the fallacy of

    a. perfection.
    b. causation.
    c. approval.
    d. shoulds.
    e. overgeneralization.

Answer: b   **Type: M**   **Page: 163**   **Knowledge**

60. When you believe that satisfaction in life is determined by forces beyond your control, you are falling for the fallacy of

    a. causation.
    b. helplessness.
    c. catastrophic expectations.
    d. approval.
    e. shoulds.

Answer: b   **Type: M**   **Page: 164**   **Knowledge**

61. According to your text, the first step in minimizing your debilitative emotions is to

    a. monitor your emotional reactions.
    b. note the activating event.
    c. record your self-talk.
    d. dispute your irrational beliefs.
    e. confront the person who caused them.

Answer: a   **Type: M**   **Page: 165**   **Knowledge**

62. Which of the following are examples of self-talk?

    a. Jim shouldn't drink three beers.
    b. Jim's always drinking.
    c. He'll have an accident.
    d. Jim makes me feel insecure.
    e. All of the above might be examples of self-talk.

Answer: e   **Type: M**   **Page: 160**   **Application**

63. Which of the following are examples of self-talk?

    a. I shouldn't have pushed so hard.
    b. I'll make her neurotic.
    c. I'll never be able to make her see my side.
    d. I can't get anyone to listen to me.
    e. All of the above might be examples of self-talk.

Answer: e   **Type: M**   **Page: 160**   **Application**

64. Blushing, sweating, and a sudden change in vocal pitch are all emotional changes classified as

   a.   proprioceptive stimuli.
   b.   nonverbal reactions.
   c.   cognitive interpretations.
   d.   physio-emotional changes.
   e.   all of the above.

   Answer: b   **Type: M**   **Page: 138**   **Knowledge**

65. An empty feeling in the pit of your stomach, tense muscles, and headache are examples of the emotional component labeled

   a.   nonverbal reactions.
   b.   cognitive interpretations.
   c.   physiological changes.
   d.   rational-emotive therapy.
   e.   environment.

   Answer: c   **Type: M**   **Page: 136**   **Comprehension**

66. Your text says we don't express our emotions very well or very frequently because

   a.   of social rules and roles.
   b.   others put us down.
   c.   we recognize so many emotions.
   d.   self-disclosure is already high enough.
   e.   of inadequate self-concepts.

   Answer: a   **Type: M**   **Pages: 147–148**   **Comprehension**

67. Which of the following improves the expression of emotion in the statement "You're making me nervous"?

   a.   Say "I feel nervous when you drive over the speed limit."
   b.   Say "Your fast driving is not making me feel very safe."
   c.   Say "I feel like taking the keys."
   d.   All of the above could improve the statement.
   e.   No improvement is needed.

   Answer: a   **Type: M**   **Pages: 149–154**   **Evaluation**

68. Which of the following best improves the emotional statement, "I'm a little upset and wonder where you get off acting like that"?

   a.   "You're driving me crazy."
   b.   "I can't figure out what to do when you won't tell me what's wrong."
   c.   "Your emotions are getting the best of you right now."
   d.   "I'm upset that our food budget for the month is spent."
   e.   The original statement is the best expression of emotion.

   Answer: d   **Type: M**   **Pages: 149–154**   **Evaluation**

69. Facilitative feelings

    a. are emotional counterfeits.
    b. happen only when you feel good.
    c. keep us from communicating effectively.
    d. contribute to effective functioning.
    e. are more common in other cultures.

    Answer: d   **Type: M**   **Page: 156**   **Comprehension**

70. Debilitative emotions

    a. are emotional counterfeits.
    b. happen only when you feel bad.
    c. keep you from feeling and communicating effectively.
    d. contribute to effective functioning.
    e. none of the above

    Answer: c   **Type: M**   **Page: 157**   **Comprehension**

71. Two things that distinguish facilitative feelings from debilitative ones are

    a. emotions and behavior.
    b. interpretation and intention.
    c. longevity and interpretation.
    d. intention and intensity.
    e. intensity and duration.

    Answer: e   **Type: M**   **Pages: 156–157**   **Knowledge**

72. Sensations activated by the movement of internal tissue are called

    a. emotional senses.
    b. internal emotions.
    c. sensational stimulation.
    d. proprioceptive stimuli.
    e. practical defenses.

    Answer: d   **Type: M**   **Page: 136**   **Knowledge**

73. The element of the communication model that is most closely involved with causing an emotion is

    a. channel.
    b. decoding.
    c. noise.
    d. environment.
    e. feedback.

    Answer: b   **Type: M**   **Pages: 8, 157**   **Synthesis**

74. The relationship between thinking and feeling described in your text involved which dimensions of the perception process?

    a. selection
    b. organization
    c. interpretation
    d. all of the above
    e. none of the above

    Answer: d   **Type: M**   **Pages: 157–158**   **Synthesis**

75. Which of the following is an example of the fallacy of causation?

    a. "My boss makes me so nervous that I can't do a good job."
    b. "I hurt Laura's feelings yesterday when I asked her to stop being so critical."
    c. "Bruce is driving me crazy with his excuses."
    d. both a and b above
    e. a, b, and c above

    Answer: e   **Type: M**   **Pages: 162–163**   **Application**

76. You're fed up with a close friend's habit of offering unsolicited advice about how to live your life. Which of the following is a useful guideline for expressing your feelings?

    a. Play it cool at first; don't let your friend know how much the advice irritates you.
    b. Demonstrate the strength of your feelings by refusing to talk with your friend for a while.
    c. Avoid bringing up this difficult subject until you can't tolerate it any longer.
    d. Don't dilute the strength of your message by sharing positive feelings about your friendship along with your irritation.
    e. Say you're annoyed by one specific piece of advice because you'd prefer to make your own decision on that matter.

    Answer: e   **Type: M**   **Pages: 149–154**   **Evaluation**

77. Self-talk can be

    a. facilitative or debilitative.
    b. a form of psychological noise.
    c. influenced by selective perception.
    d. part of a self-fulfilling prophecy.
    e. all of the above.

    Answer: e   **Type: M**   **Pages: Chs. 1–3, p. 157 Synthesis**

78. You are fed up with the way certain family members insist on knowing the details of your personal life. According to your text, what causes your feelings?

    a. the way your family phrases their questions
    b. expecting your family to respect your privacy
    c. self-fulfilling prophecies your family imposes on you
    d. lack of feedback
    e. the fallacy of perfection

    Answer: b   **Type: M**   **Page: 162**   **Analysis**

79. The statement "Bob never has a good word to say about anyone" is an example of the fallacy of

    a. shoulds.
    b. approval.
    c. overgeneralization.
    d. causation.
    e. all of the above

    Answer: c   **Type: M**   **Page: 162**   **Application**

80. Subscribing to the fallacy of catastrophic expectations can lead to

    a. self-fulfilling prophecies.
    b. erroneous perception checking.
    c. reflected appraisals.
    d. physiological noise.
    e. both c and d above.

    Answer: a   **Type: M**   **Page: 164**   **Synthesis**

81. "I feel like quitting school" is an example of

    a. a feeling statement.
    b. an emotionally counterfeit statement.
    c. an emotional intention.
    d. a contextual emotion.
    e. a self-fulfilling prophecy.

    Answer: b   **Type: M**   **Page: 152**   **Application**

82. Your brother asks about the money you got from your parents and then hangs up the telephone when you tell him. If you want to truly express your emotion, what is one good way to restate, "I feel you've been unfair"?

    a. "I think you tricked me, and I feel that's unfair."
    b. "I feel duped."
    c. "I'm disappointed you didn't ask me to explain."
    d. "You're making me mad by not letting me explain."
    e. The original statement is a good-feeling statement.

    Answer: c   **Type: M**   **Pages: 149–154**   **Synthesis**

83. What's ineffective about this feeling statement: "I feel you are lazy."

    a. It doesn't accept responsibility for a feeling.
    b. It doesn't describe the speaker's feeling.
    c. It interprets another's behavior.
    d. All of the above describe what's ineffective about the statement.
    e. There is nothing ineffective about the original statement.

    Answer: d   **Type: M**   **Pages: 149–154**   **Synthesis**

84. Revealing mixed feelings means

    a. mixing up all the feelings you have.
    b. expressing more than one feeling.
    c. sharing what you feel and what your partner feels, too.
    d. all of the above.
    e. none of the above.

    Answer: b   **Type: M**   **Page: 153**   **Comprehension**

INSTRUCTIONS for questions 85–94: Match each of the statements below with the fallacy it most clearly represents.

    a. fallacy of causation
    b. fallacy of shoulds
    c. fallacy of overgeneralization
    d. fallacy of perfection
    e. fallacy of catastrophic expectations

85. "Those interviewers made me so nervous."

    Answer: a   **Type: Matching**   **Page: 163**   **Application**

86. "You ought to keep in touch more."

    Answer: b   **Type: Matching**   **Page: 161**   **Application**

87. "I know he'll be crushed if I don't go out with him."

    Answer: a   **Type: Matching**   **Page: 163**   **Application**

88. "You never tell me how you feel."

    Answer: c   **Type: Matching**   **Page: 162**   **Application**

89. "I lost my temper with Mac last night. I've had interpersonal communication; I know better."

    Answer: d   **Type: Matching**   **Page: 160**   **Application**

90. "All you do is criticize me!"

    Answer: c   **Type: Matching**   **Page: 162**   **Application**

91. "You're driving me crazy."

    Answer: a   **Type: Matching**   **Page: 163**   **Application**

92. "You should be more patient."

    Answer: b   **Type: Matching**   **Page: 161**   **Application**

93. "You're always finishing my sentences for me."

    Answer: c   **Type: Matching**   **Page: 162**   **Application**

94.   "I know I'll make a fool of myself if I tell him how I feel."

      Answer: e   **Type: Matching**   **Page: 164**   **Application**

95.   "There is nothing good or bad but thinking makes it so." Apply this Shakespeare quote to communication in one of your relationships. Give specific examples and describe details.

      Answer   **Type: E**   **Page: 157**   **Application**

96.   Give examples of cultural, gender, and social influences on emotional expression from your own life.

      Answer   **Type: E**   **Pages: 144–148**   **Application**

97.   "When emotions begin to be shared, a relationship begins to deepen." How does this come about? Give two examples from your own experience that support this statement.

      Answer   **Type: E**   **Page: 149**   **Analysis**

98.   Report on three situations from your life that illustrate the primary and mixed emotions illustrated by Robert Plutchik's "emotion wheel."

      Answer   **Type: E**   **Page: 142**   **Application**

99.   Identify at least three irrational fallacies in the text you most commonly accept. Explain each fallacy and explain the potential harm each may cause if you fail to dispute it.

      Answer   **Type: E**   **Pages: 160–164**   **Analysis**

100.   Explain the relationship between interpersonal perception as described in Chapter Three and the rational-emotive approach to emotions in Chapter Four.

      Answer   **Type: E**   **Page: Ch. 3 and p. 157   Synthesis**

(Note: The following essay question works best as a "take-home" exam because of the time necessary to effectively complete it.)

101.   What are the guidelines suggested in your text for expressing feelings? Describe how you can apply these guidelines to your life. Give specific examples.

      Answer   **Type: E**   **Pages: 149–154**   **Application**

CHAPTER 5

LANGUAGE: BARRIER AND BRIDGE

1. The "Challenging the "S Word"" reading in Chapter Five is about cursing in schools.

   Answer: F   **Type: T**   **Page: 192**   **Recall**

2. "It's a 'girl' thing for women" argues that the word "girl" can be used as a powerful term by women.

   Answer: T   **Type: T**   **Page: 187**   **Recall**

3. "The Many Meanings of 'I Love You'" in this chapter points out how too many people think they are in love when they are just infatuated.

   Answer: F   **Type: T**   **Page: 180**   **Recall**

4. A group of synonyms such as one finds in a dictionary can completely define an object.

   Answer: F   **Type: T**   **Page: 178**   **Comprehension**

5. Because meanings rest more in people than in words, labels are unimportant.

   Answer: F   **Type: T**   **Page: 186**   **Comprehension**

6. Equivocal words are words that can be interpreted in more than one way.

   Answer: T   **Type: T**   **Page: 179**   **Knowledge**

7. Emotive words are words that sound as if they're describing something but are really announcing the speaker's attitude toward it.

   Answer: T   **Type: T**   **Page: 197**   **Knowledge**

8. Linguistic relativism is a notion that holds that our language exerts a strong influence on our perceptions.

   Answer: T   **Type: T**   **Page: 216**   **Knowledge**

9. "I'm rather upset" is more powerful language than "I'm upset."

   Answer: F   **Type: T**   **Page: 194**   **Comprehension**

10. A perfectly worded "I" statement delivered with total sincerity will ensure that the other person will not get defensive.

    Answer: F   **Type: T**   **Page: 204**   **Knowledge**

11. Language is symbolic.

    Answer: T   **Type: T**   **Page: 177**   **Knowledge**

12. Syntactic rules govern language.

    Answer: T   **Type: T**   **Page: 186**   **Knowledge**

13. Relative words gain their meaning from comparison.

    Answer: T   **Type: T**   **Page: 181**   **Knowledge**

14. The U.S. is a high-context language culture.

    Answer: F   **Type: T**   **Page: 211**   **Comprehension**

15. We use high-level abstractions to fool others but not ourselves.

    Answer: F   **Type: T**   **Page: 183**   **Knowledge**

16. The best way to move down the abstraction ladder when someone confronts you with vague language is to look up the confusing words in a dictionary.

    Answer: F   **Type: T**   **Pages: 184–185**   **Application**

17. Semantic rules are more powerful than an individual's personal meaning for words.

    Answer: T   **Type: T**   **Page: 178**   **Analysis**

18. Sign language is symbolic in nature.

    Answer: T   **Type: T**   **Page: 177**   **Knowledge**

19. Much of the awkwardness that comes with first using "I" language is due to its unfamiliarity.

    Answer: T   **Type: T**   **Page: 203**   **Knowledge**

20. Emotive words sound like statements of fact, but they're typically opinions.

    Answer: T   **Type: T**   **Page: 197**   **Knowledge**

21. Inferential statements are interpretations of behavior.

    Answer: T   **Type: T**   **Page: 196**   **Comprehension**

22. Meanings are best found by studying the words people use, not by observing how people use them.

    Answer: F   **Type: T**   **Page: 178**   **Comprehension**

23. A formal language culture will have different vocabularies for different sexes, levels of social status, or degrees of intimacy.

    Answer: T   **Type: T**   **Page: 214**   **Comprehension**

24.   "I" language statements may contain the word "I" more than once.

Answer: T   **Type: T**   **Page: 200**   **Evaluation**

25.   "No" is so clear and short that it is one of the few words that is never misinterpreted.

Answer: T   **Type: T**   **Page: 182**   **Analysis**

26.   Asking questions may be a linguistic way to avoid making a declaration.

Answer: T   **Type: T**   **Page: 207**   **Comprehension**

27.   Statements that contain the word "is" ("Kyle is an active guy") may lead to the assumption that people are unchanging.

Answer: T   **Type: T**   **Page: 181**   **Knowledge**

28.   Studies have found that females use as much cursing or profanity as males.

Answer: F   **Type: T**   **Page: 207**   **Knowledge**

29.   Women use more intensifiers than men do.

Answer: F   **Type: T**   **Page: 208**   **Knowledge**

30.   Research shows that linguistic differences are more often a function of sex roles than they are of biological sex.

Answer: T   **Type: T**   **Page: 209**   **Comprehension**

31.   Men discuss with other men the same conversation topics that women discuss with other women.

Answer: F   **Type: T**   **Page: 205**   **Knowledge**

32.   Your text confirms the stereotype that women are more likely to talk about feelings and relationships than men are.

Answer: T   **Type: T**   **Page: 206**   **Knowledge**

33.   Men talk more about sports figures and current events than women do.

Answer: T   **Type: T**   **Page: 205**   **Knowledge**

34.   Men and women report using language for different purposes.

Answer: T   **Type: T**   **Page: 206**   **Knowledge**

35.   The process of static evaluation implies that people or things are unchanging.

Answer: T   **Type: T**   **Page: 181**   **Knowledge**

36. "The Challenging the 'S Word'" reading in Chapter Five described how some people have negative associations for the word

 a. superior.
 b. saint.
 c. sport.
 d. squaw.
 e. Sunday.

 Answer: d   **Type: M**   **Page: 192**   **Recall**

37. In the "Language and Heritage" reading in Chapter Five, a woman points out that some Spanish words

 a. are not tied to culture.
 b. have caused international war.
 c. are English derivatives.
 d. describe English culture better than English does.
 e. have no direct English equivalent.

 Answer: e   **Type: M**   **Page: 215**   **Recall**

38. Chapter Five began with a biblical passage about

 a. Daniel in the lion's den.
 b. the prodigal son.
 c. the good Samaritan.
 d. the Tower of Babel.
 e. the Garden of Eden.

 Answer: d   **Type: M**   **Page: 176**   **Recall**

39. The "Many Meanings of 'I Love You'" passage in Chapter Five described

 a. a lovers' quarrel.
 b. many ways to say "I love you."
 c. the many meanings of the words "I love you."
 d. how to tell when a speaker who says "I love you" is sincere.
 e. how the term "love" has different meanings in various cultures.

 Answer: c   **Type: M**   **Page: 180**   **Recall**

40. In the "I" and "You" Language on the Job Communication Transcript, Rebecca confronts Tom about his

 a. vacation time.
 b. sexist language.
 c. frequent absences.
 d. abstractions.
 e. "you" language

 Answer: c   **Type: M**   **Page: 202**   **Recall**

41. "It's a 'girl' thing for women" in Chapter Five illustrates

 a. that who uses the term "girl" determines the reaction to it.
 b. the use of "girl" is a sexist term.
 c. that "no" is more clear to women than to girls.
 d. how inexpressive the term "girl" is.
 e. how feminists have overreacted and banned the use of the term "girl."

 Answer: a   **Type: M**   **Page: 187**   **Recall**

42. In the Looking at Diversity reading in Chapter Five, Mikako Garard describes how

 a. you have to translate a culture, not just a language, to be bilingual.
 b. diverse Australians are when they use the same English language we use with different meanings.
 c. the energy audits she conducted for Southern California Edison used low-level abstraction to better educate their customers.
 d. spinal meningitis can cause language difficulties.
 e. being trilingual has helped her in her job.

 Answer: a   **Type: M**   **Page: 212**   **Recall**

43. According to the text, one semantic problem is that much language is too

 a. wordy.
 b. sentimental.
 c. unfeeling.
 d. abstract.
 e. specific.

 Answer: d   **Type: M**   **Page: 182**   **Comprehension**

44. A behavioral description should include

 a. a dictionary definition.
 b. a microscopic analysis.
 c. only equivocal terms.
 d. all of the above.
 e. none of the above.

 Answer: e   **Type: M**   **Pages: 183–184**   **Analysis**

45. We learn to distinguish a speaker's intention when we encounter unclear statements by relying on the _____ rules of language.

 a. pragmatic
 b. ambiguous
 c. relative
 d. equivocal
 e. syntactic

 Answer: a   **Type: M**   **Page: 186**   **Knowledge**

46. In a low-context language culture, you will notice

    a. indirect expression of opinions.
    b. use of silence admired.
    c. less reliance on explicit verbal messages.
    d. self-expression valued.
    e. ambiguity admired.

    Answer: d   **Type: M**   **Page: 211**   **Comprehension**

47. Succinctness in language is most extreme in cultures where

    a. silence is valued.
    b. the language system is limited.
    c. more than one language is spoken.
    d. verbal fluency is admired.
    e. the use of equivocation is high.

    Answer: a   **Type: M**   **Page: 213**   **Knowledge**

48. All of the following statements about language are true except:

    a. Men's speech is more direct and task-oriented.
    b. Women's speech is more indirect and elaborate.
    c. Men are more likely to talk about themselves with women.
    d. Men accommodate more to topics women raise.
    e. In some cases there is no difference in male and female language.

    Answer: d   **Type: M**   **Page: 208**   **Synthesis**

49. Which of the factors below counts for the least influence on the linguistic differences in speech?

    a. gender
    b. setting
    c. expertise of the speaker
    d. social roles
    e. sex roles

    Answer: a   **Type: M**   **Page: 209**   **Synthesis**

50. On the strength of a recommendation from one of your friends, you took a class from an instructor that your friend had described as "witty, bright, and a fair grader." You fell asleep in the class and received a "D" in the course, although you thought you deserved a "B." You were a victim of misunderstanding because of

    a. emotive language.
    b. irregular words.
    c. euphemistic language.
    d. divergence.
    e. linguistics.

    Answer: a   **Type: M**   **Page: 197**   **Application**

51. Which of the following is the highest-level abstraction?

   a. complaining
   b. complaining about chores
   c. complaining about my housekeeping
   d. reminding me to wash the dishes
   e. reminding me about chores I haven't done

   Answer: a   **Type: M**   **Page: 182**   **Application**

52. Which of the following is the lowest-level abstraction?

   a. paying attention to me every day
   b. letting me know you appreciate me
   c. saying "thanks" when I help with your work
   d. paying attention to me
   e. giving me more time

   Answer: c   **Type: M**   **Page: 182**   **Evaluation**

53. Which of the following is the best example of highly abstract language?

   a. "Turn to page 116 and do the exercise at the bottom of the page."
   b. "My car wouldn't start this morning; I wish I had never bought it."
   c. "John is a patriotic person."
   d. "Can you play tennis?"
   e. "My favorite course is Interpersonal Communication."

   Answer: c   **Type: M**   **Page: 182**   **Application**

54. When we study semantics, we learn that

   a. words mean a lot in and of themselves.
   b. the labels we attach to our experiences can shape the attitudes we hold.
   c. words typically can be interpreted in only one way.
   d. meanings rest more in words than in the people who use them.

   Answer: b   **Type: M**   **Page: 178**   **Comprehension**

55. In cultures that stress formality in language,

   a. using correct grammar is most important.
   b. language use defines social position.
   c. the people talk less.
   d. there are fewer real friendships.
   e. the people are too stiff to really communicate.

   Answer: b   **Type: M**   **Page: 214**   **Comprehension**

56. Equivocal words

    a. have more than one commonly accepted definition.
    b. are low-level abstractions.
    c. mean the same to all people and are thus redundant.
    d. have meanings one person can guess at but another can't.
    e. have no known nonverbal signals to accompany them.

    Answer: a   **Type: M**   **Page: 179**   **Knowledge**

57. When I refer to my math classmates and say they're a "bunch of good guys," I may have caused a misunderstanding in that I used

    a. equivocal words.
    b. emotive words.
    c. semantic words.
    d. behavioral interpretations.
    e. a euphemism.

    Answer: b   **Type: M**   **Page: 197**   **Knowledge**

58. Which of the following is the least abstract definition of a successful college experience?

    a. a better understanding of Western civilization
    b. completion of the requirements listed on page 24 of the college catalog with a grade-point average of 2.0 or higher
    c. the ability to express oneself clearly, understand principles of the arts and sciences, and have some expertise in a chosen field of study
    d. both intellectual and social adjustment
    e. the ability to contribute to society

    Answer: b   **Type: M**   **Page: 182**   **Analysis**

59. One of the problems we run into when we use abstract language is that we

    a. tend to avoid finding the generalizations we need for understanding.
    b. may clarify things for others instead of ourselves.
    c. may send too clear a message
    d. may confuse ourselves.

    Answer: d   **Type: M**   **Page: 183**   **Comprehension**

60. Using high-level abstractions may be helpful when the abstractions

    a. let us talk about the similarities between several objects or events.
    b. act as a verbal shorthand.
    c. avoid confrontation with others.
    d. all of the above
    e. High-level abstractions are never helpful.

    Answer: d   **Type: M**   **Page: 182**   **Comprehension**

61. A speaker's willingness to take responsibility for his/her thoughts or feelings can be indicated by the use of

  a. singular terms.
  b. "I" language.
  c. "you" language.
  d. consequence terms.
  e. euphemisms.

  Answer: b   **Type: M**   **Page: 200**   **Analysis**

62. "People from the East Coast are rude." Which of the following abstraction problems is illustrated by this statement?

  a. stereotyping
  b. confusing others
  c. confusing yourself
  d. being too frank
  e. bicoastalism

  Answer: a   **Type: M**   **Page: 182**   **Application**

63. Which of the following statements avoids high abstractions?

  a. "You're the best friend I've ever had."
  b. "I think you've just been terrific."
  c. "I appreciated you loaning us that pan on Monday."
  d. "You are so thoughtful."
  e. "I love the way you always come through for me."

  Answer: c   **Type: M**   **Page: 184**   **Application**

64. Which of the following is a way to avoid the abstraction in the statement "I've got to be a better student"?

  a. "I'm going to spend two hours a day studying."
  b. "I'm going to try harder."
  c. "I'm going to get some help from some places on campus."
  d. "My mother and father will be happier if I'm a better student."
  e. "Instructors like students who try hard."

  Answer: a   **Type: M**   **Page: 184**   **Evaluation**

65. A behavioral description should include

  a. who is involved.
  b. in what circumstances the behavior occurs.
  c. what behaviors are involved.
  d. all of the above.
  e. none of the above.

  Answer: d   **Type: M**   **Page: 184**   **Comprehension**

66. Which of the following is the least abstract statement?

    a. "I love dinner parties."
    b. "I love eating out in all the cities of the United States."
    c. "I like to have eight people over for a six-course French meal including a chocolate mousse dessert."
    d. "The eight friends had forty-eight dollars between them to eat a healthy dinner last night."
    e. "The chocolate cake at Piero's is an ultimate delight."

    Answer: c   **Type: M**   **Page: 184**   **Evaluation**

67. If I say "here the drink bring," I have violated a(n) _____ rule of our language.

    a. initial
    b. syntactic
    c. median
    d. semantic
    e. final

    Answer: b   **Type: M**   **Page: 186**   **Knowledge**

68. Syntactic rules of language govern

    a. the ways in which symbols can be arranged.
    b. the ways in which speakers respond to symbols.
    c. the words that become slang.
    d. the creation of new tactics.
    e. the way that semanticists create meaning.

    Answer: a   **Type: M**   **Page: 186**   **Knowledge**

69. Linguistic relativism is a concept that signifies that

    a. language exerts a strong influence on perceptions.
    b. language is relative.
    c. language determines culture.
    d. truth is a relative cultural experience.
    e. everything is relative.

    Answer: a   **Type: M**   **Page: 216**   **Knowledge**

70. Making an inference is a reasonable thing to do relationally as long as

    a. you make a number of them.
    b. you wait for the other to infer also.
    c. the other person understands you.
    d. you identify the inference to the other person.
    e. you first describe the fact that led to the inference.

    Answer: e   **Type: M**   **Page: 196**   **Synthesis**

71. Which of the following statements is a fact?

    a. "It's clear you shouldn't have said that."
    b. "Fact number one: you said a dumb thing."
    c. "It's a fact that playing mind games always backfires."
    d. "I heard you say you weren't interested."
    e. "You should have thought about the result of saying you weren't interested before you opened your mouth."

Answer: d   **Type: M**   **Page: 196**   **Knowledge**

72. Which of the following is the highest-level abstraction?

    a. Jake Adams
    b. human being
    c. man
    d. farmer
    e. wheat farmer

Answer: b   **Type: M**   **Page: 182**   **Evaluation**

73. Which of the following is the lowest-level abstraction?

    a. car
    b. Chevy
    c. 1986 Chevy Nova
    d. blue Chevy
    e. reliable car

Answer: c   **Type: M**   **Page: 182**   **Evaluation**

74. "Californians love to surf." Which of the following abstraction problems is illustrated by this statement?

    a. stereotyping
    b. confusing others
    c. confusing yourself
    d. static evaluation
    e. none of the above

Answer: a   **Type: M**   **Page: 182**   **Analysis**

75. Words that have more than one dictionary definition are called

    a. emotive language.
    b. relative words.
    c. equivocal words.
    d. fiction terms.
    e. semantic distracters.

Answer: c   **Type: M**   **Page: 179**   **Knowledge**

76. If you take an "easy" class your friend recommended and find it "hard," you have had semantic problems due to

    a. euphemistic language.
    b. relative words.
    c. equivocal words.
    d. fiction terms.
    e. semantic distracters.

    Answer: b   **Type: M**   **Page: 181**   **Knowledge**

77. You promise to return your friend's tape "soon" and your friend gets mad when you don't return it that day. You originally meant "soon" to be the end of the week. You and your friend experienced a semantic problem due to

    a. emotive language.
    b. relative words.
    c. equivocal words.
    d. euphemisms.
    e. semantic distracters.

    Answer: b   **Type: M**   **Page: 181**   **Application**

78. A culture is unavoidably shaped and reflected by the language its members speak. This concept is

    a. high-context culture.
    b. low-context culture.
    c. cultural anthropology.
    d. cognitive determinism.
    e. linguistic determinism.

    Answer: e   **Type: M**   **Page: 214**   **Comprehension**

79. "You can't trust a woman." Which of the following errors is illustrated by this statement?

    a. stereotyping
    b. confusing denotation and connotation
    c. the fallacy of causation
    d. static evaluation
    e. semantic distraction

    Answer: a   **Type: M**   **Page: 182**   **Application**

80. Using language that incorrectly represents people as unchanging (e.g., "Frank is selfish") can lead to

    a. psychological noise.
    b. the fallacy of overgeneralization.
    c. self-fulfilling prophecies.
    d. selective perception.
    e. all of the above.

    Answer: e   **Type: M**   **Page: 181**   **Synthesis**

81. You think Erin is "arrogant." Your friend thinks she has a lot of "self-confidence." An argument over who is right would revolve around

    a. syntactic rules.
    b. relative terms.
    c. emotive language.
    d. sequential placement.
    e. linguistic determinism.

    Answer: c   **Type: M**   **Page: 197**   **Evaluation**

82. Misunderstandings that revolve around emotive, equivocal, and relative language can all be clarified by

    a. clearer punctuation of perceptual events.
    b. more interpersonal and less impersonal communication.
    c. replacing abstract terms with concrete ones.
    d. static definitions.
    e. sequential placement.

    Answer: c   **Type: M**   **Pages: 179–181, 197**   **Synthesis**

83. You tell a friend "I wish you'd be direct instead of hinting around," but your friend responds by denying that she/he hints. One way to help resolve the issue is to

    a. describe the hinting according to the dictionary.
    b. give a behavioral description of your mother's hinting so he/she gets the idea.
    c. specifically describe the friend's hinting when it occurs.
    d. describe all at once the many times that the troublesome behavior occurs.

    Answer: c   **Type: M**   **Page: 184**   **Evaluation**

84. Which of the following is the clearest behavioral description?

    a. "I wish you were as friendly as you used to be to people we meet at parties."
    b. "I'd like you to invite the Molitors over this weekend."
    c. You always look so glum these days—cheer up."
    d. "I wish you'd warm up around my friends."
    e. "You've changed."

    Answer: b   **Type: M**   **Page: 184**   **Evaluation**

85. Semantic misunderstandings often arise because of

    a. differing psychological environments.
    b. sloppy encoding by the sender.
    c. distorted perceptions of the receiver.
    d. failure to use perception checking.
    e. all of the above.

    Answer: e   **Type: M**   **Page: 178**   **Analysis**

86. How could you increase the power of the statement "I, uh, think I'd be a little happier if you could make it on time. Okay?"?

    a. Revise the sequential placement.
    b. Use perception checking.
    c. Use more disclaimers.
    d. Add a tag question.
    e. None of the above increases the power of the statement.

    Answer: e   **Type: M**   **Page: 194**   **Evaluation**

87. Which of the following illustrates stereotyping?

    a. Women comprise less than 10 percent of that population.
    b. Old people get senile.
    c. Disabled workers claim over $1 million per year in benefits.
    d. Forty percent of the wealthiest people in the U.S. give 20 percent of their income to charity.

    Answer: b   **Type: M**   **Page: 182**   **Application**

88. An "I" language statement must contain

    a. a description of the other person's behavior.
    b. a description of the other person's feelings.
    c. the consequences of the speaker's behavior.
    d. an analysis of the other person's behavior.
    e. supportive comments about the other person.

    Answer: a   **Type: M**   **Page: 200**   **Analysis**

89. What's missing from this "I" language statement? "When you hung up without saying where we'd meet, I felt confused and so I went to the wrong place."

    a. It doesn't describe the other person's behavior.
    b. It doesn't describe the speaker's feelings.
    c. It doesn't describe the consequences the other's behavior has for the speaker.
    d. It doesn't describe the speaker's interpretation of the behavior.
    e. This "I" language statement is fine just the way it is.

    Answer: d   **Type: M**   **Page: 200**   **Knowledge**

INSTRUCTIONS for questions 90–99: Identify each of the following statements as fact or inference.

    a. inference
    b. fact

90. You are trying to hurt me.

    Answer: a   **Type: Matching**   **Page: 196**   **Evaluation**

91. You told Jimmy that I didn't want to go out with him.

    Answer: b   **Type: Matching**   **Page: 196**   **Evaluation**

92.   Jim is so cute and helpful.

   Answer: a   **Type: Matching**   **Page: 196**   **Evaluation**

93.   Jim wrote me a letter to help me get that job.

   Answer: b   **Type: Matching**   **Page: 196**   **Evaluation**

94.   Your children are disruptive.

   Answer: a   **Type: Matching**   **Page: 196**   **Evaluation**

95.   Your children interrupted me when I spoke.

   Answer: b   **Type: Matching**   **Page: 196**   **Evaluation**

96.   The school board president was arrested for drunken driving.

   Answer: b   **Type: Matching**   **Page: 196**   **Evaluation**

97.   Their new apartment is more comfortable than the old one.

   Answer: a   **Type: Matching**   **Page: 196**   **Evaluation**

98.   Liz's outfit has many colors in it.

   Answer: b   **Type: Matching**   **Page: 196**   **Evaluation**

99.   Dan's language skills are very developed.

   Answer: a   **Type: Matching**   **Page: 216**   **Evaluation**

100.   "Language is power." Discuss this statement, using (a) an explanation of the types of powerful/powerless language given in your text, and (b) examples of these types of language in your own life.

   Answer   **Type: E**   **Page: 194**   **Analysis**

101.   Using "I" language patterns from the text, create five "I" language statements you could actually deliver to people important in your life. Identify the three parts of each of your complete "I" statements.

   Answer   **Type: E**   **Page: 200**   **Synthesis**

102.   Compare and contrast your use of language with that of someone else you know, pointing out the similarities or differences in 1) verbal communication style (direct/indirect, elaborate/succinct, formal/informal) and 2) worldview. Cite specific examples.

   Answer   **Type: E**   **Pages: 210–216**   **Synthesis**

103. Using low-level abstractions, describe two ways in which you presently communicate successfully or two ways in which you would like to communicate better in interpersonal situations. For each goal, be sure to describe the people involved, the circumstances in which the communication takes place, and the current or desired behaviors.

    Answer   **Type: E**   **Pages: 184–185**   **Synthesis**

104. Describe what abstract language is and how you use unnecessarily abstract language that causes communication problems. Give at least five examples. Tell how you could lower the level of abstraction in each of the examples you have given or provide reasons why the higher-level abstraction is justified and relationally beneficial.

    Answer   **Type: E**   **Pages: 182–185**   **Synthesis**

105. In your own words, explain the statement "meanings rest more in people than in words." Cite examples from your own experience.

    Answer   **Type: E**   **Pages: 178–186**   **Application**

(Note: The following essay questions work best as "take-home" exams because of the time necessary to effectively complete them.)

106. Tape-record two separate 10- to 15-minute conversations you have with a man and a woman who are important in your life. Describe these conversations briefly in terms of content and style. Compare the conversations and comment on any variables involved, using terms and research from your text that address the issue of gender and language.

    Answer   **Type: E**   **Pages: 205–208**   **Synthesis**

107. The text describes some ways in which men and women use language both differently and similarly. Cite a major research finding in each of the following areas and cite examples from your life that reflect these findings or contradict them: a) content, b) reasons for communicating, c) conversational style, and d) nongender variables.

    Answer   **Type: E**   **Pages: 206–209**   **Synthesis**

CHAPTER 6

NONVERBAL COMMUNICATION:
MESSAGES WITHOUT WORDS

1. "The Way You Talk Can Hurt You?" reading in Chapter Six claims that women lose influence by using a rising intonation at the end of declarative sentences.

    Answer: T   **Type: T**   **Page: 253**   **Recall**

2. "The Way You Talk Can Hurt You?" reading in Chapter Six calls for men to indicate more cooperation in their language by using rising intonation.

    Answer: F   **Type: T**   **Page: 253**   **Recall**

3. In the Sherlock Holmes story in Chapter Six, Watson points out that Holmes was the first nonverbal researcher to define paralanguage.

    Answer: F   **Type: T**   **Page: 222**   **Recall**

4. One study reported in the nonverbal communication chapter revealed that rapists sometimes use the postural clues of potential victims to choose those they believe are easy to intimidate.

    Answer: T   **Type: T**   **Page: 245**   **Recall**

5. In "The Look of a Victim" story in Chapter Six, prisoners convicted of assault revealed how many times they had mugged men based on their clothing.

    Answer: F   **Type: T**   **Page: 246**   **Recall**

6. Results of the "ugly room" experiment, described in the environment section of the nonverbal chapter, showed that subjects showed a greater desire to work in the ugly room because they didn't have any other distractions.

    Answer: F   **Type: T**   **Page: 261**   **Recall**

7. One study in the nonverbal chapter reported that rapists select their victims on the basis of the way they wear their hair.

    Answer: F   **Type: T**   **Page: 245**   **Recall**

8. According to the text, you can't not communicate.

    Answer: T   **Type: T**   **Page: 225**   **Comprehension**

9.   Nonverbal communication is usually specific and clear.

Answer: F   **Type: T**   **Page: 237**   **Comprehension**

10. Nonverbal communication is not as effective at conveying thoughts or ideas as it is at conveying relational messages.

Answer: T   **Type: T**   **Page: 232**   **Comprehension**

11. Once you increase your awareness of nonverbal messages, you can "read" another person's nonverbal behavior accurately in most situations.

Answer: F   **Type: T**   **Page: 239**   **Comprehension**

12. Your text defines nonverbal communication as "those messages expressed by other than linguistic means."

Answer: T   **Type: T**   **Page: 223**   **Knowledge**

13. Nonverbal and verbal behaviors operate together to create messages.

Answer: T   **Type: T**   **Page: 233**   **Comprehension**

14. In social transactions, the higher status person is generally the more rigid, tense-appearing one, whereas the one with lower status is usually more relaxed.

Answer: F   **Type: T**   **Page: 245**   **Knowledge**

15. Research indicates that people are quite accurate at judging facial expressions for surprise, fear, anger, disgust, happiness, and sadness.

Answer: T   **Type: T**   **Page: 247**   **Knowledge**

16. In laboratory settings, subjects are better judges of positive facial expressions than they are of negative ones.

Answer: T   **Type: T**   **Page: 238**   **Comprehension**

17. Gestures can be intentional or unintentional.

Answer: T   **Type: T**   **Page: 245**   **Synthesis**

18. Research reveals that increased use of manipulators is often a sign of discomfort.

Answer: T   **Type: T**   **Page: 245**   **Knowledge**

19. In many instances, the use of touch increases liking and boosts compliance.

Answer: T   **Type: T**   **Page: 254**   **Knowledge**

20. People penetrate our "spatial bubble" by both physical and visual invasion.

Answer: T   **Type: T**   **Pages: 247, 257**   **Application**

21. Generally, facing someone directly signals your interest in that person.

Answer: T   **Type: T**   **Page: 243**   **Knowledge**

22. Research shows that people who question deceptive communicators get no better at detecting their lies.

Answer: T   **Type: T**   **Page: 236**   **Knowledge**

23. Most communication scholars don't define American Sign Language as nonverbal communication.

Answer: T   **Type: T**   **Page: 223**   **Knowledge**

24. Nonverbal communication can be very revealing, but it can have so many possible meanings that it's foolish to think your interpretation will always be correct.

Answer: T   **Type: T**   **Page: 241**   **Comprehension**

25. Some people are more skillful than others at accurately decoding nonverbal behavior.

Answer: T   **Type: T**   **Page: 239**   **Knowledge**

26. Your text defines nonverbal communication as any type of communication that isn't expressed by speech.

Answer: F   **Type: T**   **Page: 223**   **Comprehension**

27. Different emotions show most clearly in various parts of the face.

Answer: T   **Type: T**   **Page: 247**   **Knowledge**

28. According to your text, some researchers claim that over 90 percent of the emotional impact of a message comes from nonverbal sources.

Answer: T   **Type: T**   **Page: 223**   **Knowledge**

29. According to your text, research has demonstrated that over 60 percent of the emotional impact of a message comes from verbal sources.

Answer: F   **Type: T**   **Page: 223**   **Comprehension**

30. When we are interested in something or someone, the pupils of our eyes usually get smaller.

Answer: F   **Type: T**   **Page: 248**   **Knowledge**

31. A low degree of gesturing may be as significant an indicator of double messages as a high degree of gesturing.

Answer: T   **Type: T**   **Page: 247**   **Knowledge**

32. Stammering and saying "uh" are actually nonverbal behaviors termed disfluencies.

Answer: T   **Type: T**   **Page: 250**   **Knowledge**

33. Researchers have found nonverbal convergence impossible when dealing with members of different cultures.

    Answer: F   **Type: T**   **Page: 230**   **Comprehension**

34. Paralinguistic elements always accompany the spoken word.

    Answer: T   **Type: T**   **Page: 250**   **Comprehension**

35. Nonverbal behavior can initiate interaction or serve as feedback to prior messages.

    Answer: T   **Type: T**   **Pages: 225–234**   **Synthesis**

36. Many nonverbal behaviors are governed by cultural rules.

    Answer: T   **Type: T**   **Page: 226**   **Knowledge**

37. Silence or pauses count as nonverbal communication.

    Answer: T   **Type: T**   **Page: 250**   **Comprehension**

38. Patterns of eye contact are fairly consistent across cultures.

    Answer: F   **Type: T**   **Page: 227**   **Comprehension**

39. Emblems are nonverbal behaviors that have the same meaning to all members of a particular culture or co-culture.

    Answer: T   **Type: T**   **Page: 245**   **Knowledge**

40. It is possible to recognize paralinguistic messages, even if you don't understand the language being spoken.

    Answer: T   **Type: T**   **Page: 250**   **Comprehension**

41. According to research cited in your text, touch and health are not related.

    Answer: F   **Type: T**   **Page: 254**   **Knowledge**

42. One way to signal a desire to avoid involvement when forced into intimate distance with another is to position yourself in an indirect body orientation.

    Answer: T   **Type: T**   **Page: 243**   **Comprehension**

43. Researchers have found that the face and eyes are capable of only five basic expressions.

    Answer: F   **Type: T**   **Page: 247**   **Knowledge**

44. Pupil dilation can be a sign of interest.

    Answer: T   **Type: T**   **Page: 248**   **Knowledge**

45. Disfluencies are one type of paralanguage.

    Answer: T   **Type: T**   **Page: 250**   **Comprehension**

46. According to your text, people usually get more social meaning from what others do than from what they say.

   Answer: T   **Type: T**   **Page: 223**   **Comprehension**

47. If you get within one foot of someone else in U.S. culture, you've invaded their intimate zone, according to researcher Edward Hall.

   Answer: T   **Type: T**   **Page: 259**   **Evaluation**

48. There are more nonverbal than verbal messages available to you in a communication exchange.

   Answer: T   **Type: T**   **Page: 225**   **Analysis**

49. Verbal messages have clear beginnings and endings.

   Answer: T   **Type: T**   **Page: 241**   **Knowledge**

50. Nonverbal messages are more continuous, while verbal messages are more discrete.

   Answer: T   **Type: T**   **Page: 241**   **Knowledge**

51. Verbal messages are more deliberate than nonverbal messages.

   Answer: T   **Type: T**   **Page: 242**   **Knowledge**

52. Nonverbal cues are especially likely to carry weight when they contradict a speaker's words.

   Answer: T   **Type: T**   **Page: 242**   **Knowledge**

53. When you notice nonverbal deception cues, you can be sure the person is lying.

   Answer: F   **Type: T**   **Page: 239**   **Comprehension**

54. Deception studies have found that deceivers are more likely to be found out when they feel strongly about the information being hidden.

   Answer: T   **Type: T**   **Page: 236**   **Knowledge**

55. If deceivers feel confident and not guilty, their deception is more likely to be found out.

   Answer: F   **Type: T**   **Page: 236**   **Knowledge**

56. In the excerpt from the Sherlock Holmes story in Chapter Six, Holmes points out that Watson

   a. listens but fails to see.
   b. sees but does not observe.
   c. can't observe well because he doesn't communicate.
   d. fails to solve cases because he pays too much attention to nonverbal messages.
   e. watches but fails to listen.

   Answer: b   **Type: M**   **Page: 222**   **Recall**

57. The "unliving rooms" described in this chapter are rooms where

    a. no one is allowed to touch one another.
    b. people feel unloved.
    c. the surroundings discourage users from relaxing.
    d. no one has been for days.
    e. some researchers can communicate with the dead.

    Answer: c   **Type: M**   **Page: 261**   **Recall**

58. The Looking at Diversity reading in Chapter Six ("Nonverbal Stereotyping") features a black man who says he is frequently

    a. mistaken for white when he wears business suits.
    b. able to impress women with his knowledge of classical music.
    c. asked to speak to black groups because he knows how to behave nonverbally.
    d. arrested because of his color.
    e. a violence suspect because of his race.

    Answer: e   **Type: M**   **Page: 240**   **Recall**

59. In the Sherlock Holmes story in this chapter, Holmes notices that Watson

    a. had been out in vile weather.
    b. has put on weight.
    c. has a careless servant.
    d. all of the above
    e. none of the above

    Answer: d   **Type: M**   **Page: 222**   **Recall**

60. "The Look of a Victim" story in this chapter points out that victims of assault may set themselves up as easy targets because of

    a. their clothing.
    b. the way they walk.
    c. their hairstyles.
    d. wearing makeup.
    e. the fact that each victim had looked at the attacker beforehand.

    Answer: b   **Type: M**   **Page: 246**   **Recall**

61. Researchers who watched films of New York Mayor Fiorello LaGuardia with the sound turned off found that they could tell

    a. which language he was speaking by noting the changes in his nonverbal behavior.
    b. when he was going to end each speech by his gestures.
    c. how angry he was by his facial expressions.
    d. what he was saying as well as how he felt about it.
    e. all of the above.

    Answer: a   **Type: M**   **Page: 226**   **Recall**

62. When researchers compared black women in all-black groups to white women in all-white groups, they found that

    a. all the women engaged in similar nonverbal behaviors.
    b. the black women had more intense feelings than the white.
    c. the white women exhibited more emblems and manipulators.
    d. the black women interrupted more and were nonverbally more expressive.
    e. all of the above

    Answer: d   **Type: M**   **Page: 228**   **Recall**

63. "The Look of a Victim" in the nonverbal chapter summarizes

    a. a fairy tale about chronemics.
    b. the nonverbal behavior of traffic accident victims.
    c. the "muggability rating" of New York pedestrians.
    d. the clothing that leads to date rape.

    Answer: c   **Type: M**   **Page: 246**   **Recall**

64. Studies of nonverbal communication across cultures reveal that

    a. smiles and laughter are a universal signal of positive emotions.
    b. sour expressions convey displeasure in some cultures and pleasure in others.
    c. the expression of feelings is discouraged in most cultures.
    d. all facial expressions are inborn.

    Answer: a   **Type: M**   **Page: 227**   **Synthesis**

65. The design and environment of rooms

    a. communicate information about the owner's personality.
    b. shape the interaction that takes place there.
    c. communicate information about the interests of the owner.
    d. b and c above
    e. all of the above

    Answer: e   **Type: M**   **Page: 261**   **Synthesis**

66. Kinesics is the study of

    a. personal distances.
    b. verbal and nonverbal behavior.
    c. body position and motion.
    d. environmental stress.
    e. clothing and color.

    Answer: c   **Type: M**   **Page: 240**   **Knowledge**

67. Proxemics is the study of

    a. the way people and animals use space.
    b. the way people use words to transmit messages.
    c. the way people use facial expressions.
    d. the way people use silence.
    e. the way people use vocal cues.

    Answer: a   **Type: M**   **Page: 257**   **Knowledge**

68. The many ways the voice communicates—including tone, speed, pitch, number and length of pauses, volume, etc.—are called

    a. paralanguage.
    b. vocalics.
    c. noncommunicators.
    d. nonvocals.
    e. proxemics.

    Answer: a   **Type: M**   **Page: 250**   **Knowledge**

69. The nonverbal researchers cited in your text claim that, when we consider the actual meaning involved in communication situations, verbal messages

    a. carry less meaning than nonverbal ones.
    b. carry more meaning than nonverbal ones.
    c. aren't really listened to.
    d. are too full of nonverbal signals.
    e. define the communication situation.

    Answer: a   **Type: M**   **Page: 223**   **Comprehension**

70. The main reason we miss many nonverbal clues contained in posture messages is that

    a. people don't stand up straight.
    b. the clues don't stand on their own.
    c. they aren't very obvious.
    d. sitting and standing aren't important clues.
    e. the clues are so blatantly obvious that people ignore them.

    Answer: c   **Type: M**   **Page: 244**   **Knowledge**

71. The first of Edward T. Hall's proxemic zones, the closest distance, is

    a. social distance.
    b. skin distance.
    c. intimate distance.
    d. touching distance.
    e. eye distance.

    Answer: c   **Type: M**   **Page: 258**   **Knowledge**

72. Nonverbally, women _____ more than men.

    a. make less eye contact
    b. smile less
    c. are less vocally expressive
    d. gesture more
    e. require more personal space

    Answer: d   **Type: M**   **Page: 230**   **Comprehension**

73. Deceptive nonverbal communication

    a. is always aimed at taking advantage of the recipient.
    b. may simply be a polite way to express an idea that would be difficult to handle if expressed in words.
    c. is more common among well-educated people.
    d. illustrates why we should always use clear messages.
    e. is termed congruency.

    Answer: b   **Type: M**   **Page: 237**   **Synthesis**

74. Interpretation of nonverbal messages (decoding ability) is more accurate

    a. with age and training.
    b. among introverts.
    c. among dogmatists.
    d. among men.
    e. all of the above

    Answer: a   **Type: M**   **Page: 238**   **Comprehension**

75. Psychologist Albert Mehrabian's studies of nonverbal posture behaviors has found that

    a. we are generally unaware of posture.
    b. different facial expressions help posture interpretation.
    c. we should use unambiguous postural cues.
    d. tension and relaxation of muscles can indicate status differences.
    e. posture is not important to body image.

    Answer: d   **Type: M**   **Page: 245**   **Comprehension**

76. All of the following statements are true except:

    a. The eyes can communicate positive and negative attitudes.
    b. Nonverbal messages of the face and eyes are the easiest to read.
    c. Even the pupils of the eyes can communicate messages.
    d. The eyes can indicate dominance and submission.
    e. The eyes send involvement messages.

    Answer: b   **Type: M**   **Pages: 247–248**   **Knowledge**

77. All of the following are characteristics of nonverbal behavior except:

    a. Nonverbal communication is culture-bound.
    b. Nonverbal behavior is clear and unambiguous.
    c. Nonverbal communication is primarily relational.
    d. All nonverbal behavior has communicative value.
    e. Nonverbal communication serves many functions.

    Answer: b   **Type: M**   **Pages: 225–237**   **Knowledge**

78. All of the following are true about touch except:

    a. Touch can be of life-and-death importance to a child.
    b. Touch can signal a variety of relationships.
    c. Touch can be a way to communicate both negative and positive feelings.
    d. Touch can increase a child's mental functioning.
    e. Touch in any of its forms can have positive effects.

    Answer: e   **Type: M**   **Pages: 252–255**   **Synthesis**

79. Which of the following statements is true?

    a. Nonverbal messages can repeat or accent verbal messages.
    b. Nonverbal messages can substitute for verbal messages.
    c. Nonverbal messages can complement and regulate verbal messages.
    d. Nonverbal messages can contradict verbal messages.
    e. Nonverbal messages can relate to verbal messages in all of the ways mentioned above.

    Answer: e   **Type: M**   **Pages: 233–234**   **Comprehension**

80. People's nonverbal behavior generally expresses

    a. relational messages.
    b. what they think.
    c. no communication at all.
    d. indifference.
    e. more about what they think than they are able to say.

    Answer: a   **Type: M**   **Page: 231**   **Comprehension**

81. When you become aware of nonverbal messages in your everyday life, you should interpret them as

    a. facts.
    b. clues that need to be checked out.
    c. more reliable indicators of thinking than verbal messages.
    d. ways to understand meanings.
    e. double meanings.

    Answer: b   **Type: M**   **Page: 239**   **Comprehension**

82.   When our nonverbal behavior is unintentional,

    a.   others disregard it.
    b.   others attach more significance to it.
    c.   others can't make interpretations based on it.
    d.   others respond with their own unintentional behaviors.
    e.   others recognize it and make interpretations based on it.

Answer: e　　　　**Type: M**　　　　**Page: 241**　　　　**Comprehension**

83.   The study of the way people and animals use space is termed

    a.   paralanguage.
    b.   space technology.
    c.   kinesics.
    d.   proxemics.
    e.   none of the above.

Answer: d　　　　**Type: M**　　　　**Page: 257**　　　　**Knowledge**

84.   The nonverbal ways the voice communicates are termed

    a.   paralanguage.
    b.   nonverbal toners.
    c.   prekinesics.
    d.   pitches.
    e.   chronemics.

Answer: a　　　　**Type: M**　　　　**Page: 250**　　　　**Knowledge**

85.   Hall's Distance Zones are

    a.   personal, impersonal, social, public.
    b.   intimate, personal, social, public.
    c.   intimate, nonintimate, social, public.
    d.   open, blind, hidden, unknown.
    e.   none of the above.

Answer: b　　　　**Type: M**　　　　**Pages: 258–260**　　　　**Knowledge**

86.   Most adaptors (self-touching behaviors) are

    a.   unconscious.
    b.   signs of deception.
    c.   excitement cues.
    d.   attempts to attract others.
    e.   signs of vulnerability.

Answer: a　　　　**Type: M**　　　　**Page: 245**　　　　**Knowledge**

87. Nonverbal communication is related to perception in that

    a. people who perceive better exhibit more nonverbal behaviors.
    b. we can't perceive most nonverbal behaviors.
    c. we perceive only what our own nonverbal behaviors are.
    d. cultural factors influence how we interpret many nonverbal behaviors.
    e. cultural perception and nonverbal behavior are identical terms.

    Answer: d   **Type: M**   **Ch. 3 and Page 226**   **Synthesis**

88. Using stammering or "uh, um, er" in conversation is the nonverbal behavior called

    a. affect displays.
    b. microexpressions.
    c. illustrators.
    d. disfluencies.
    e. macroexpressions.

    Answer: d   **Type: M**   **Page: 250**   **Knowledge**

89. The eyes typically send messages of

    a. involvement and avoidance.
    b. primarily negative attitudes.
    c. deception.
    d. degree of arousal.

    Answer: a   **Type: M**   **Page: 248**   **Comprehension**

90. The nonverbal term for the combination of two or more expressions of emotion in different parts of the face is

    a. multiexpressions.
    b. complex indicators.
    c. emo-mixes.
    d. affect blends.
    e. emotion mergers.

    Answer: d   **Type: M**   **Page: 247**   **Knowledge**

91. If you see someone smiling, you could interpret this communication to mean

    a. the other is friendly.
    b. the other is happy.
    c. the other wants to communicate.
    d. the other is faking something.
    e. any of the above

    Answer: e   **Type: M**   **Page: 241**   **Application**

92. Your friend insists that she is interested in what you are saying, but she keeps looking out the window while you speak. She is most probably

    a. telling a lie.
    b. bored with the conversation.
    c. noticing something out the window.
    d. daydreaming.
    e. Any of the above are equally possible.

    Answer: e   **Type: M**   **Page: 241**   **Application**

93. Nonverbal communication serves the functions of

    a. repeating and substituting.
    b. complementing and accenting.
    c. regulating and contradicting.
    d. all of the above.
    e. none of the above.

    Answer: d   **Type: M**   **Pages: 233–234**   **Knowledge**

94. In our culture, nodding your head up and down is a deliberate nonverbal behavior with a very precise meaning of "yes." According to your text, this is termed a(n)

    a. facilitator.
    b. interlocutor.
    c. emblem.
    d. nonverbalator.
    e. encoder.

    Answer: c   **Type: M**   **Page: 245**   **Synthesis**

95. All of the following are true about nonverbal communication across cultures except that

    a. distance patterns vary across cultures.
    b. patterns of eye contact vary around the world.
    c. emblems have precise and distinct meanings within cultural groups.
    d. amounts of touch needed emerges as a culture-universal.
    e. smiles, laughter, and sour expressions are universal signals of positive or negative emotion.

    Answer: d   **Type: M**   **Page: 226**   **Synthesis**

96. The nonverbal function equivalent to using italics in print is called

    a. complementing.
    b. accenting.
    c. regulating.
    d. contradicting.
    e. substituting.

    Answer: b   **Type: M**   **Page: 234**   **Comprehension**

97. Which of the following is an example of what social scientists call an emblem?

    a. waving your hand
    b. leaning back in your chair
    c. crossing your legs
    d. brushing your hair
    e. brushing your teeth

    Answer: a **Type: M** **Page: 245** **Application**

98. Research reveals that increased use of manipulators is often a sign of

    a. discomfort.
    b. power.
    c. shyness.
    d. dogmatism.
    e. inferiority.

    Answer: a **Type: M** **Page: 245** **Comprehension**

99. Vocal intonation patterns, audible breaths, eye contact patterns, and pauses in a conversation are nonverbal behaviors that illustrate the nonverbal function of

    a. substituting.
    b. regulating.
    c. accenting.
    d. repeating.
    e. complementing.

    Answer: b **Type: M** **Page: 234** **Application**

100. Apply the research cited in the nonverbal chapter to your life by indicating which effect the following message would have: Your friend says "I'm really interested in you" while he or she is looking at TV.

    a. You believe the words.
    b. You believe that the speaker is nervous.
    c. You believe the speaker may not be too interested in you since she's/he's not looking at you.
    d. You believe that since there is a good TV program on, you should watch it.
    e. You believe that the speaker has just finished a book on nonverbal communication.

    Answer: c **Type: M** **Page: 242** **Application**

101.   All of the following are true about the voice and communication except:

a.   Communicators who speak loudly and without hesitations are viewed as more
confident than those who pause and speak quietly.
b.   Younger-sounding communicators whose language is accent-free are rated as more
competent than older-sounding communicators.
c.   Some vocal factors influence the way a speaker is perceived.
d.   Accents that identify a speaker's membership in a group lead to more positive
evaluations of that person if the group is a prestigious one.
e.   People with more attractive voices are rated more highly than those whose speech
sounds less attractive.

Answer: b   **Type: M**   **Page: 250**   **Comprehension**

102.   All of the following behaviors have communicative value except

a.   closed eyes.
b.   walking out of a room.
c.   sitting forward.
d.   an expressionless face.
e.   All of the above do have communicative value.

Answer: e   **Type: M**   **Page: 225**   **Analysis**

103.   The nonverbal behavior of smiling at a friend as you say "come on over here" is an
example of the nonverbal function called

a.   substituting.
b.   regulating.
c.   complementing.
d.   contradicting.
e.   accenting.

Answer: c   **Type: M**   **Page: 233**   **Application**

104.   If you don't want a friend to know you are unhappy with your relationship, the best
thing to do is

a.   avoid eye contact.
b.   say less than usual.
c.   stay away from the friend more than usual.
d.   keep your voice free of emotion.
e.   none of the above.

Answer: e   **Type: M**   **Page: 236**   **Analysis**

105.   Nonverbal regulators can signal

a.   turn-taking.
b.   the desire to end a conversation.
c.   an invitation to respond.
d.   all of the above.
e.   none of the above.

Answer: d   **Type: M**   **Page: 234**   **Knowledge**

106. Nonverbal evidence of lying is most likely to occur when the deceiver

    a. has no strong feelings about the deception.
    b. has not rehearsed the deception.
    c. does not feel anxious or guilty about the lies.
    d. has lack of emotional involvement with the deception.
    e. doesn't know people are watching.

    Answer: b   **Type: M**   **Page: 236**   **Comprehension**

107. Adaptors are

    a. deceptive nonverbal behaviors.
    b. nonverbal coaches or teachers.
    c. one category of gestures.
    d. rare in some cultures.
    e. none of the above.

    Answer: c   **Type: M**   **Page: 245**   **Knowledge**

108. In nonverbal communication, studies of leakage deal with

    a. innate behaviors.
    b. illness behaviors.
    c. environmental issues.
    d. deception signals.
    e. perceptions of illness.

    Answer: d   **Type: M**   **Page: 234**   **Application**

109. Someone biting his/her fingernails may be communicating

    a. nervousness.
    b. anticipation.
    c. shyness.
    d. thoughtfulness.
    e. any of the above.

    Answer: e   **Type: M**   **Page: 239**   **Evaluation**

110. All of the following are true about nonverbal communication except:

    a. Nonverbal behaviors reach us one at a time, whereas verbal messages reach us all at once.
    b. Nonverbal communication is continuous with no clear beginning or ending.
    c. Nonverbal communication is more ambiguous than verbal communication.
    d. Nonverbal signals are much more powerful than verbal messages when they are delivered at the same time.
    e. Nonverbal messages aren't as deliberate as verbal messages.

    Answer: a   **Type: M**   **Pages: 240–242**   **Comprehension**

INSTRUCTIONS for questions 111–116: Match each description below with the term it best describes.

    a. chronemics
    b. emblem
    c. verbal communication
    d. nonverbal communication
    e. disfluency

111.   Usually expresses our thoughts best

      Answer: c   **Type: Matching**   **Page: 231**   **Knowledge**

112.   Usually expresses our feelings best

      Answer: d   **Type: Matching**   **Page: 231**   **Knowledge**

113.   Study of use and structure of time

      Answer: a   **Type: Matching**   **Page: 262**   **Knowledge**

114.   Waving, shaking head or finger

      Answer: b   **Type: Matching**   **Page: 245**   **Comprehension**

115.   Stammering

      Answer: e   **Type: Matching**   **Page: 250**   **Knowledge**

116.   Arriving early for an appointment

      Answer: a   **Type: Matching**   **Page: 262**   **Comprehension**

INSTRUCTIONS for questions 117–124: Match each description below with the term it best describes.

    a. illustrators
    b. touching
    c. affect blends
    d. proxemics
    e. kinesics

117.   Study of the use of space

      Answer: d   **Type: Matching**   **Page: 257**   **Knowledge**

118.   Study of body motion

      Answer: e   **Type: Matching**   **Page: 242**   **Knowledge**

119.   Combination of facial expressions

      Answer: c   **Type: Matching**   **Page: 247**   **Knowledge**

120.   Nonverbal behaviors that accompany and support spoken words

      Answer: a   **Type: Matching**   **Page: 245**   **Knowledge**

121.   Hitting, punching, patting, and pinching

   Answer: b   **Type: Matching**   **Page: 252**   **Comprehension**

122.   Stepping closer to indicate intimacy

   Answer: d   **Type: Matching**   **Page: 257**   **Comprehension**

123.   Smiling and looking quizzical at the same time

   Answer: c   **Type: Matching**   **Page: 247**   **Comprehension**

124.   Pointing to major terms written on the board during a lecture.

   Answer: a   **Type: Matching**   **Page: 245**   **Comprehension**

125.   Imagine that you have been commissioned to design a new campus center. What sort of communication should take place there? What kinds of furnishings and decorations would you suggest to increase the likelihood of this communication occurring? What messages would your choice of designs and decorations communicate?

   Answer   **Type: E**   **Page: 261**   **Evaluation**

126.   One characteristic of nonverbal communication is "all behavior has communicative value." Describe two incidents from your experience which illustrate both deliberate and unintentional meaning derived from nonverbal communication in these two incidents. Identify the nonverbal behaviors that occurred. Identify the meanings you did/did not intend to convey and the meanings that were conveyed from your perspective and that of your partner in each incident.

   Answer   **Type: E**   **Page: 225**   **Analysis**

127.   Using at least two of the types of nonverbal communication described in your text, and referring to your own experience, describe an incident which illustrates how nonverbal behavior can be ambiguous. How could you or the other person involved reduce the ambiguity of that situation?

   Answer   **Type: E**   **Page: 237**   **Application**

128.   Describe two interpersonal situations from your experience in which nonverbal behavior accented or contradicted the message being expressed verbally. Be sure that your descriptions of both the verbal message and the nonverbal behaviors are specific. Avoid obvious situations (i.e., yelling reinforces words like "I'm angry").

   Answer   **Type: E**   **Page: 234**   **Application**

129.   Use the list of differences between verbal and nonverbal communication in Chapter Six to analyze a recent conversation you have had with someone important to you. Describe the verbal and nonverbal messages and which channels were best suited to convey various messages.

   Answer   **Type: E**   **Pages: 240–242**   **Analysis**

CHAPTER 7

LISTENING: MORE THAN MEETS THE EAR

1. The average listener is capable of hearing speech at rates of up to 600 words per minute.

    Answer: T   **Type: T**   **Page: 279**   **Knowledge**

2. When we listen to an average speaker, we are listening to between 100 and 150 words per minute.

    Answer: T   **Type: T**   **Page: 279**   **Knowledge**

3. There is no single "best" listening style to use in all situations.

    Answer: T   **Type: T**   **Page: 307**   **Comprehension**

4. A good listener will always state her own opinion so the other person knows where she stands on the issue.

    Answer: F   **Type: T**   **Page: 293**   **Comprehension**

5. You should do more paraphrasing than any other type of listening.

    Answer: F   **Type: T**   **Page: 305**   **Comprehension**

6. We spend more time listening than in any other type of communication.

    Answer: T   **Type: T**   **Page: 268**   **Knowledge**

7. It's impossible to listen effectively all of the time.

    Answer: T   **Type: T**   **Page: 277**   **Knowledge**

8. During careful listening, your heart rate will quicken and your body temperature will rise.

    Answer: T   **Type: T**   **Page: 269**   **Knowledge**

9. Speaking has more apparent advantages than listening does.

    Answer: T   **Type: T**   **Page: 280**   **Knowledge**

10. Like defensiveness, listening is often reciprocal.

    Answer: T   **Type: T**   **Pages: 270**   **Synthesis**

11. Questioning is one type of listening to help others.

    Answer: T   **Type: T**   **Page: 297**   **Knowledge**

12. One characteristic of effective paraphrasing is its tentative nature.

    Answer: T   **Type: T**   **Page: 296**   **Synthesis**

13. Your text recommends paraphrasing whenever someone wants your help.

    Answer: F   **Type: T**   **Page: 305**   **Comprehension**

14. Paraphrasing is the most appropriate listening style in the classroom.

    Answer: F   **Type: T**   **Page: 285**   **Synthesis**

15. Studies show that good listeners keep eye contact and react with appropriate facial
    expressions.

    Answer: T   **Type: T**   **Page: 270**   **Knowledge**

16. According to the text, the most helpful way of responding to a problem is to offer
    good, specific advice.

    Answer: F   **Type: T**   **Page: 293**   **Comprehension**

17. Speaking is an active process; listening is a passive activity.

    Answer: F   **Type: T**   **Page: 271**   **Comprehension**

18. Paraphrasing is a valuable communication tool because it enables the people who
    practice it to share more about themselves with others.

    Answer: F   **Type: T**   **Page: 305**   **Comprehension**

19. Listening is an innate ability. Most people become good listeners as they mature.

    Answer: F   **Type: T**   **Page: 281**   **Comprehension**

20. If senders express themselves clearly, there is little need for feedback.

    Answer: F   **Type: T**   **Page: 270**   **Comprehension**

21. Listening behaviors such as insulated listening, pseudolistening, and selective listening
    are often reasonable responses to a deluge of relatively worthless information.

    Answer: T   **Type: T**   **Page: 276**   **Comprehension**

22. Because prompting involves using silences, it is not classified as a listening response.

    Answer: F   **Type: T**   **Page: 301**   **Knowledge**

23. Prompting is a more passive listening style than advising.

    Answer: T   **Type: T**   **Page: 301**   **Evaluation**

24. Paraphrasing is a good listening style to use if you want to ease back mentally and be entertained.

     Answer: F   **Type: T**   **Page: 303**   **Evaluation**

25. A questioning response is not really a form of feedback.

     Answer: F   **Type: T**   **Page: 285**   **Synthesis**

26. Even if you give accurate advice to a person, that advice may not be helpful.

     Answer: T   **Type: T**   **Page: 293**   **Knowledge**

27. Accurate analysis of a problem may arouse defensiveness.

     Answer: T   **Type: T**   **Page: 294**   **Knowledge**

28. Sometimes asking questions of a person with a problem only leads to a long digression that confuses matters.

     Answer: T   **Type: T**   **Page: 297**   **Knowledge**

29. When you use paraphrasing as a helping tool, your reflection should usually contain both thoughts and feelings.

     Answer: T   **Type: T**   **Page: 302**   **Knowledge**

30. Questioning and paraphrasing are both forms of feedback.

     Answer: T   **Type: T**   **Pages: 297 302**   **Synthesis**

31. Paraphrasing is recommended as a good listening style both for informational listening and listening to help.

     Answer: T   **Type: T**   **Page: 286**   **Comprehension**

32. Counterfeit questions are aimed at understanding others.

     Answer: F   **Type: T**   **Page: 285**   **Comprehension**

33. Analyzing can be one helpful way to help a speaker consider alternative meanings.

     Answer: T   **Type: T**   **Page: 296**   **Knowledge**

34. You actually need to speak more than listen when you listen for information in order to get all the details.

     Answer: F   **Type: T**   **Page: 284**   **Evaluation**

35. Advice given in a respectful, caring way, has been identified as a key ingredient in keeping platonic male–female friendships strong.

     Answer: T   **Type: T**   **Page: 294**   **Knowledge**

36. While paraphrasing responses can be helpful, they are useful only when they accurately reflect the other person's message.

    Answer: F   **Type: T**   **Page: 289**   **Synthesis**

37. Of the many different elements in the listening process, hearing is the physiological dimension.

    Answer: T   **Type: T**   **Page: 269**   **Comprehension**

38. According to your text, people usually try their best to listen but their effectiveness is limited primarily by biological factors.

    Answer: F   **Type: T**   **Pages: 277–282**   **Comprehension**

39. When you are paraphrasing, you need to repeat what the speaker has said word for word.

    Answer: F   **Type: T**   **Page: 288**   **Comprehension**

40. Informational paraphrasing focuses on the ideas a speaker has expressed.

    Answer: T   **Type: T**   **Page: 285**   **Comprehension**

41. Prompting is a more passive approach to problem-solving than advising or judging.

    Answer: T   **Type: T**   **Page: 301**   **Comprehension**

42. It is possible to use a helping response style that is actually unhelpful.

    Answer: T   **Type: T**   **Page: 307**   **Synthesis**

43. Since all listening judgments are negative, we should avoid them at all cost.

    Answer: F   **Type: T**   **Page: 294**   **Comprehension**

44. If your long-winded friend isn't "getting to the point," it's best to interrupt and ask him or her what the main or key idea is.

    Answer: F   **Type: T**   **Page: 285**   **Evaluation**

45. You should rotate your styles of listening after one or two responses so that you don't become bored by any one style.

    Answer: F   **Type: T**   **Page: 307**   **Evaluation**

46. You should use the styles of listening that help the other person and not worry about whether these styles feel comfortable to you.

    Answer: F   **Type: T**   **Page: 307**   **Evaluation**

47. In Paraphrasing on the Job transcript in Chapter Seven, Mark listens to Jill about

    a. dating problems.
    b. her parents.
    c. their boss.
    d. her roommate.
    e. relocating.

    Answer: c   **Type: M**   **Page: 306**   **Recall**

48. In the "Finding Common Ground through Listening" reading in Chapter Seven,

    a. geologists and city administrators discover new solutions through listening.
    b. pro-choice and pro-life groups uncover a shared concern through listening.
    c. teens and parents listen to each other to minimize rebellion.
    d. doctors listen to patients better to diagnose their illnesses.
    e. gardeners and their clients understand expectations better through listening.

    Answer: b   **Type: M**   **Page: 291**   **Recall**

49. The listening program described in Chapter Seven, "They Learn to Aid Customers," trained

    a. prostitutes.
    b. cosmetologists.
    c. teachers.
    d. parents.
    e. ministers.

    Answer: b   **Type: M**   **Page: 295**   **Recall**

50. In the Looking at Diversity reading in this chapter, Bruce Anderson wants to

    a. solve inner city problems through listening.
    b. train others to know what it's like to be deaf.
    c. provide listening aids in churches and courtrooms.
    d. eliminate overly loud music that leads to hearing problems.
    e. teach students who are hard of hearing and deaf.

    Answer: e   **Type: M**   **Page: 272**   **Recall**

51. According to a newspaper account in your text, one professor identified the percentage of students actually listening to a lecture by

    a. observing nonverbal cues.
    b. distributing a questionnaire.
    c. giving pop quizzes.
    d. occasionally making nonsensical statements.
    e. firing a gun.

    Answer: e   **Type: M**   **Page: 279**   **Recall**

52. According to a study of college students and their communication activities, about 30 percent of their communication time was spent

    a. writing.
    b. speaking.
    c. engaging in face-to-face listening.
    d. reading.
    e. engaging in listening to mass communication media.

    Answer: c   **Type: M**   **Page: 268**   **Recall**

53. All of the following are ineffective listening styles mentioned in the text except

    a. ambushing.
    b. insulated listening.
    c. stage hogging.
    d. pseudolistening.
    e. signal listening.

    Answer: e   **Type: M**   **Pages: 274–277**   **Knowledge**

54. While we are capable of hearing speech at rates up to 600 words per minute, the average person speaks between

    a. 400 and 500 words per minute
    b. 200 and 275 words per minute
    c. 100 and 150 words per minute
    d. 50 and 70 words per minute
    e. 20 and 30 words per minute

    Answer: c   **Type: M**   **Page: 279**   **Knowledge**

55. The process of using questioning and paraphrasing messages is a type of

    a. linear communication.
    b. insensitive listening.
    c. selective perception.
    d. defensive behavior.
    e. feedback.

    Answer: e   **Type: M**   **Pages: 10, 288**   **Synthesis**

56. Two kinds of listening to help are

    a. analyzing and supporting.
    b. informational and helpful.
    c. simple and complex.
    d. facilitative and debilitative.
    e. verbatim and restatement.

    Answer: a   **Type: M**   **Pages: 296, 298**   **Comprehension**

57. All of the following are reasons why it is difficult to listen all the time except:

    a. We hear so many verbal messages.
    b. We are often wrapped up in personal concerns.
    c. We comprehend words at a slower rate than people speak them.
    d. We have many physical distractions.
    e. We think speaking has more advantages than listening.

    Answer: c   **Type: M**   **Pages: 277–282**   **Comprehension**

58. Giving only the appearance of being attentive is termed

    a. pseudolistening.
    b. selective listening.
    c. defensive listening.
    d. insensitive listening.
    e. fake listening.

    Answer: a   **Type: M**   **Page: 275**   **Knowledge**

59. Which of the following are styles of listening to help?

    a. advising, judging, analyzing, questioning, and supporting
    b. erupting, advising, sharing, withholding, and evaluating
    c. nonlistening, pseudolistening, evaluating, questioning, and advising
    d. feedback, encoding, decoding, and channel selection
    e. informing, facilitating, sensitizing, and sharing

    Answer: a   **Type: M**   **Pages: 293–298**   **Comprehension**

60. The advantage of paraphrasing to help is that

    a. you can clarify your partner's concerns.
    b. you can suggest the solution that's best for your partner.
    c. you can use the clear message format (behavior, interpret, etc.).
    d. you can share your own experiences and ideas.
    e. you can focus on what you think is most relevant.

    Answer: a   **Type: M**   **Page: 305**   **Comprehension**

61. According to your text, advice is

    a. only to be used when paraphrasing fails.
    b. helpful when it is correct or accurate.
    c. best when preceded by your analysis of a situation.
    d. not necessarily helpful to others just because it worked for you.
    e. less helpful than either supporting or judging response styles.

    Answer: d   **Type: M**   **Page: 293**   **Synthesis**

62. Which is the best helping paraphrase response to the following statement? "My boss keeps kidding me about how we should have an affair. I don't know what to do. Sometimes I think he's just joking, and sometimes I think it's a real proposition."

    a. "Either way it's sexual harassment, which is illegal. You shouldn't let him get away with it!"
    b. "So you can't figure out his motives . . . is that it?"
    c. "You sound upset by this."
    d. "You sound worried and confused because you're not sure if he's coming on to you or not?"
    e. "That's a common problem these days. I can see why you're upset, and I don't blame you."

    Answer: d   **Type: M**   **Page: 302**   **Analysis**

63. Imagine you've been listening for some time to a friend talk about whether or not to drop out of school. Which is the best helpful paraphrasing response?

    a. "You're confused because there are as many reasons to stay as there are to leave, huh?"
    b. "Which alternative sounds best to you?"
    c. "When you're this confused, it's best to go with your heart."
    d. "You do sound mixed up. Maybe you ought to hold off making a decision for a while."
    e. "Tell me more. I think we can get to the bottom of this if we talk it out. I'm listening."

    Answer: a   **Type: M**   **Page: 302**   **Analysis**

64. You meet a friend at the supermarket who asks how you are doing. You say, "I'm simply at wits' end—too busy." Which of the following from your friend would qualify as an insensitive listening response?

    a. "Will you come help me study for my math test?"
    b. "So your wits are being tried?"
    c. "Sounds like you are really busy."
    d. "So you're feeling stressed because you've got too much to do?"

    Answer: a   **Type: M**   **Page: 277**   **Application**

65. You meet a friend at the supermarket and ask how he is doing. He replies "I'm OK— just stressed with all these finals." Which of the following is the best helping paraphrasing response you can make?

    a. "Yeah, I know what you mean."
    b. "So you're stressed, huh?"
    c. "You'll be fine; you always get good grades."
    d. "Bet you're wishing you hadn't taken 18 units, huh?"
    e. "So you're managing most things just fine, but will be relieved when finals are over?"

    Answer: e   **Type: M**   **Page: 302**   **Application**

66. When you use paraphrasing as a helping tool, your reflection should contain

    a. thoughts.
    b. feelings.
    c. analysis.
    d. both a and b above.
    e. both b and c above.

    Answer: d   **Type: M**   **Page: 302**   **Comprehension**

67. When you try to reflect the underlying message in a statement, you are engaging in

    a. judging.
    b. questioning.
    c. paraphrasing.
    d. prompting.
    e. pseudolistening.

    Answer: c   **Type: M**   **Page: 289**   **Comprehension**

68. Which of the following bodily changes occurs during careful listening?

    a. heart rate quickens
    b. respiration increases
    c. body temperature rises
    d. all of the above
    e. none of the above

    Answer: d   **Type: M**   **Page: 279**   **Comprehension**

69. Which of the following is the best helpful paraphrase to "I'm really bummed out about my apartment situation."

    a. "So you're bummed out, huh?"
    b. "Your apartment situation is bad?"
    c. "You're depressed because you haven't found a place to live yet?"
    d. "You should really get a new place; I agree."
    e. "It will all work out by next month."

    Answer: c   **Type: M**   **Page: 302**   **Evaluation**

70. Constructive criticism is a kind of listening response that falls into the category termed

    a. advising.
    b. judging.
    c. analyzing.
    d. supporting.
    e. questioning.

    Answer: b   **Type: M**   **Page: 294**   **Comprehension**

71. Before you meet with your professor, you think that she will talk "over your head." When you actually speak with her, you have a difficult time understanding what she is saying. Based on the information given above, the most likely cause of your listening problem is

    a. lack of effort.
    b. lack of training.
    c. faulty assumptions.
    d. rapid thought.
    e. preoccupation.

    Answer: c   Type: M   Page: 280   Application

72. Your roommate gives the appearance of listening to you, but you can tell from her responses that her mind is elsewhere. You could call her listening style in this instance

    a. stage hogging.
    b. insulated listening.
    c. pseudolistening.
    d. defensive listening.
    e. ambushing.

    Answer: c   Type: M   Page: 275   Application

73. Which of the following is the best helping paraphrase response for the statement: "I can't stand that class! The lectures are a waste of time, and the tests are full of nit-picking questions. I'm not learning anything."

    a. "Sounds like you're fed up with the class."
    b. "Sounds like you're thinking about dropping the class."
    c. "Sounds like the class has nit-picking tests and is a waste of time."
    d. "Sounds like you resent spending so much time on information you don't consider useful."
    e. "Sounds like you're fed up with school."

    Answer: d   Type: M   Page: 302   Application

74. Paraphrasing can be considered a form of

    a. perception checking.
    b. nonverbal communication.
    c. assertive communication.
    d. bypassing.
    e. behavioral description.

    Answer: a   Type: M   Page: 288   Synthesis

75. The ability of a listener to think faster than a speaker can talk

    a. often contributes to poor listening.
    b. allows the listener to understand the speaker's ideas better.
    c. creates the potential for psychological noise in the listener.
    d. all of the above
    e. none of the above

    Answer: d   **Type: M**   **Page: 279**   **Comprehension**

76. The tentative nature of paraphrasing thoughts and feelings means that it is

    a. open-minded.
    b. longer.
    c. objective.
    d. brief.
    e. subjective

    Answer: a   **Type: M**   **Page: 288**   **Synthesis**

77. "I think that the reason you're so confused is that you're trying to make everyone else happy and forgetting your own happiness." This statement is what type of listening response?

    a. supporting
    b. advising
    c. questioning
    d. paraphrasing
    e. analyzing

    Answer: e   **Type: M**   **Page: 296**   **Application**

78. "From what you've said, it sounds like you're mad at your boss for expecting you to drop your personal plans whenever he wants you to work. Is that right?" This statement is what type of response?

    a. supporting
    b. judging
    c. questioning
    d. paraphrasing
    e. analyzing

    Answer: d   **Type: M**   **Page: 302**   **Application**

79. "Sure it's unfair. But you shouldn't let that stop you. Life is unfair, so you're crazy to let it bother you." This statement is what type of response?

    a. supporting
    b. judging
    c. questioning
    d. paraphrasing
    e. parroting

    Answer: b   **Type: M**   **Page: 294**   **Application**

80. Paraphrasing

    a. is a form of sending.
    b. is a form of receiving.
    c. is a form of feedback.
    d. illustrates the transactional nature of communication.
    e. all of the above

    Answer: e   **Type: M**   **Pages: 10, 288**   **Synthesis**

81. All of the following are described in the text as helping responses except

    a. analyzing.
    b. judging.
    c. repeating.
    d. supporting.
    e. paraphrasing.

    Answer: c   **Type: M**   **Pages: 293–301**   **Comprehension**

82. "I just can't decide whether I can afford to move out on my own. Do you think I'll be able to handle it financially?" Which of the following is a prompting response to this statement?

    a. "I guess you're worried that you can't make it ."
    b. "I don't know, really. Do you think you will?"
    c. "You know best because it is your money."
    d. "I can't imagine why you"d spend all that money on rent when you can live at home for free."
    e. "If your parents could just help you out a little, then you could make it."

    Answer: b   **Type: M**   **Page: 301**   **Application**

83. Which of the following is an informational paraphrase to the statement, "You've got to get those reports in on time or it looks bad for both of us."

    a. "Sounds like you're upset with me."
    b. "Could you help me out by reminding me when the deadlines are?"
    c. "Are you saying you're going to fire me if I don't?"
    d. "Because I didn't get the Murphy report done by last Friday, you and I are both in trouble?"
    e. "Those guys in upper management are too uptight about deadlines."

    Answer: d   **Type: M**   **Page: 288**   **Application**

84. When choosing the best listening style, it is important to consider

    a. the situation.
    b. the other person.
    c. yourself.
    d. both a and b above.
    e. a, b, and c above.

    Answer: e   **Type: M**   **Page: 307**   **Comprehension**

INSTRUCTIONS for questions 85–110: Match each statement with the helping listening style it characterizes.

    a. paraphrasing
    b. judging
    c. supporting
    d. advising
    e. analyzing

85. "That's a terrible idea!"

    Answer: b   Type: Matching   Page: 294   Analysis

86. "You ought to give it a try. You've got nothing to lose."

    Answer: d   Type: Matching   Page: 293   Analysis

87. "You're really afraid of failing, aren't you?"

    Answer: e   Type: Matching   Page: 296   Analysis

88. "Don't let it get you down. You're doing a great job."

    Answer: c   Type: Matching   Page: 298   Analysis

89. "Sure it's discouraging now, but it will be over soon."

    Answer: c   Type: Matching   Page: 298   Analysis

90. "So you're upset because Chris didn't pay you back?"

    Answer: a   Type: Matching   Page: 302   Analysis

91. "You"ll never know what he thinks unless you ask."

    Answer: d   Type: Matching   Page: 293   Analysis

92. "Have you ever thought about just giving her what she wants?"

    Answer: d   Type: Matching   Page: 293   Analysis

93. "I can't believe it! He's really a jerk for saying that."

    Answer: b   Type: Matching   Page: 294   Analysis

94. "So you're hoping they'll call, but you're not sure what you'll say if they do?"

    Answer: a   Type: Matching   Page: 302   Analysis

95. "Of course you get pushed around. That's what happens when you don't tell people what you want."

    Answer: b   Type: Matching   Page: 294   Analysis

96. "If you can't be honest, you're not a real friend."

    Answer: b   Type: Matching   Page: 294   Analysis

97. "Sounds like you're mad at me for embarrassing you. Is that right?"

     Answer: a   **Type: Matching**   **Page: 302**   **Analysis**

98. "You've always done fine in the past. Don't worry; you can do it this time, too."

     Answer: c   **Type: Matching**   **Page: 298**   **Analysis**

99. "You'd be a lot happier if you stopped blaming everyone else for your problems."

     Answer: b   **Type: Matching**   **Page: 294**   **Analysis**

100. "You're only doing that to get back at him for cheating on you."

     Answer: e   **Type: Matching**   **Page: 296**   **Analysis**

101. "Don't try so hard and you'll probably do better."

     Answer: d   **Type: Matching**   **Page: 293**   **Analysis**

102. "Your problem isn't being too mean; you're afraid of being too nice!"

     Answer: e   **Type: Matching**   **Page: 296**   **Analysis**

103. "The reason you're insecure is that money means a lot to you."

     Answer: e   **Type: Matching**   **Page: 296**   **Analysis**

104. "Don't give up. You'll get it this next time."

     Answer: c   **Type: Matching**   **Page: 298**   **Analysis**

105. "Your sister has a strong hold on you, and that's why you're afraid to face your parents."

     Answer: e   **Type: Matching**   **Page: 296**   **Analysis**

106. "Are you saying that you're hesitant to take a math class for fear of failing?"

     Answer: a   **Type: Matching**   **Page: 302**   **Analysis**

107. "Have you tried just talking to her about it?"

     Answer: d   **Type: Matching**   **Page: 293**   **Analysis**

108. "I think you're still unsure of yourself because of all the moving you did as a child."

     Answer: e   **Type: Matching**   **Page: 296**   **Analysis**

109. "I think it's a good idea and you're a good person."

     Answer: b   **Type: Matching**   **Page: 294**   **Analysis**

110. "Hey, he didn't leave you the last time this happened; he won't this time."

     Answer: c   **Type: Matching**   **Page: 298**   **Analysis**

111. We have all been selective, insulated, defensive, insensitive, and ambushing listeners. Give an example of each type of listening from your own personal experience. Illustrate any misunderstandings that developed as a result of your listening behavior.

      Answer   **Type: E**   **Pages: 275–277**   **Analysis**

112. Briefly describe two informational listening situations in which you have been involved. Evaluate each of the six suggestions for informational listening in your text in light of your two situations. Give examples in each category to illustrate how you listened effectively or how you might have improved your informational listening. Be specific.

      Answer   **Type: E**   **Pages: 282–289**   **Evaluation**

113. Describe an unsuccessful communication transaction in which you used a poor listening style to receive information. Discuss the advantages and disadvantages of using paraphrasing to improve the reception of the information.

      Answer   **Type: E**   **Page: 287**   **Synthesis**

114. Describe the style(s) of listening you use most often when helping others. How successful are these styles? What makes them successful or unsuccessful? What might you do to increase your effectiveness as a helpful listener?

      Answer   **Type: E**   **Pages: 293–302**   **Evaluation**

115. In your own words, describe what paraphrasing is and how it is used to help others solve their problems. Use real or hypothetical examples and concrete specific language to explain and illustrate your answer.

      Answer   **Type: E**   **Page: 302**   **Synthesis**

116. Recount an interpersonal situation in which you failed to listen effectively. Describe the factors which caused you to listen poorly. What could you have done to change those factors?

      Answer   **Type: E**   **Pages: 277–282**   **Evaluation**

CHAPTER 8

COMMUNICATION AND RELATIONAL DYNAMICS

1. In Chapter Eight's "Looking at Diversity" reading, Kelly Vodden talks about how the Internet hinders relational development.

   Answer: F **Type: T** **Page: 327** **Recall**

2. According to Chapter Eight, a study of truthfulness shows that over half of an individual's daily statements are totally honest.

   Answer: F **Type: T** **Page: 352** **Recall**

3. Over 90 percent of subjects in "lying" experiments chose to equivocate rather than lie.

   Answer: T **Type: T** **Page: 357** **Recall**

4. In the "Is Misleading Your Spouse Fraud or Tact?" reading in Chapter Eight, Ronald Askew sued his ex-wife for fraud because she admittedly concealed the fact that she had never been sexually attracted to him.

   Answer: T **Type: T** **Page: 355** **Recall**

5. People with especially high or low self-esteem find "perfect" people more attractive than people who are competent but flawed.

   Answer: T **Type: T** **Page: 316** **Knowledge**

6. Self-disclosure is more effective when it is used frequently by a communicator.

   Answer: F **Type: T** **Page: 348** **Comprehension**

7. According to Chapter Eight, we are usually attracted to people who are similar to us.

   Answer: T **Type: T** **Page: 314** **Comprehension**

8. To be good at self-disclosure you need to disclose frequently and steadily to keep up your skill.

   Answer: F **Type: T** **Page: 348** **Comprehension**

9. Small talk typically occurs during the initiating stage of an interpersonal relationship.

   Answer: F **Type: T** **Page: 325** **Knowledge**

10. The experimenting stage of interpersonal relationships is characterized by small talk.

    Answer: T   **Type: T**   **Page: 325**   **Knowledge**

11. Disliking is a clear signal that an interpersonal relationship does not exist.

    Answer: F   **Type: T**   **Page: 318**   **Synthesis**

12. We can categorize interpersonal relationships as intimate or not by the place in which they occur.

    Answer: F   **Type: T**   **Page: 327**   **Synthesis**

13. Self-disclosure must be frequent to be effective.

    Answer: F   **Type: T**   **Page: 348**   **Comprehension**

14. According to Chapter Eight, we are more attracted to people who are good at what they do but admit their mistakes.

    Answer: T   **Type: T**   **Page: 316**   **Knowledge**

15. The terminating stage of an interpersonal relationship can be quite short or drawn out over time.

    Answer: T   **Type: T**   **Page: 330**   **Knowledge**

16. Any healthy relationship will go through all the ten stages of interpersonal relationships from initiating to terminating, as described in Chapter Eight of your text.

    Answer: F   **Type: T**   **Page: 330**   **Knowledge**

17. Clichés, the outer circle of the self-disclosure model in your text, are the most revealing type of communication.

    Answer: F   **Type: T**   **Page: 339**   **Knowledge**

18. The most revealing level of self-disclosure usually involves talking about feelings.

    Answer: T   **Type: T**   **Page: 340**   **Knowledge**

19. Bringing up feelings like "I feel uncomfortable when you drop by without calling" is not appropriate to self-disclosure situations.

    Answer: F   **Type: T**   **Page: 343**   **Comprehension**

20. We usually remain attracted to others we believe are like us, even if they behave in an offensive manner.

    Answer: F   **Type: T**   **Page: 316**   **Knowledge**

21. When we find others offensive, there is a tendency for us to dislike them more if we also see them as similar to ourselves.

    Answer: T   **Type: T**   **Page: 316**   **Knowledge**

22. After we get to know others, their liking for us becomes less of a factor in our attraction toward them.

    Answer: T   **Type: T**   **Page: 316**   **Synthesis**

23. Reciprocal liking builds attractiveness.

    Answer: T   **Type: T**   **Page: 316**   **Knowledge**

24. People are judged as attractive when they match the amount and content of their self-disclosure to the self-disclosure of others.

    Answer: T   **Type: T**   **Page: 316**   **Knowledge**

25. The experimenting stage of interpersonal relationships is characterized by the exchange of biographical information and "niceties."

    Answer: T   **Type: T**   **Page: 325**   **Knowledge**

26. A well-documented conclusion from research is that one act of self-disclosure usually begets another from the other party.

    Answer: T   **Type: T**   **Page: 346**   **Knowledge**

27. When we self-disclose to strangers, it is usually for reciprocity or identity formation.

    Answer: T   **Type: T**   **Page: 346**   **Comprehension**

28. It is quite possible to have a wide range of satisfying relationships without having much intimacy at all.

    Answer: T   **Type: T**   **Page: 322**   **Knowledge**

29. Social circles merge and the relational partners take on a new relational identity in the intensifying stage of relationships.

    Answer: F   **Type: T**   **Page: 328**   **Comprehension**

30. The strongest influence on why people disclose seems to be how well they know the other person.

    Answer: T   **Type: T**   **Page: 345**   **Knowledge**

31. Intimacy can come from intellectual sharing alone.

    Answer: T   **Type: T**   **Page: 318**   **Comprehension**

32. In interpersonal relationships, the rule is: The more self-disclosure the better.

    Answer: F   **Type: T**   **Page: 349**   **Comprehension**

33. The Johari Window model suggests that the amount of intimacy in a relationship is determined by the most open person.

    Answer: F   **Type: T**   **Page: 343**   **Comprehension**

34. In most instances, the relational stage of bonding generates social support for the relationship.

     Answer: T   **Type: T**   **Page: 328**   **Knowledge**

35. Differentiation in relationships is always negative, since it is part of the "coming apart" process.

     Answer: F   **Type: T**   **Page: 329**   **Comprehension**

36. The circumscribing stage of interpersonal relationships involves total avoidance of the other.

     Answer: F   **Type: T**   **Page: 331**   **Comprehension**

37. Since they are honest and true, comments to another like "I've always thought you were a bit flaky" have constructive effects in self-disclosure.

     Answer: F   **Type: T**   **Page: 349**   **Comprehension**

38. Many long-term relationships aren't characterized by a constant exchange of intimate details.

     Answer: T   **Type: T**   **Page: 344**   **Comprehension**

39. The deepest and most effective self-disclosure will include much detail about your past life.

     Answer: F   **Type: T**   **Page: 339**   **Comprehension**

40. Lies may help us avoid embarrassment.

     Answer: T   **Type: T**   **Page: 350**   **Comprehension**

41. The initiating stage of interpersonal relationships is usually brief.

     Answer: T   **Type: T**   **Page: 325**   **Comprehension**

42. Communication during the initiating stage of interpersonal relationships is usually characterized by lengthy investigations into the personality of the parties involved.

     Answer: F   **Type: T**   **Page: 325**   **Comprehension**

43. Self-disclosure on both sides is usually necessary for the development of an interpersonal relationship.

     Answer: T   **Type: T**   **Page: 346**   **Comprehension**

44. According to your text, the value and ease of self-disclosure is increased by including a third party in your discussion.

     Answer: F   **Type: T**   **Page: 344**   **Comprehension**

45. Hints are more direct than equivocal statements.

     Answer: T   **Type: T**   **Page: 357**   **Comprehension**

46. Most lies are told for the benefit of the recipient.

    Answer: F   **Type: T**   **Page: 352**   **Comprehension**

47. All self-disclosure leads to liking or attractiveness.

    Answer: F   **Type: T**   **Page: 316**   **Comprehension**

48. Research shows that people are judged as attractive in proportion to the amount to which they disclose themselves to others, no matter what the situation.

    Answer: F   **Type: T**   **Page: 317**   **Comprehension**

49. Your text makes the case that hints, benign lies, and equivocations are sometimes ethical alternatives to telling the truth.

    Answer: T   **Type: T**   **Page: 358**   **Synthesis**

50. Self-disclosure is more effective when it is used in the context of a positive relationship.

    Answer: T   **Type: T**   **Page: 345**   **Knowledge**

51. Self-disclosure of personal thoughts and feelings may be inappropriate and risky in the work setting.

    Answer: T   **Type: T**   **Page: 348**   **Application**

52. Good listening skills are necessary aspects of your self-disclosure skills because you have to listen well to others in order to match the content and amount of your self-disclosure to theirs.

    Answer: T   **Type: T**   **Page: 349**   **Synthesis**

53. Most self-disclosure is reciprocal.

    Answer: T   **Type: T**   **Page: 346**   **Comprehension**

54. You should avoid making disclosing statements that contain negative messages.

    Answer: F   **Type: T**   **Page: 349**   **Comprehension**

55. Self-disclosure can have the effect of an attack on the other person.

    Answer: T   **Type: T**   **Page: 349**   **Comprehension**

56. The best way to develop a positive interpersonal relationship is usually to begin that relationship by revealing a great amount of highly personal information about yourself.

    Answer: F   **Type: T**   **Page: 344**   **Knowledge**

57. People sometimes self-disclose to create a good impression.

    Answer: T   **Type: T**   **Page: 346**   **Knowledge**

58. According to the text, real self-disclosure does not involve attempts at control of the other.

    Answer: F   **Type: T**   **Page: 347**   **Comprehension**

59. If research in the text is accurate, your relationship will be likely to end if you discover your partner has told you a serious lie.

    Answer: T   **Type: T**   **Page: 354**   **Synthesis**

60. Physical intimacy is obviously the best type of relational intimacy.

    Answer: F   **Type: T**   **Page: 318**   **Evaluation**

61. The "Blind" window of the Johari model represents things about yourself that another may know about you, but you do not.

    Answer: T   **Type: T**   **Page: 342**   **Knowledge**

62. The "Unknown" window of the Johari model represents things about yourself that another knows but you do not.

    Answer: F   **Type: T**   **Page: 342**   **Comprehension**

63. The social penetration model represents both the breadth and the depth of your self-disclosure with another person.

    Answer: T   **Type: T**   **Page: 339**   **Knowledge**

64. Just because we have revealed many different kinds of facts to another doesn't mean that we have an intimate relationship.

    Answer: T   **Type: T**   **Page: 340**   **Comprehension**

65. We form many relationships with others because they are like us in some ways and different from us in others.

    Answer: T   **Type: T**   **Page: 314**   **Comprehension**

66. Attraction to others is greatest when we perceive we are similar to them in a high percentage of important areas like goals and beliefs.

    Answer: T   **Type: T**   **Page: 314**   **Comprehension**

67. Differences strengthen a relationship when they are complementary.

    Answer: T   **Type: T**   **Page: 314**   **Knowledge**

68. Social exchange theory suggests that self-disclosure is an outdated semi-economic model of relationships.

    Answer: F   **Type: T**   **Page: 324**   **Comprehension**

CHAPTER EIGHT   COMMUNICATION AND RELATIONAL DYNAMICS   **207**

69. The fact that we are attracted to competent people means that we need to appear flawless to others.

    Answer: F   **Type: T**   **Page: 316**   **Analysis**

70. Self-disclosure tends to draw people closer as long as the messages are perceived to be appropriate.

    Answer: T   **Type: T**   **Page: 349**   **Knowledge**

71. Constant self-disclosure is a useful goal for those of us trying to improve a relationship.

    Answer: F   **Type: T**   **Page: 348**   **Comprehension**

72. Not all self-disclosure draws people closer.

    Answer: T   **Type: T**   **Page: 348**   **Synthesis**

73. Research shows that deception threatens relationships.

    Answer: T   **Type: T**   **Page: 354**   **Knowledge**

74. Some lies are designed to make the relationship grow.

    Answer: T   **Type: T**   **Page: 352**   **Knowledge**

75. Circumscribing is the stage in the relationship process during which partners become emotionally closer.

    Answer: F   **Type: T**   **Page: 329**   **Knowledge**

76. Dialectical tensions exist in relationships when two incompatible forces or pressures exist at the same time.

    Answer: T   **Type: T**   **Page: 332**   **Comprehension**

77. If a communicator is truly competent, he/she will be able to resolve the conflicting needs involved in dialectical tensions competently.

    Answer: F   **Type: T**   **Page: 334**   **Analysis**

78. If faced with a choice to tell a face-saving lie or deliver an equivocal message, most people will tell the lie.

    Answer: F   **Type: T**   **Page: 356**   **Knowledge**

79. In the Chapter Eight Communication Transcript, Ramon
    a. self-discloses to Julie about his father.
    b. admits he can't swim.
    c. and Julie discover that they were born in the same town through self-disclosure.
    d. discloses some inappropriate information to Julie.
    e. and Julie become great friends because of self-disclosure.

    Answer: d   **Type: M**   **Page: 351**   **Recall**

80. According to your text, there are three alternatives to self-disclosure:

    a. white lies, equivocation, and hinting.
    b. empathy, evasion, and evaluation.
    c. strategy, straightforwardness, and spontaneity.
    d. lying, circling, and confessing.
    e. stroking, withholding, and sandbagging.

    Answer: a   **Type: M**   **Pages: 350–357**   **Knowledge**

81. According to your text, all of the following are reasons to be somewhat deceitful in relationships except

    a. to guide social interaction.
    b. to empower others.
    c. to save face.
    d. to avoid conflict.
    e. to expand or reduce relationships.

    Answer: b   **Type: M**   **Pages: 352–353**   **Synthesis**

82. You've just delivered a speech to your classmates. None of them liked your speech very much. According to your text, which of the following is the response you are most likely to hear from them when you ask how you did?

    a. "You did a great job."
    b. "I'm nervous about my speech tomorrow."
    c. "I don't think it was a very good speech."
    d. "You made some interesting points."

    Answer: d   **Type: M**   **Page: 356**   **Application**

83. The Johari Window is an important device to help explore the role

    a. coding plays in communication.
    b. interpretation plays in clarifying understanding.
    c. feedback plays in negative relationships.
    d. self-disclosure plays in communication.
    e. affection needs play in strong relationships.

    Answer: d   **Type: M**   **Page: 343**   **Knowledge**

84. According to the text, which of the following is good advice about self-disclosure?

    a. Wait for the other person to open up before you do.
    b. The more self-disclosure, the better.
    c. Self-disclosure is "safest" in twosomes, and not around others.
    d. Most relationships are characterized by almost constant amounts of self-disclosure.
    e. It's best to accompany each piece of negative self-disclosure with a compliment to soften any hurt.

    Answer: c   **Type: M**   **Pages: 344–345**   **Synthesis**

85. After studying the Johari Window, one can draw the logical conclusion that

    a. we must all try to "open up" our "blind" areas.
    b. the risk involved in self-disclosure keeps interpersonal relationships from succeeding.
    c. communicating will make us more "open."
    d. some amount of self-disclosure is necessary for the success of any interpersonal relationship.
    e. no conclusions can be drawn.

    Answer: d   **Type: M**   **Page: 343**   **Analysis**

86. The social penetration model by Altman and Taylor

    a. shows ways in which a relationship can be more or less intimate.
    b. suggests how relationships can operate on superficial or more personal levels.
    c. defines a relationship in terms of its breadth and depth.
    d. helps identify why certain relationships are strong or weak.
    e. all of the above

    Answer: e   **Type: M**   **Page: 339**   **Analysis**

87. According to the text, we are usually attracted to people who

    a. like us.
    b. are high self-disclosers.
    c. are perfect.
    d. approve of us even in ways we know are inaccurate.

    Answer: a   **Type: M**   **Page: 314**   **Comprehension**

88. To qualify as self-disclosure, a statement must

    a. involve feelings.
    b. be intentional, significant, and not otherwise known.
    c. be reciprocated by the same type of statement from a partner.
    d. involve intimate information.
    e. be shared privately.

    Answer: b   **Type: M**   **Page: 337**   **Comprehension**

89. "I've never been out of this state" is an example of self-disclosure at which of the following levels?

    a. cliché
    b. fact
    c. opinion
    d. feeling
    e. interpretation

    Answer: b   **Type: M**   **Page: 340**   **Application**

90. "It's nice to meet you" is an example of self-disclosure at which of the following levels?

    a. cliché
    b. fact
    c. opinion
    d. feeling
    e. interpretation

    Answer: a   **Type: M**   **Page: 339**   **Application**

91. "I'm worried that you won't follow through on your commitment" is an example of self-disclosure at which of the following levels?

    a. cliché
    b. fact
    c. opinion
    d. feeling
    e. interpretation

    Answer: d   **Type: M**   **Page: 340**   **Application**

92. "I don't think you're telling the truth" is an example of self-disclosure at which of the following levels?

    a. cliché
    b. fact
    c. opinion
    d. feeling
    e. interpretation

    Answer: c   **Type: M**   **Page: 340**   **Application**

93. In most relationships, the amount of self-disclosure will

    a. increase over time.
    b. decrease with age.
    c. stabilize and then stop.
    d. become more one-sided as trust develops.
    e. become greater as the communication ability of both interactants developed from classes like this one increases.

    Answer: a   **Type: M**   **Page: 345**   **Knowledge**

94. The Johari Window suggests that

    a. both breadth and depth are important.
    b. the amount of self-disclosure in a relationship is usually determined by the least disclosing person.
    c. self-disclosure is a self-fulfilling prophecy.
    d. risk should be considered when self-disclosing.
    e. not all self-disclosure is interpersonal.

    Answer: b   **Type: M**   **Page: 343**   **Analysis**

95. Quadrants of the Johari Window are

   a. open, narrow, blind, unknown.
   b. open, hidden, blind, unknown.
   c. broad, narrow, blind, unknown.
   d. open, hidden, neutral, unknown.
   e. open, closed, neutral, unknown.

   Answer: b   **Type: M**   **Page: 342**   **Knowledge**

96. Which of the following best fits the definition of self-disclosure given in this class?

   a. telling your romantic partner about your feelings toward him/her
   b. telling your college teacher about past grades
   c. telling your mother your weight
   d. telling your family physician about your health
   e. telling anyone anything about you

   Answer: a   **Type: M**   **Page: 337**   **Application**

97. According to Knapp's model of interaction stages, symbolic public gestures that show the world that a relationship exists usually occur in which stage in interpersonal relationships?

   a. experimenting
   b. intensifying
   c. bonding
   d. integrating
   e. circumscribing

   Answer: c   **Type: M**   **Page: 328**   **Knowledge**

98. When the target of self-disclosure is a friend, the most frequent reason people give for volunteering personal information is

   a. to get to know the other better.
   b. relationship maintenance and enhancement.
   c. defensiveness reduction.
   d. self-validation.
   e. manipulation.

   Answer: b   **Type: M**   **Page: 346**   **Knowledge**

99. With strangers as the target of self-disclosure, the most common reason people give for disclosing is

   a. defensiveness reduction.
   b. manipulation.
   c. reciprocity.
   d. relationship maintenance.
   e. relationship enhancement.

   Answer: c   **Type: M**   **Page: 346**   **Knowledge**

100. Which of the following changes does not typically occur in the intensifying stage of interpersonal relationships?

    a. Forms of address become more informal.
    b. The parties begin to take on an identity as a social unit.
    c. Feelings of commitment are directly expressed.
    d. Increased familiarity leads to verbal shortcuts.
    e. The parties begin to refer to themselves as "we."

    Answer: b　　　　**Type: M**　　　　**Page: 326**　　　　**Synthesis**

101. Social exchange theory suggests that we often seek out people who can give us

    a. rewards greater than or equal to the costs we encounter in dealing with them.
    b. more self-esteem.
    c. relational rewards rather than physical ones.
    d. something in exchange for what we give them.
    e. both relational and physical things without demanding anything of us.

    Answer: a　　　　**Type: M**　　　　**Page: 324**　　　　**Knowledge**

102. The relative size of each area in our personal Johari Windows

    a. remains relatively constant.
    b. is dependent on our gender.
    c. becomes larger as we mature.
    d. changes according to our relationship with the other person.

    Answer: d　　　　**Type: M**　　　　**Page: 343**　　　　**Comprehension**

103. "This was a rotten idea" is an example of self-disclosure at which of the following levels?

    a. cliché
    b. fact
    c. opinion
    d. feeling
    e. interpretation

    Answer: c　　　　**Type: M**　　　　**Page: 340**　　　　**Application**

104. "Why don't you go ahead and visit your friends without me this weekend. I'll stick around and catch up on my studies." This statement typifies which relational stage?

    a. integrating
    b. differentiating
    c. bonding
    d. terminating
    e. intensifying

    Answer: b　　　　**Type: M**　　　　**Page: 329**　　　　**Application**

105. When two opposing or incompatible forces exist simultaneously in an interpersonal relationship, the struggle to achieve these opposing goals creates what is called a

   a.   collectivistic tension.
   b.   differentiating end state.
   c.   counterfeit goal state.
   d.   dialectical tension.
   e.   proximity problem.

   Answer: d   **Type: M**   **Page: 332**   **Knowledge**

106. Conflicting desires for connection and independence in an interpersonal relationship lead to the

   a.   connection–autonomy dialectic.
   b.   cohesion–revolt dialectic.
   c.   predictability–novelty dialectic.
   d.   openness–privacy dialectic.

   Answer: a   **Type: M**   **Page: 332**   **Knowledge**

107. Conflicting desires for both intimacy and the lack of it in an interpersonal relationship lead to the

   a.   connection–autonomy dialectic.
   b.   cohesion–revolt dialectic.
   c.   predictability–novelty dialectic.
   d.   openness–privacy dialectic.

   Answer: d   **Type: M**   **Page: 334**   **Knowledge**

108. Of all the strategies for managing dialectical tensions, _____ is the least functional.

   a.   denial
   b.   disorientation
   c.   alternation
   d.   segmentation

   Answer: a   **Type: M**   **Page: 334**   **Knowledge**

INSTRUCTIONS for questions 109–114: Match the statement below with the term it best describes.

   a.   self-disclosure
   b.   Knapp's staircase model
   c.   Johari Window
   d.   social penetration
   e.   exchange

109. Model to explore the role of self-disclosure in relationships

   Answer: c   **Type: Matching**   **Page: 337**   **Knowledge**

110. Model to examine breadth and depth of relationships

   Answer: d   **Type: Matching**   **Page: 324**   **Knowledge**

111. Explains stages in relationships

   Answer: b   **Type: Matching**   **Page: 324**   **Knowledge**

112. Voluntarily revealing personal information

   Answer: a   **Type: Matching**   **Page: 337**   **Knowledge**

113. Theory explaining costs and rewards in relationships

   Answer: e   **Type: Matching**   **Page: 324**   **Knowledge**

114. Discuss the relationship between risk and trust. Evaluate how these two are related to self-disclosure. Apply this discussion to a relationship in which you are involved.

   Answer   **Type: E**   **Pages: 344–345**   **Evaluation**

115. Referring to the reasons for deceit outlined in your chapter, analyze a current relationship you are in according to the degrees of truthfulness and deceit. Are you satisfied with the level of honesty? Explain your answer.

   Answer   **Type: E**   **Pages: 350–354**   **Analysis**

116. Using the social penetration model in your text, describe the breadth and depth of one important interpersonal relationship you have. Explain why you are satisfied/unsatisfied with this relationship.

   Answer   **Type: E**   **Page: 339**   **Synthesis**

117. Describe one important relationship in which you are involved in terms of the stages of interpersonal relationships found in your text. Give specific behavioral examples that illustrate your relationship is in a particular stage. Give a history of your relationship as it relates to the stages of relationships found in your text and speculate as to the next stage you will move to or the stage at which you have stabilized.

   Answer   **Type: E**   **Pages: 324–329**   **Evaluation**

118. Draw a Johari Window describing your relationship with an important person in your life. Comment on which parts of yourself you keep in the "hidden" area, and explain your reasons for doing so. Describe the benefits and costs of not disclosing these parts of your personality. Next, look at the size of the "blind" area model. Is the blind area large or small because of the amount of feedback you get from the other person, or because of the way you react to the feedback you do get? How would a window describing your partner's relationship with a mutual friend look similar to yours? Different? Explain. Are you satisfied with the kind of relationship your windows describe? If not, what could you do to change it?

   Answer   **Type: E**   **Page: 343**   **Evaluation**

119.   Pick two people you know—one with whom you want to strengthen your relationship, and one to whom you are not particularly attracted. Using the interpersonal attraction variables in the text, analyze the reasons why you want/don't want to form a relationship with each person.

Answer   **Type: E**   **Pages: 314–322**   **Analysis**

120.   Discuss three types of intimacy in a relationship that is important to you. Explain your satisfaction with the intimacy or distance in each area. Relate any other factors (change, independence, culture, gender, etc.) that affect your intimacy in this relationship.

Answer   **Type: E**   **Pages: 317–322**   **Evaluation**

CHAPTER 9

IMPROVING COMMUNICATION CLIMATES

1. In the "Police Work and Facework" reading in Chapter Nine, Lorenzo Duarte describes how being respectful to a criminal suspect led to the suspect's confession and the arrest of others.

    Answer: T   **Type: T**   **Page: 386**   **Recall**

2. Defensiveness is often a self-perpetuating cycle.

    Answer: T   **Type: T**   **Page: 374**   **Synthesis**

3. When your partner criticizes you, the best thing you can do is ignore the criticism so you won't get defensive.

    Answer: F   **Type: T**   **Page: 387**   **Comprehension**

4. Remarks about a specific subject (i.e., appearance, intelligence, honesty) that make one person defensive might arouse little or no defensiveness in another.

    Answer: T   **Type: T**   **Page: 375**   **Analysis**

5. You are most likely to become defensive when you are confronted with a face-threatening act.

    Answer: T   **Type: T**   **Page: 375**   **Knowledge**

6. Most of the times we become defensive is because we are threatened physically.

    Answer: F   **Type: T**   **Page: 375**   **Comprehension**

7. People become defensive when they perceive they are being threatened.

    Answer: T   **Type: T**   **Page: 375**   **Comprehension**

8. Gibb's research identified behaviors that are likely to bring about defensiveness, but it neglected to identify any alternative behaviors that could be supportive.

    Answer: F   **Type: T**   **Page: 380**   **Knowledge**

9. Once a progressive spiral has been established in a relationship, it is likely to continue indefinitely.

    Answer: F   **Type: T**   **Page: 374**   **Knowledge**

10. You should agree with a critic only when your perceptions match his/hers.

   Answer: F   **Type: T**   **Page: 395**   **Comprehension**

11. Your text recommends agreeing with criticisms that are untrue about you, since doing so will help you recognize ways you can improve.

   Answer: F   **Type: T**   **Page: 394**   **Comprehension**

12. It is possible to disagree with another person in a confirming way.

   Answer: T   **Type: T**   **Page: 371**   **Comprehension**

13. When you respond nondefensively to criticism, you can agree with the truth of what the critic is saying.

   Answer: T   **Type: T**   **Page: 394**   **Knowledge**

14. In order to deal effectively with criticism, it is necessary to acknowledge and accept the other's criticism.

   Answer: F   **Type: T**   **Page: 394**   **Comprehension**

15. The most damaging kind of disconfirming response is disagreeing with the other person.

   Answer: F   **Type: T**   **Page: 372**   **Knowledge**

16. Communication climates are a function of the tasks people perform rather than the way the people feel about one another.

   Answer: F   **Type: T**   **Page: 368**   **Comprehension**

17. Messages shaping the communication climate of a relationship can be both verbal and nonverbal.

   Answer: T   **Type: T**   **Page: 368**   **Comprehension**

18. Defensiveness in human communication is usually reciprocal.

   Answer: T   **Type: T**   **Page: 373**   **Synthesis**

19. Endorsement is the strongest type of confirming message.

   Answer: T   **Type: T**   **Page: 371**   **Knowledge**

20. The Gibb categories define behaviors that improve or hurt the communication climate.

   Answer: T   **Type: T**   **Page: 380**   **Comprehension**

21. Sometimes people become defensive when confronted with accusations they know are true.

   Answer: T   **Type: T**   **Page: 375**   **Comprehension**

22. Because it is always a kind of relational message, metacommunication is likely to arouse defensiveness.

    Answer: F   **Type: T**   **Page: 375**   **Synthesis**

23. Tangential responses are one type of disconfirming message.

    Answer: T   **Type: T**   **Page: 370**   **Knowledge**

24. Just recognizing the other person is so easy that most people don't see it as very confirming.

    Answer: F   **Type: T**   **Page: 369**   **Evaluation**

25. An acknowledgment statement is more confirming than a recognition statement.

    Answer: T   **Type: T**   **Page: 371**   **Evaluation**

26. Incongruent responses contain two messages that seem to deny or contradict each other.

    Answer: T   **Type: T**   **Page: 370**   **Knowledge**

27. Since ambiguous responses leave your partner unsure of your position, they would likely be interpreted as disconfirming.

    Answer: T   **Type: T**   **Page: 370**   **Comprehension**

28. An impervious response sends a disconfirming message because the other person is not responded to.

    Answer: T   **Type: T**   **Page: 370**   **Knowledge**

29. Whereas acknowledging others means you are interested in their ideas, endorsement means that you agree with them.

    Answer: T   **Type: T**   **Page: 371**   **Knowledge**

30. Even if you don't intend to ignore others, they might perceive you as avoiding them and get defensive.

    Answer: T   **Type: T**   **Page: 375**   **Knowledge**

31. We often reduce cognitive dissonance by using defense mechanisms.

    Answer: T   **Type: T**   **Page: 376**   **Comprehension**

32. When coping with criticism, it isn't a good idea to ask what else is wrong because it just brings up too much material to handle at one time.

    Answer: F   **Type: T**   **Page: 391**   **Comprehension**

33. Asking if anything else is bothering your critic won't help you cope with criticism because it encourages more defensiveness.

    Answer: F   **Type: T**   **Page: 391**   **Comprehension**

34. Descriptive statements avoid telling the other persons what they have done that you don't like.

    Answer: F   **Type: T**   **Page: 380**   **Knowledge**

35. A controlling message can be verbal or nonverbal.

    Answer: T   **Type: T**   **Page: 381**   **Comprehension**

36. Behavior that fits into Gibb's category of "strategy" attempts to manipulate the other into doing what you want.

    Answer: T   **Type: T**   **Page: 382**   **Knowledge**

37. What Gibb describes as "spontaneity" means saying the first thing that comes into your mind.

    Answer: F   **Type: T**   **Page: 382**   **Comprehension**

38. A support climate usually results from the expression of empathy.

    Answer: T   **Type: T**   **Page: 382**   **Comprehension**

39. You have to use the Gibb category of "superiority" now and then because not all of us have the same talents.

    Answer: F   **Type: T**   **Page: 383**   **Knowledge**

40. Provisional statements often include words like "perhaps" and "from my perspective."

    Answer: T   **Type: T**   **Page: 385**   **Application**

41. Your text contained a humorous list of advice from Dave Barry about how to _____ effectively.

    a. confirm
    b. argue
    c. avoid
    d. agree
    e. disconfirm

    Answer: b   **Type: M**   **Page: 384**   **Recall**

42. Communication climates typically

    a. are confirming.
    b. are negative.
    c. are defensive or supportive.
    d. grow progressively better.
    e. get worse with time.

    Answer: c   **Type: M**   **Page: 368**   **Comprehension**

43. All of the following are disconfirming messages except

    a. interrupting the other person.
    b. giving ambiguous responses.
    c. ignoring the other person.
    d. using a problem-oriented approach.
    e. responding with clichés.

    Answer: d   **Type: M**   **Page: 370**   **Synthesis**

44. All of the following are defense mechanisms except

    a. verbal aggression.
    b. compensation.
    c. displacement.
    d. apathy.
    e. interpretation.

    Answer: e   **Type: M**   **Page: 376**   **Comprehension**

45. The most visible way disconfirming messages reinforce one another, as when one attack leads to another and another, is termed a(n)

    a. escalatory conflict spiral.
    b. de-escalatory conflict spiral.
    c. cognitive dissonance reaction.
    d. impervious dyad.
    e. pillow-talk incident.

    Answer: a   **Type: M**   **Page: 374**   **Knowledge**

46. The text suggested that you may react nondefensively to criticism by

    a. asking for a "time-out."
    b. guessing about the specifics of a critic's remarks.
    c. criticizing yourself.
    d. giving the reasons for your behavior.
    e. telling the critic to stop.

    Answer: b   **Type: M**   **Page: 388**   **Comprehension**

47. Your instructor tells you how poor your writing ability is and how wrong it is for you not to work harder on it. That instructor used the Gibb category of

    a. description.
    b. evaluation.
    c. problem orientation.
    d. equality.
    e. provisionalism.

    Answer: b   **Type: M**   **Page: 380**   **Application**

48. According to research findings about defensiveness, when one person in a dyad acts in a defensive manner

    a. a counterattack is appropriate.
    b. the partner will be supportive.
    c. a defensive spiral usually results.
    d. perceptions are not realistic.
    e. self-disclosure usually takes place.

Answer: c   **Type: M**   **Page: 380**   **Knowledge**

49. Another term which describes the Gibb defensive category of neutrality would be

    a. understanding.
    b. aggressive perception.
    c. positive/negative balance.
    d. displaced loyalty.
    e. indifference.

Answer: e   **Type: M**   **Page: 382**   **Knowledge**

50. Use of "you" language as described in the text usually indicates that the speaker is

    a. making a sincere effort to describe the other person's point of view.
    b. being spontaneous.
    c. being evaluative.
    d. acting in a descriptive manner.
    e. acting in an empathetic manner.

Answer: c   **Type: M**   **Page: 380**   **Comprehension**

51. Defensiveness is

    a. an emotion.
    b. accompanied by physiological symptoms.
    c. usually reciprocal.
    d. often unconscious.
    e. all of the above.

Answer: e   **Type: M**   **Page: 375**   **Analysis**

52. None of Gibb's categories of defensive behaviors arouse defensiveness unless

    a. the receiver of the message perceives them as threatening.
    b. the sender of the message intends to start a defensive spiral.
    c. both partners in the communication get defensive.
    d. the matching supportive behavior is ignored by the sender of the message.
    e. the self-concepts of both partners are threatened.

Answer: a   **Type: M**   **Page: 375**   **Comprehension**

53. Evaluative language is also described as

    a. "me" language.
    b. "it" language.
    c. "you" language.
    d. "neutral" language.
    e. "supportive" language.

    Answer: c   **Type: M**   **Page: 380**   **Knowledge**

54. The term that describes the quality of a personal relationship is

    a. mood.
    b. tone.
    c. climate.
    d. environment.
    e. foundation.

    Answer: c   **Type: M**   **Page: 368**   **Knowledge**

55. This chapter states that a defensive communicator protects his/her

    a. interpretations.
    b. sense data.
    c. perceived self.
    d. presenting self.
    e. none of the above

    Answer: d   **Type: M**   **Page: 375**   **Knowledge**

56. Gibb's categories provide a useful way for us to examine our

    a. self-concept.
    b. patterns of self-disclosure.
    c. defensive and supportive behaviors.
    d. manipulative behaviors.
    e. perceptual differences.

    Answer: c   **Type: M**   **Page: 380**   **Comprehension**

57. The communication climate in a relationship is determined by the

    a. roles each person has in the relationship.
    b. similarities of the parties.
    c. degree to which each person feels valued.
    d. amount of self-disclosure that occurs.
    e. listening and perceptual skills that each individual brings to the relationship.

    Answer: c   **Type: M**   **Page: 368**   **Knowledge**

58. A confirming response typically

    a. criticizes the other.
    b. agrees with or acknowledges the other.
    c. reveals deception.
    d. recognizes manipulation.
    e. controls the other.

    Answer: b   **Type: M**   **Page: 369**   **Comprehension**

59. People who act in accordance with Gibb's category of equality communicate that

    a. everyone is equal in every way.
    b. while they may have greater talent in some areas, all have just as much worth as human beings.
    c. all human beings are created with the capacity to be equal in all areas.
    d. all of the above
    e. none of the above

    Answer: b   **Type: M**   **Page: 383**   **Comprehension**

60. "I've done all the research I need to about my business; I don't need to know anything else" is an example of the Gibb defensive category of

    a. evaluation.
    b. control.
    c. superiority.
    d. certainty.
    e. strategy.

    Answer: d   **Type: M**   **Page: 383**   **Application**

61. Communicators can resolve cognitive dissonance by

    a. revising the self-concept in the face of criticism.
    b. ignoring the dissonant information.
    c. distorting the dissonant information.
    d. attacking the source of dissonant information.
    e. all of the above.

    Answer: e   **Type: M**   **Page: 376**   **Comprehension**

62. Jenny says, "Beth, I'm really upset about how we divide the cooking chores." Beth retorts, "Speaking of cooking, my secretary brought in great cookies today." Beth's response is an example of a(n)

    a. impervious response.
    b. interrupting response.
    c. irrelevant response.
    d. impersonal response.
    e. tangential response.

    Answer: e   **Type: M**   **Page: 370**   **Application**

63. Robin asks her boss if she can take Friday afternoon off to clear up some legal problems. Her boss replies, "Seems like everybody has problems these days." The boss's reply is an example of a(n)

    a. impervious response.
    b. interrupting response.
    c. irrelevant response.
    d. tangential response.
    e. impersonal response.

Answer: e　　　　**Type: M**　　　　**Page: 370**　　　　**Application**

64. Molly asks her mother if she'll help her go through her wardrobe to see what needs to be thrown out. Mother replies, "Throwing out things is a great idea; help me with cleaning out this refrigerator, won't you?" Mother's reply is an example of a(n)

    a. impervious response.
    b. interrupting response.
    c. irrelevant response.
    d. tangential response.
    e. impersonal response.

Answer: d　　　　**Type: M**　　　　**Page: 370**　　　　**Application**

65. Carmen receives a message to return Jack's phone call, but she doesn't. Her response could be classified as

    a. impervious.
    b. interrupting.
    c. irrelevant.
    d. tangential.
    e. impersonal.

Answer: a　　　　**Type: M**　　　　**Page: 370**　　　　**Application**

66. "You drink too much" is an example of the Gibb defensive category of

    a. evaluation.
    b. control.
    c. strategy.
    d. neutrality.
    e. superiority.

Answer: a　　　　**Type: M**　　　　**Page: 380**　　　　**Application**

67. Which of the following statements is the best supportive alternative to the accusation "You just don't try hard enough."

    a. "You should try harder."
    b. "You give up too easily."
    c. "I'm worried you'll fail with two D's."
    d. "You should study two hours every night."
    e. "It's time we had a talk about trying."

Answer: c　　　　**Type: M**　　　　**Page: 380**　　　　**Analysis**

68. Ambiguous responses

    a. are conversational "take aways."
    b. are unrelated to what the other person has just said.
    c. ignore the other person's attempt to communicate.
    d. contain messages with more than one meaning.
    e. interrupt the other person.

    Answer: d　　　　**Type: M**　　　　**Page: 370**　　　　**Knowledge**

69. Disconfirming responses loaded with clichés and other statements that never truly respond to the speaker are called

    a. impervious.
    b. interrupting.
    c. irrelevant.
    d. tangential.
    e. impersonal.

    Answer: e　　　　**Type: M**　　　　**Page: 370**　　　　**Knowledge**

70. An old friend flashes you a smile across the room. You turn away. You have just given a disconfirming response categorized as

    a. impervious.
    b. interrupting.
    c. irrelevant.
    d. tangential.
    e. impersonal.

    Answer: a　　　　**Type: M**　　　　**Page: 370**　　　　**Application**

71. Agreeing with a critic's perception of your behavior involves

    a. telling the critic she/he's right.
    b. saying you think she/he might interpret it that way.
    c. agreeing with the specifics of the criticism.
    d. all of the above.
    e. none of the above.

    Answer: b　　　　**Type: M**　　　　**Page: 395**　　　　**Application**

72. Which of the following is a nondefensive response to the criticism, "You've really messed up that account now"?

    a. "Tell me what, in your mind, I did that upset you."
    b. "Not taking Mr. Kimble to dinner endangers the account?"
    c. "So you're upset that the account may be lost?"
    d. "Losing that account might really hurt our department?"
    e. All of the above respond nondefensively to that criticism.

    Answer: e　　　　**Type: M**　　　　**Pages: 387–395**　　　　**Analysis**

73. An inconsistency between two conflicting pieces of information about one's self, attitudes, or behavior has been termed

    a. a defensive spiral.
    b. a supportive spiral.
    c. cognitive dissonance.
    d. an ambiguous response.
    e. intrapersonal conflict.

Answer: c   **Type: M**   **Page: 376**   **Knowledge**

74. Psychological devices that resolve dissonance by maintaining a positive presenting image at the risk of distorting reality are called

    a. reaction formations.
    b. confirming responses.
    c. defense mechanisms.
    d. self-fulfilling prophecies.
    e. climate adjusters.

Answer: c   **Type: M**   **Page: 376**   **Comprehension**

75. If others start criticizing you, one productive way to respond is to

    a. tell them to stop the criticism.
    b. point out that criticism is not productive.
    c. criticize them to show them how it feels.
    d. ask them for more details about what the criticism involves.
    e. just back off; there's no effective way to deal with this kind of "no-win" situation.

Answer: d   **Type: M**   **Page: 388**   **Comprehension**

76. You can often respond nondefensively to criticism by agreeing

    a. with the critic's truthful statements.
    b. with the critic's judgment.
    c. with the critic's perception of the situation.
    d. both a and b above
    e. both a and c above

Answer: e   **Type: M**   **Pages: 394–395**   **Comprehension**

77. All of the following are nondefensive responses to criticism recommended by your text except

    a. asking for more details about the criticism.
    b. paraphrasing the speaker's comments.
    c. asking about the consequences of your behavior.
    d. accepting the speaker's comments, even if you disagree.
    e. guessing about the details of the criticism.

Answer: d   **Type: M**   **Pages: 387–391**   **Knowledge**

78. Defensive counterattacks take the form of

    a. verbal aggression and sarcasm.
    b. description and neutrality.
    c. facilitation and compromise.
    d. assertion and aggression.
    e. all of the above.

    Answer: a   **Type: M**   **Page: 376**   **Knowledge**

79. If you emphasize how good you are in sports when someone criticizes your academic performance, you've used the defensive reaction called

    a. displacement.
    b. rationalization.
    c. repression.
    d. regression.
    e. compensation.

    Answer: e   **Type: M**   **Page: 377**   **Application**

80. Becoming defensive can be

    a. a way to prepare for self-disclosure.
    b. a way to avoid change.
    c. easy to change in ourselves and others once we recognize it.
    d. unavoidable in most instances.
    e. always undesirable.

    Answer: b   **Type: M**   **Page: 378**   **Comprehension**

81. Communication climates are a function of

    a. the way people feel about one another.
    b. the tasks people perform.
    c. individual personality characteristics.
    d. Gibb's functional theories.
    e. time, place, and context.

    Answer: a   **Type: M**   **Page: 368**   **Comprehension**

82. Which of the following could be a description of the communication climate of this classroom?

    a. cold and tense
    b. learning 35 pages per class
    c. composed of 28 students
    d. engaging in many activities
    e. having 14 females and 14 males

    Answer: a   **Type: M**   **Page: 368**   **Application**

83. Jim's boss at the bank criticizes the way Jim handled a new account. Jim says nothing to his boss, but he's very short-tempered with his roommate that evening. Which defense mechanism is Jim most likely using?

    a.   apathy
    b.   displacement
    c.   verbal aggression
    d.   regression
    e.   repression

    Answer: b   **Type: M**   **Page: 370**   **Application**

84. A defense mechanism that is characterized by a pretense of not caring is called

    a.   repression.
    b.   displacement.
    c.   compensation.
    d.   apathy.
    e.   none of the above.

    Answer: d   **Type: M**   **Page: 370**   **Knowledge**

85. Just for fun, you flirted with an attractive person at a party last night. You know your partner is hurt, so you arrange a dinner at a favorite restaurant. You are most likely using the defense mechanism of

    a.   verbal aggression.
    b.   compensation.
    c.   rationalization.
    d.   apathy.
    e.   displacement.

    Answer: b   **Type: M**   **Page: 370**   **Application**

86. Defense mechanisms are

    a.   always undesirable.
    b.   often a way to fool oneself as well as others.
    c.   a cultural phenomenon.
    d.   habits we can change easily.
    e.   all of the above.

    Answer: b   **Type: M**   **Page: 376**   **Comprehension**

87. In general, defense mechanisms

    a.   are psychological devices.
    b.   enable us to build better relationships.
    c.   protect us from liars.
    d.   enable us to resolve conflicts.

    Answer: a   **Type: M**   **Page: 376**   **Comprehension**

88. Defensiveness is most likely to occur when

    a.   an individual's presenting image is attacked.
    b.   an individual's Johari Window is attacked.
    c.   another person is problem-oriented.
    d.   sender and receiver are experiencing identical environments.
    e.   facilitative emotions are being exchanged.

    Answer: a   **Type: M**   **Page: 375**   **Comprehension**

INSTRUCTIONS for questions 89–93: Match each description below with the appropriate defense mechanism.

    a.   verbal aggression
    b.   compensation
    c.   rationalization
    d.   repression
    e.   regression

89. Stressing a strength in one area to cover up a perceived shortcoming in another area

    Answer: b   **Type: Matching**   **Page: 377**   **Knowledge**

90. Denying the existence of an unpleasant fact

    Answer: d   **Type: Matching**   **Page: 378**   **Knowledge**

91. Accusing a critic of the same fault another person claims you are guilty of

    Answer: a   **Type: Matching**   **Page: 376**   **Knowledge**

92. Offering a logical but untrue explanation of your behavior

    Answer: c   **Type: Matching**   **Page: 377**   **Knowledge**

93. Playing helpless to avoid facing attack

    Answer: e   **Type: Matching**   **Page: 378**   **Knowledge**

INSTRUCTIONS for questions 94–98: Match each defense mechanism with its description.

    a.   rationalization
    b.   sarcasm
    c.   apathy
    d.   physical avoidance
    e.   displacement

94. Disguising an attack with a barbed, humorous message

    Answer: b   **Type: Matching**   **Page: 376**   **Application**

95. Laughing off a close friend's criticism even though it bothers you

    Answer: c   **Type: Matching**   **Page: 378**   **Application**

96. Attacking your roommate after being criticized by your boss

   Answer: e　　　**Type: Matching**　　　**Page: 378**　　　**Application**

97. Blaming your lack of exercise on a desire to conserve your energy

   Answer: a　　　**Type: Matching**　　　**Page: 377**　　　**Application**

98. Steering clear of someone who points out your flaws

   Answer: d　　　**Type: Matching**　　　**Page: 378**　　　**Application**

INSTRUCTIONS for questions 99–104: Match the following Gibb supportive behaviors with their defensive-arousing counterpart.

   a. strategy
   b. superiority
   c. neutrality
   d. control
   e. certainty
   f. evaluation

99. Empathy

   Answer: c　　　**Type: Matching**　　　**Page: 380**　　　**Knowledge**

100. Provisionalism

   Answer: e　　　**Type: Matching**　　　**Page: 380**　　　**Knowledge**

101. Problem orientation

   Answer: d　　　**Type: Matching**　　　**Page: 383**　　　**Knowledge**

102. Equality

   Answer: b　　　**Type: Matching**　　　**Page: 383**　　　**Knowledge**

103. Description

   Answer: f　　　**Type: Matching**　　　**Page: 380**　　　**Knowledge**

104. Spontancity

   Answer: a　　　**Type: Matching**　　　**Page: 382**　　　**Knowledge**

INSTRUCTIONS for questions 105–109: Match the terms below with their descriptions.

   a. cognitive dissonance
   b. disconfirming response
   c. communication climate
   d. defense mechanism
   e. confirming response

105. Term describing the emotional tone of an interpersonal relationship

   Answer: c　　　**Type: Matching**　　　**Page: 368**　　　**Knowledge**

106.   Inconsistency between two or more bits of information involving oneself

    Answer: a   **Type: Matching**   **Page: 376**   **Knowledge**

107.   Psychological device to resolve conflicting thoughts about ourselves

    Answer: d   **Type: Matching**   **Page: 376**   **Knowledge**

108.   Message that communicates value for another

    Answer: e   **Type: Matching**   **Page: 369**   **Knowledge**

109.   Message that communicates lack of support for another

    Answer: b   **Type: Matching**   **Page: 372**   **Knowledge**

INSTRUCTIONS for questions 110–114: Match the type of disconfirming response with its behavioral description.

    a.   impervious
    b.   tangential
    c.   interrupting
    d.   impersonal
    e.   irrelevant

110.   Shelley says, "Let's decide what we're doing this weekend after I get paid tomorrow," and you reply, "I'm really excited about getting an 'A' on my test."

    Answer: e   **Type: Matching**   **Page: 370**   **Analysis**

111.   Vince says, "I'm so tired," and you reply, "Boy, everybody's got problems today."

    Answer: d   **Type: Matching**   **Page: 370**   **Analysis**

112.   You see Denise smile at you, but you turn away.

    Answer: a   **Type: Matching**   **Page: 370**   **Analysis**

113.   You begin talking before Lana is finished.

    Answer: c   **Type: Matching**   **Page: 370**   **Analysis**

114.   Gail asks how your roommate is feeling; you tell her about your own health.

    Answer: b   **Type: Matching**   **Page: 370**   **Analysis**

115.   Describe two of your important relationships in terms of communication climate. What factors contribute to the overall climate in each relationship? Describe confirming and disconfirming behaviors for each relationship that lead you to your overall assessment.

    Answer   **Type: E**   **Pages: 368–372**   **Analysis**

116.   How do defensive behaviors work in the sphere of work relationships? Given your knowledge of Gibb's categories, what advice would you give to a manager?

    Answer   **Type: E**   **Pages: 380–385**   **Application**

117. Pretend you have explained the Gibb categories of defensive and supportive behaviors to someone who knows you well. Ask this person which of the Gibb categories you use. Record the responses, giving a specific example for each category.

Answer   **Type: E**   **Pages: 380–385**   **Synthesis**

118. Pick the two defense mechanisms you most commonly use. For each, describe (a) a recent incident when you used it, (b) the part of your self-concept you were protecting, and (c) the consequences of your defensiveness. If you haven't used defense mechanisms recently, answer this question with defense mechanisms you have used in the past. Be specific.

Answer   **Type: E**   **Page: 376**   **Synthesis**

119. Describe an important relationship in which you are involved in terms of a positive or negative "spiral" of behavior. Indicate how behaviors over the past six months (or any defined segment of time) have tended to "beget" similar behaviors in your relationship. Comment on the future direction of your spiral.

Answer   **Type: E**   **Page: 374**   **Evaluation**

120. Describe two incidents during the past year in which you were criticized. For each incident, describe the situation and what led up to the criticism, how you handled the criticism, and how you might handle this criticism differently now that you have the information from this chapter. Give actual quotes of how you would respond to criticism this time. If you wouldn't handle this criticism differently, describe how your original response handled the criticism effectively. Comment on the probable outcomes of each incident if you handled the criticism more effectively.

Answer   **Type: E**   **Pages: 387–395**   **Evaluation**

121. Define cognitive dissonance. Give five examples from your life that illustrate this concept in action. Label any defensive behaviors you use to cope with cognitive dissonance.

Answer   **Type: E**   **Pages: 376**   **Synthesis**

CHAPTER 10

MANAGING INTERPERSONAL CONFLICTS

1. In the "Crazymaker" reading in this chapter, psychologist George Bach describes passive-aggressive behaviors.

   Answer: T   **Type: T**   **Page: 411**   **Recall**

2. Research cited in the text states that strong marriages are characterized by productive expressions of conflict, among other things.

   Answer: T   **Type: T**   **Page: 405**   **Recall**

3. Destructive fights often start because the initiator confronts a partner who isn't ready for a confrontation.

   Answer: T   **Type: T**   **Page: 414**   **Knowledge**

4. Handling conflict assertively guarantees that you'll get what you want.

   Answer: F   **Type: T**   **Page: 413**   **Comprehension**

5. Interdependence must exist between two parties in order for a conflict to exist.

   Answer: T   **Type: T**   **Page: 404**   **Knowledge**

6. A conflict can exist only when both parties are aware of a disagreement.

   Answer: T   **Type: T**   **Page: 403**   **Knowledge**

7. According to Chapter Ten, stating your intentions is an important element of a clear message.

   Answer: T   **Type: T**   **Page: 420**   **Knowledge**

8. Avoidance and accommodation are both forms of nonassertive behavior.

   Answer: T   **Type: T**   **Page: 407**   **Comprehension**

9. One key to the win-win approach to conflict resolution is to look for the single best solution at the beginning of your conversation.

   Answer: F   **Type: T**   **Page: 441**   **Comprehension**

10. Win-lose or win-win outcomes to conflicts can often be products of self-fulfilling prophecies.

    Answer: T   **Type: T**   **Page: 434**   **Analysis**

11. The text says that "counting to ten" applies to win-win problem solving.

    Answer: T   **Type: T**   **Page: 436**   **Analysis**

12. As long as one person in the relationship is aware of the disagreement, a conflict exists.

    Answer: F   **Type: T**   **Page: 403**   **Knowledge**

13. The win-win approach to conflict resolution requires parties to reach a solution through compromise.

    Answer: F   **Type: T**   **Page: 437**   **Knowledge**

14. "You can live happily ever after" is the ultimate theme of *Looking Out/Looking In*.

    Answer: F   **Type: T**   **Page: 447**   **Comprehension**

15. With enough skill you should be able to use win-win problem solving successfully in almost any conflict.

    Answer: F   **Type: T**   **Page: 436**   **Knowledge**

16. When people express hostility in obscure ways, "passive aggression" occurs.

    Answer: T   **Type: T**   **Page: 409**   **Knowledge**

17. The win-win approach to conflict resolution requires each party to compromise by giving up something he or she wants.

    Answer: F   **Type: T**   **Page: 437**   **Knowledge**

18. In win-win problem solving, it's important to request specific change from your partner as early as possible in the "fight."

    Answer: F   **Type: T**   **Page: 438**   **Comprehension**

19. In order to communicate clearly, you should use all the elements of a clear message each time you speak.

    Answer: F   **Type: T**   **Page: 422**   **Application**

20. The clear message format should always be used in the order given in your text for best results.

    Answer: F   **Type: T**   **Page: 422**   **Analysis**

21. It's OK to reword the clear message format to suit your own particular style of speaking.

    Answer: T   **Type: T**   **Page: 422**   **Analysis**

22. You shouldn't have to repeat the clear message format if you express yourself clearly in the first place.

    Answer: F   **Type: T**   **Page: 422**   **Analysis**

23. In a survey of conflict views of college men and women, women were described as being

   a. more concerned with maintaining the relationship during a conflict.
   b. more concerned with power in the conflict.
   c. more interested in the content of the conflict.
   d. more ego-involved in the conflict than men.
   e. all of the above.

   Answer: a   **Type: M**   **Page: 429**   **Recall**

24. Complementary and symmetrical conflict styles have been shown to produce

   a. marriages that got back together after conflict.
   b. couples who find other mates while getting divorced.
   c. a greater percentage of divorces that are settled amicably.
   d. both "good" results as well as "bad" ones.
   e. divorces that only have the facade of politeness.

   Answer: d   **Type: M**   **Page: 425**   **Comprehension**

25. According to the study of successful marital conflict styles described in your text, happily married couples were found to handle conflict by

   a. using perception checking and admitting their defensiveness when it occurred.
   b. using paraphrasing to draw out the real reasons why the partner was angry.
   c. avoiding the expression of anger.
   d. realizing how silly the conflict was and making up.
   e. expressing negative emotions freely to help them clear the air.

   Answer: a   **Type: M**   **Page: 405**   **Recall**

26. One study reported in your text revealed that college students in romantic relationships who believe that conflicts are destructive

   a. are more likely to neglect the relationship than couples with less negative attitudes.
   b. are more likely to quit the relationship than couples with less negative attitudes.
   c. are less likely to see a solution to the conflict.
   d. are less likely to seek out win-win solutions than other couples.
   e. all of the above

   Answer: e   **Type: M**   **Page: 446**   **Recall**

27. An uncontrolled, spontaneous "explosion"—a "Vesuvius"—is

   a. encouraged by your text as a first step to solving conflict.
   b. therapeutic when you feel it's impossible to be relational and your partner understands what you're doing.
   c. a great way of eliminating defensive behaviors by "clearing the air."
   d. one way to make sure your partner will listen to you.
   e. all of the above.

   Answer: b   **Type: M**   **Page: 446**   **Recall**

28. Over 20 years of marriage and conflict research finds that unhappy married couples

    a. are more concerned with defending themselves than with being problem-oriented.
    b. listen carefully to one another.
    c. have empathy for their partners instead of sympathy.
    d. use "I" language too much.
    e. disclose too much

    Answer: a   **Type: M**   **Page: 405**   **Comprehension**

29. Intention statements can communicate

    a. where you stand on an issue.
    b. requests of others.
    c. descriptions of how you plan to act in the future.
    d. a, b, and c above.
    e. only interpretations of behavior.

    Answer: d   **Type: M**   **Page: 421**   **Comprehension**

30. Win-win problem solving is seldom used because

    a. there is a lack of awareness of it.
    b. emotional reflexes prevent constructive solutions.
    c. it requires both persons' cooperation.
    d. win-win problem solving is actually the most used problem-solving style of all.
    e. a, b, and c above

    Answer: e   **Type: M**   **Page: 438**   **Comprehension**

31. A person who buys a piece of new furniture, finds it damaged, and says nothing because he doesn't want to confront the retailer, is engaging in the personal conflict style of

    a. nonassertion.
    b. direct aggression.
    c. indirect communication.
    d. assertion.
    e. none of the above

    Answer: a   **Type: M**   **Page: 406**   **Application**

32. You're angry that your neighbor's cat uses your child's sandbox as a litter box, so you deposit a collection of sand and droppings on your neighbor's front porch. You've engaged in the personal conflict style described as

    a. nonassertion.
    b. direct aggression.
    c. indirect communication.
    d. assertion.
    e. passive aggression.

    Answer: b   **Type: M**   **Page: 408**   **Application**

33. In order for a conflict to exist, two interdependent parties must perceive

    a. incompatible goals.
    b. scarce rewards.
    c. interference from the other party in achieving their goals.
    d. a, b, and c above.
    e. both a and c above.

    Answer: d   **Type: M**   **Pages: 403–404**   **Knowledge**

34. You are upset with your friend Laura because she's borrowed some clothes and not returned them. You badmouth Laura to some mutual friends, telling them Laura is "undependable." You've engaged in the personal conflict style described as

    a. nonassertion.
    b. direct aggression.
    c. passive aggression.
    d. assertion.

    Answer: c   **Type: M**   **Page: 409**   **Application**

35. When people deliver subtle aggressive messages (involving feelings of resentment, anger, or rage that they aren't able or willing to express directly), and they still maintain the front of kindness, they are engaging in what psychologist George Bach calls

    a. defense arousal.
    b. nonverbal conflict.
    c. "trick or treat" messages.
    d. crazymaking.
    e. one-up conflict resolution.

    Answer: d   **Type: M**   **Page: 409**   **Knowledge**

36. A possible pitfall of using passive aggression is that

    a. the object of your indirect aggression may just miss the point.
    b. a short-range "win" may lose in the long run.
    c. you deny yourself and the other party a chance of building any kind of honest relationship.
    d. All of the above are possible pitfalls involved with the use of passive aggression.
    e. Passive aggression really has no pitfalls.

    Answer: d   **Type: M**   **Page: 409**   **Comprehension**

37. Conflict rituals are

    a. inherently wrong.
    b. the best way to solve the variety of conflicts that are part of any relationship.
    c. almost always positive.
    d. unacknowledged but repeating patterns of dealing with conflict.
    e. all of the above.

    Answer: d   **Type: M**   **Page: 427**   **Comprehension**

38. The "ownership" of a problem almost always belongs to

    a. the person who brings it up.
    b. the person to whom the complaint is directed.
    c. the person with the lowest amount of self-disclosure.
    d. the person with the greatest amount of passive aggressive behavior.
    e. the most assertive person.

Answer: a   **Type: M**   **Page: 438**   **Comprehension**

39. You and your partner's pattern of managing disagreements that repeats itself over time is called your

    a. relational conflict style.
    b. cognitive dissonance pattern.
    c. harmony/disharmony pattern.
    d. "Vesuvius."
    e. clear message format.

Answer: a   **Type: M**   **Page: 427**   **Knowledge**

40. Which of the following is the best example of a specific intention clearly stated to a partner?

    a. "I want you to be honest with me."
    b. "I want more understanding from you."
    c. "I need to talk about our relationship."
    e. "I want two hours to myself to read."

Answer: e   **Type: M**   **Page: 421**   **Application**

41. Since a record of pure objective information would simply describe an event without saying what it means, we should remember that when we attach meaning to behavior, we are

    a. labeling.
    b. making our intentions known.
    c. interpreting.
    d. expressing our feelings.
    e. using all of the above.

Answer: c   **Type: M**   **Page: 416**   **Comprehension**

42. Which of the following is an accurate feeling statement?

    a. "I feel like you're angry at me."
    b. "I feel like going home now."
    c. "I feel embarrassed when I do poorly on tests."
    d. "I feel you ought to be more careful."
    e. All of the above are feeling statements.

Answer: c   **Type: M**   **Page: 448**   **Evaluation**

43. "Crazymakers" are

    a. undiagnosed schizophrenics who use aggressive behaviors.
    b. disguised forms of aggression.
    c. people who have been driven to distraction by noncommunicative partners.
    d. humorous greeting cards that express aggression.
    e. none of the above.

    Answer: b   **Type: M**   **Page: 409**   **Comprehension**

44. All of the following are true about conflict except

    a. conflict is natural.
    b. every relationship of any depth at all has conflict.
    c. conflict can be beneficial.
    d. people typically have similar conflict styles.

    Answer: d   **Type: M**   **Pages: 402–405**   **Synthesis**

45. A communicator who describes behavior is using

    a. objective information.
    b. crazymakers.
    c. paraphrasing.
    d. abstract descriptions.
    e. all of the above.

    Answer: a   **Type: M**   **Page: 415**   **Comprehension**

46. Studies of different cultures and conflict reveal that

    a. assertiveness is valued worldwide.
    b. North Americans avoid confrontation more than other cultures studied.
    c. individualistic cultures are less assertive than collective ones.
    d. the assertiveness appropriate in North America would be rude and insensitive in collectivist cultures.
    e. all of the above are true.

    Answer: d   **Type: M**   **Page: 431**   **Comprehension**

47. One of the best methods to use to describe your problem and needs to a partner during conflict resolution is

    a. paraphrasing.
    b. perception checking.
    c. the clear message format.
    d. emotional description.
    e. high-level abstractions.

    Answer: c   **Type: M**   **Page: 415**   **Knowledge**

48. All of the following are behavioral descriptions except

    a. "I notice you're frowning."
    b. "I saw you walk out of the party."
    c. "Your behavior shows me you're angry."
    d. "You've shouted the last three times we've discussed money."
    e. "You haven't said 'I love you' in over a week."

    Answer: c   **Type: M**   **Page: 415**   **Application**

49. Which of the following is an interpretation?

    a. "I got an 'A' on my history paper."
    b. "My boyfriend is jealous."
    c. "I sure appreciate your help."
    d. "Would you tell me what you mean by that?"
    e. All of the above are interpretations.

    Answer: b   **Type: M**   **Page: 416**   **Application**

50. A consequence statement can describe

    a. what happens to you, the speaker.
    b. what happens to the person you're addressing or to others.
    c. why you're bothered or pleased by another's behavior.
    d. what happens without moralizing about it.
    e. all of the above.

    Answer: e   **Type: M**   **Page: 419**   **Synthesis**

51. In working toward a win-win solution, you should do all of the following except

    a. identify and define the conflict.
    b. generate a number of possible solutions.
    c. evaluate the alternative solutions.
    d. push for the solution that you have proposed.
    e. follow up on the solution.

    Answer: d   **Type: M**   **Pages: 438–442**   **Synthesis**

52. Studies of intimate and aggressive relational conflict styles find that

    a. the pattern partners choose may reveal a great deal about the kind of relationship they have chosen.
    b. the intimate-nonaggressive style fails to handle problems.
    c. intimate-aggressive partners avoid conflicts.
    d. intimacy and aggression are opposites and thus not productive topics for study.
    e. intimacy and aggression work best in symmetrical relationships.

    Answer: a   **Type: M**   **Page: 456**   **Comprehension**

53. A win-win "fight" is recommended as a positive way of handling conflict because it

   a. allows for clear expression of differences and wants.
   b. guarantees that your demands will be met.
   c. lets dyads express conflict by nonharmful physical aggression.
   d. allows for spontaneous expression of feelings.
   e. forces one partner to come to see the other's needs.

   Answer: a   **Type: M**   **Pages: 426**   **Synthesis**

54. You hint to your partner that you've been feeling neglected lately by mentioning how many nice things your friend's partner has done. You've used the personal conflict style called

   a. indirect communication.
   b. nonassertive behavior.
   c. direct aggression.
   d. passive aggression.
   e. assertion.

   Answer: a   **Type: M**   **Page: 410**   **Application**

55. According to your text, the elements of a clear message are

   a. feeling, interpretation, assertion, and consequence.
   b. behavior, interpretation, feeling, assertion, and intention.
   c. behavior, assertion, aggression, and interpretation.
   d. behavior, interpretation, feeling, consequence, and intention.
   e. assertion, aggression, negotiation, interpretation, and intention.

   Answer: d   **Type: M**   **Pages: 415–421**   **Synthesis**

56. In order to decide which conflict style you should use, you should consider

   a. the situation.
   b. the receiver.
   c. your goals.
   d. a, b, and c above.
   e. the other person's conflict style most of all.

   Answer: d   **Type: M**   **Page: 414**   **Comprehension**

INSTRUCTIONS for questions 57–61: Match each of the following crazymakers with its description.

   a. mind reader
   b. crisis tickler
   c. guilt maker
   d. pseudoaccommodator
   e. avoider

57. When this person's partner brings up a problem, she pretends to be busy with the laundry.

   Answer: e   **Type: Matching**   **Page: 411**   **Comprehension**

58.   This person pretends that there's nothing wrong when his partner brings up a conflict.

   Answer: d   **Type: Matching**   **Page: 411**   **Comprehension**

59.   This person handles conflict by trying to make her partner feel responsible for causing her discomfort.

   Answer: c   **Type: Matching**   **Page: 411**   **Comprehension**

60.   This person almost brings what's bothering him to the surface, but never quite comes out and expresses himself.

   Answer: b   **Type: Matching**   **Page: 411**   **Comprehension**

61.   Instead of expressing her feelings honestly, this person explains what her partner "really" means or what's "really wrong."

   Answer: a   **Type: Matching**   **Page: 411**   **Comprehension**

INSTRUCTIONS for questions 62–66: Match each of the following crazymakers with its description.

   a.   distractor
   b.   subject changer
   c.   beltliner
   d.   blamer
   e.   contract tyrannizer

62.   Whenever the conversation approaches an area of conflict, this person steers the conversation to another topic.

   Answer: b   **Type: Matching**   **Page: 411**   **Comprehension**

63.   Mad about the fact that his girlfriend went out with someone else, this person attacks her for being a poor student.

   Answer: a   **Type: Matching**   **Page: 411**   **Comprehension**

64.   This person insists that agreements cannot be changed from what was agreed previously.

   Answer: e   **Type: Matching**   **Page: 411**   **Comprehension**

65.   This person is more interested in finding fault than in solving conflict.

   Answer: d   **Type: Matching**   **Page: 411**   **Comprehension**

67.   This person uses intimate knowledge of his partner to hurt her where he knows she will be most sensitive.

   Answer: c   **Type: Matching**   **Page: 411**   **Comprehension**

INSTRUCTIONS for questions 68–71: Match each of the following crazymakers with its description.

    a. joker
    b. withholder
    c. gunnysacker
    d. trivial tyrannizer
    e. trapper

68. This person asks for something in a conflict and then attacks his partner for the very thing he requested that she do.

Answer: e	Type: Matching	Page: 411	Comprehension

69. This person does things that she knows really bother her partner instead of honestly sharing her resentments.

Answer: d	Type: Matching	Page: 411	Comprehension

70. This person makes a collection of his resentments and then pours all the pent-up hostilities out at once.

Answer: c	Type: Matching	Page: 411	Comprehension

71. This person withdraws affection, help, or favors to punish her partner instead of expressing her anger directly.

Answer: b	Type: Matching	Page: 411	Comprehension

72. This person uses humor to disguise aggressive feelings.

Answer: a	Type: Matching	Page: 411	Comprehension

INSTRUCTIONS for questions 73–112: Identify each of the following statements within quotation marks as according to the clear message format.

    a. feeling
    b. behavior
    c. interpretation
    d. consequence
    e. intention

73. "I feel like leaving now."

Answer: e	Type: Matching	Page: 421	Application

74. "Whenever we fight, both of us wind up regretting it."

Answer: d	Type: Matching	Page: 419	Application

75. "I feel you're not being fair."

Answer: c	Type: Matching	Page: 416	Application

76. "You've never used language like that before."

   Answer: b   **Type: Matching**   **Page: 415**   Application

77. "You're certainly touchy today."

   Answer: c   **Type: Matching**   **Page: 416**   Application

78. "I sure am grateful for your help."

   Answer: a   **Type: Matching**   **Page: 418**   Application

79. "I just want you to know how I feel."

   Answer: e   **Type: Matching**   **Page: 421**   Application

80. "I want that twenty dollars you owe me."

   Answer: e   **Type: Matching**   **Page: 421**   Application

81. "You're smoking again after you said you were quitting."

   Answer: b   **Type: Matching**   **Page: 415**   Application

82. "I feel like calling her up right now."

   Answer: e   **Type: Matching**   **Page: 421**   Application

83. "I don't think you like me."

   Answer: c   **Type: Matching**   **Page: 416**   Application

84. "I'm going to eat out tonight."

   Answer: e   **Type: Matching**   **Page: 421**   Application

85. "Because we were five minutes late, we couldn't be seated until intermission."

   Answer: d   **Type: Matching**   **Page: 419**   Application

86. "You seem pretty sure of yourself."

   Answer: c   **Type: Matching**   **Page: 416**   Application

87. "I'm uncomfortable about that."

   Answer: a   **Type: Matching**   **Page: 418**   Application

88. "You're overreacting to that."

   Answer: c   **Type: Matching**   **Page: 416**   Application

89. "I want to study tonight."

   Answer: e   **Type: Matching**   **Page: 421**   Application

90. "You're just trying to set me against her."

      Answer: c   **Type: Matching**   **Page: 416**   Application

91. "I'm glad you're coming."

      Answer: a   **Type: Matching**   **Page: 418**   Application

92. "Quit teasing me!"

      Answer: e   **Type: Matching**   **Page: 421**   Application

93. "I can tell you're upset."

      Answer: c   **Type: Matching**   **Page: 416**   Application

94. "You're wearing that shirt I like."

      Answer: b   **Type: Matching**   **Page: 415**   Application

95. "You haven't popped your gum all evening."

      Answer: b   **Type: Matching**   **Page: 415**   Application

96. "I hope you'll visit again soon."

      Answer: e   **Type: Matching**   **Page: 421**   Application

97. "Since you're here, I've decided to relax."

      Answer: d   **Type: Matching**   **Page: 419**   Application

98. "Give me that book."

      Answer: e   **Type: Matching**   **Page: 421**   Application

99. "You're asking me to do something that's too difficult."

      Answer: c   **Type: Matching**   **Page: 416**   Application

100. "I know you wore that outfit to please me."

      Answer: c   **Type: Matching**   **Page: 416**   Application

101. "You should study more often."

      Answer: c   **Type: Matching**   **Page: 416**   Application

102. "I'm really burned up about that bill."

      Answer: a   **Type: Matching**   **Page: 418**   Application

103. "You think this studying is easy for me."

      Answer: c   **Type: Matching**   **Page: 416**   Application

104. "I feel you should pay half."

     Answer: e   **Type: Matching**   **Page: 421**   **Application**

105. "Because you helped me and I felt relieved, I had time to cook for you."

     Answer: d   **Type: Matching**   **Page: 419**   **Application**

106. "Let's go to the movies."

     Answer: e   **Type: Matching**   **Page: 421**   **Application**

107. "I don't think you really mean that."

     Answer: c   **Type: Matching**   **Page: 416**   **Application**

108. "Ever since you said that I was wrong, I've been afraid to ask your opinion."

     Answer: d   **Type: Matching**   **Page: 419**   **Application**

109. "Tell me the truth."

     Answer: e   **Type: Matching**   **Page: 421**   **Application**

110. "That's not fair."

     Answer: c   **Type: Matching**   **Page: 416**   **Application**

111. "She's holding a grudge."

     Answer: c   **Type: Matching**   **Page: 416**   **Application**

112. "I wish you'd call more often."

     Answer: e   **Type: Matching**   **Page: 421**   **Application**

113. Explain a current conflict you are having with a friend or loved one. Apply the win-win method to arrive at a solution using all six steps as though you were speaking to your partner.

     Answer   **Type: E**   **Pages: 438–442**   **Synthesis**

114. In a short essay, defend or refute the following statement: "Conflict is a destructive behavior."

     Answer   **Type: E**   **Page: 405**   **Evaluation**

115. Do you think it is a good idea to "give in" or "give up" in a conflict? If you answered "yes," describe the circumstances that would warrant giving in. If you answered "no," explain why not.

     Answer   **Type: E**   **Page: 414**   **Evaluation**

116. Imagine a conflict which cannot be solved. What have you learned about interpersonal communication that might enable you to cope with unresolvable conflict?

     Answer   **Type: E**   **Pages: 1–447**   **Evaluation**

117. Pick the two crazymakers you use most often. For each, describe the circumstances in which the crazymaker is used, the function which the crazymaker serves, the consequences of using the crazymaker, and any alternative behavior which would be more constructive.

     Answer   **Type: E**   **Page: 411**   **Evaluation**

118. "In order for there to be winners, there have to be losers." Discuss this statement by examining an interpersonal conflict in which you have been involved.

     Answer   **Type: E**   **Pages: 433–436**   **Synthesis**

119. Using the clear message format from Chapter Ten (behavior, interpretation, feeling, consequence, and intention), write one gripe, request, appreciation, or some other message that you could share with a person who is important to you at this time in your life. (Don't use the message you already composed when we discussed this method in class.)

     Answer   **Type: E**   **Pages: 415–421**   **Synthesis**

PART FOUR

INTERPERSONAL COMMUNICATION EXERCISES FOR SPECIFIC VOCATIONS

CHAPTER 3

PERCEPTION:
WHAT YOU SEE IS WHAT YOU GET

LEGAL ASSISTANT STUDIES
Guarding Against Perceptual Errors

Think about these two personalities/characters:

Case One:

John Farrell, 35 years old, engineer at Sandia Labs, graduate of UNM, father of two daughters, ages 5 and 7, lives in N. E. Heights, drives a 1988 Volvo station wagon. Wife is an accountant at Sunwest Bank.

Now interject that John has been arrested for drunk driving. How does that change your perception?

Case Two:

Lynda Wolcott, 33 years old, buyer for Mervyn's department store, attractive mother of three, John (age 9), Amanda (age 7), and Anthony (age 4). Married to Tom for ten years. Tom is an attorney. Own home in Sandia Heights. Children attend Georgia O'Keeffe grade school.

Now interject that Lynda has been arrested for drunk driving. How does that change your perception?

INSTRUCTOR NOTE: Point out that one of the comments heard most often from beginning paralegals is that they had no clue about client complexities. It is sometimes hard to believe that problems happen to everyone and one cannot be judgmental in the legal profession.

CHAPTER 4

EMOTIONS

LEGAL ASSISTANT STUDIES
Components of Emotion

How would you likely react in each of the following situations? What emotions might you feel? What would be the best way to express them?

1. You have been asked to interview a client. Client has been charged with sexual abuse of a child. You enter the office. He (the client) is quite attractive, very charming, and a college graduate.

2. The client you are interviewing describes throwing her two-year-old daughter against the wall. The statement is expressed with no emotion.

3. It is 2:30 P.M. You are trying to complete a document that must be filed with the court by 4:00 P.M. The attorney you work with just found out that she lost a case that has been pending for three years. An outraged client has just called demanding to speak to you. Your significant other just called to remind you of dinner arrangements. She is on hold.

4. You are interviewing a husband and wife who have lost their five-year-old daughter in a car accident. The mother breaks down in uncontrollable sobbing during the interview. She cannot stop.

5. You are asked by the attorney you work with to complete a research project. You must contact the client to ask a few questions. After introducing yourself as the paralegal, the client asks why the attorney is no longer doing the work and states that it is not acceptable to him that a paralegal do the legal work that he hired a lawyer to do.

6. You are interviewing a client in the hospital. The client is a woman who has allegedly been severely beaten by her boyfriend. You enter the hospital room to meet the client, encountering a situation worse than you could ever have imagined.

7. You are asked to pick up a client your attorney has accepted pro bono (no charge). You are to take the client to a Social Security hearing. You go to the door and enter the apartment. The apartment is infested with cockroaches. The client has two young children under age three.

CHAPTER 5

LANGUAGE: BARRIER AND BRIDGE

LEGAL ASSISTANT STUDIES
Check Your Abstractions

1. Women lawyers are _____.

2. Men lawyers are _____.

3. Conflict is _____.

4. People who seek legal assistance are _____.

5. Clients are _____.

6. People who become paralegals are _____.

7. People who are sued are _____.

8. People who commit crimes are _____.

9. Problems are _____.

10. Judges are _____.

CHAPTER 6

NONVERBAL COMMUNICATION:
MESSAGES WITHOUT WORDS

NURSES

1. Which of these nonverbal codes have the greatest potential to enhance your image and credibility with patients, family members, and other members of the medical profession: physical appearance, kinesics (body orientation, gestures, posture), facial expression and eyes, vocalics, silence, touch, proxemics, use of time, scents, the environment?

2. List two specific ways that you could use the information on nonverbal communication to be perceived as professional and credible to patients, family members, and other members of the medical profession.

4. In your opinion, what are the two nonverbal codes that nurses tend to give little attention to? Why?

HEALTH OCCUPATIONS STUDENT WORKSHEET
Additional Questions for Those in Health Occupations to Consider

1. Read what your text says about the distances at which we communicate (Hall's work). So much of your work is carried on at the intimate distance, yet the person is often someone you have just met. What effect does this have on the interaction?

2. Usually we get a lot of feedback from another person's facial expression. When communicating with patients who have physiological and muscular problems that prevent their full facial expressions, what are some difficulties persons in health occupations encounter?

   What assumptions do we make about those who don't respond? How do we feel?

3. Discuss the relative importance of verbal and nonverbal behavior in your career.

HEALTH OCCUPATIONS INSTRUCTOR NOTES
Additional Questions for Those in Health Occupations to Consider

1. Read what your text says about the distances at which we communicate (Hall's work). So much of your work is carried on at the intimate distance, yet the person is often someone you have just met. What effect does this have on the interaction?
People often interpret close proximity as intimacy or as a threat. Some patients may be uncomfortable because closeness is usually only experienced by them with those with whom they are intimate. Others may be uncomfortable because they perceive a threat when someone is that physically close to them. Be aware of other nonverbal reactions of the patients to try to determine their level of comfort.

2. Usually we get a lot of feedback from another person's facial expression. When communicating with patients who have physiological and muscular problems that prevent their full facial expressions, what are some difficulties persons in health occupations encounter?
To illustrate this, try to have one student role-play a person who shows absolutely no facial expression, or no change in expression, while the other student tries to perform some care or get some initial history. Let students discuss the tendency to stop our own expressions when we don't get positive feedback from others.

What assumptions do we make about those who don't respond? How do we feel? Even though we know cognitively that this person can't respond, we may feel offended and that may reflect in our own attempts to overcompensate and be over-animated or to stop our own expressions.

3. Discuss the relative importance of verbal and nonverbal behavior in your career.
Get students to focus on the fact that regardless of what they say, it is how they say it and how they act that patients/clients remember. Bedside manner is almost entirely a nonverbal communication component. A pharmacist who won't take time with anyone, a nurse who doesn't have time for patients give nonverbal cues that register as to how much worth the patient feels he/she has in the eyes of this person. Nervous gestures and mannerisms may make patients feel that way; calming gestures and voice may have that effect on patients. How patients feel about their care may have more to do with nonverbal than verbal behavior.

NURSES

I. PERSONAL APPEARANCE creates the first impression and influences subsequent communication.
   A. In the first four minutes people notice our race, gender, age, and appearance. As a nurse, what are some attributions or judgments patients, family members, and other members of the medical profession may make about you based on your
      1. race?
      2. gender?
      3. age?

     4. appearance?

  B. Dress includes artifacts and clothing
      1. Artifacts are objects we have or wear or carry with us or keep beside us. What are some artifacts that might enhance your credibility and trustworthiness? What are some things that others in your profession may see with, on, or beside you that would lessen your credibility? Examples: equipment, jewelry, tools, cases, glasses, instruments.
         a. items that would enhance credibility

         b. items that might lessen credibility

  C. Clothing may indicate our perception of the physical, social, or cultural context. It may communicate similarities, group identification, or status and power. Give some examples of how dress could reflect professionalism and be appropriate for the job(s) being performed.
      1.

      2.

      3.

      4.

II. BODY MOVEMENT includes body orientation, posture, gestures, emblems, regulators.
  A. How could your posture indicate formality or informality?

  B. How could you indicate your perception of your status? of the other person's status?

  C. What are some regulators that you might use in your job?
      1.

      2.

  D. How could your body orientation communicate
      1. inclusion or exclusion?

      2. approach or avoidance?

      3. liking or disliking?

III. FACE AND EYE BEHAVIORS can have a variety of meanings attached to them. What are some ways a nurse can effectively use
  A. facial expressions?

B. eye contact, movement, expression?

IV. VOCALICS or PARALANGUAGE refers not to what is said, but how it is said. How can each of these be used effectively by a nurse?
   A. pitch

   B. rate

   C. volume

   D. tone

   E. pauses

V. SILENCE communciates at various levels and has various meanings attached to it, depending on the context.
   A. The absence of verbal communication does not mean there is no communication occurring. How does a nurse use silence effectively?

   B. Silence can be interpreted in various and sometimes opposite ways. Give an example of a time when the silence of a nurse or patient might be interpreted in each of the opposing ways.
      1. Comfort/Discomfort

      2. Submission/Control

      3. Liking/Disliking

VI. TOUCH is a particularly powerful way to communicate.
   A. Cultures may be high-contact or low-contact cultures.

   B. Touch may communicate opposite emotions and relationships.

      1. caring, concern, intimacy

      2. control, power, dominance
   C. Harassment issues involve touch in the workplace. What kinds of touch and in what situations might this be an issue?

VII. PROXEMICS is the study of the distances that we use to communicate. Edward T. Hall describes various distances at which we typically communicate. Give an example of a time when each distance would be appropriate (or inappropriate) in your job.

   A. Examples of appropriate use of
      1. intimate distance (0–18″)

      2. personal distance (18″–4′)

      3. social distance (4′–12′)

      4. public distance (over 12′)

   B. Examples of inappropriate use of
      1. intimate distance (0–18″)

      2. personal distance (18″–4′)

      3. social distance (4′–12′)

      4. public distance (over 12′)

   C. Personal space and territoriality are different; territoriality refers to claims of physical spaces. Write some rules to avoid invasion of others' territoriality in your profession.
      1. Don't pick up another's stethoscope and use it.

      2.

      3.

      4.

   D. What are some examples of invasion of a patient's territory that are unavoidable in doing your job? How can you remain sensitive to the patient in spite of your necessary invasion?
      1.

      2.

      3.

VIII. CHRONEMICS refers to the meaning attached to time. People may attach different meanings to your actions depending upon their own perception of time and your actions with regard to time.
- A. How do the people you will deal with view time? How important is time to them?
  1. Monochronic tends to stick to schedule, be time-conscious.

  2. Polychronic tends to be less clock-oriented, working on many projects, but not on a strict schedule.

- B. Consider the chronological context of your communication with people. How long will you know many of the people you deal with?

- C. Discuss your use of informal time. What do the words a little while, soon, later, early, for a while mean in your profession in different contexts? Give some examples.

IX. SCENTS AND SMELLS often create powerful messages, and people attach a lot of meaning to them. Give some examples of this in your profession.

X. The ENVIRONMENT may signal to us how to act and how to interact. Consider the environments in which you will work. How does the environment itself communicate to people? What does it communicate?
- A. Whether a conversation is considered public or private may be signaled by the environment.

- B. The pleasantness of the environment may influence length and quality of interaction.

- C. Status or formality may be perceived from the environment.

CHAPTER 9

IMPROVING COMMUNICATION CLIMATES

DEFENSIVENESS
Computer Programming Student Worksheet

Your text describes how each of the items on the left contributes to defensiveness. As a computer programmer or systems analyst, what are some situations or times on the job when others would display evaluation, control, etc. toward you, thereby creating a greater potential for you to feel defensive? List a type of situation for each item. These are potential problems. On the right, list ways you could respond that would not increase the amount of defensiveness.

Evaluation

Control

Strategy

Neutrality

Superiority

Certainty

Computer Programming Instructor Notes

Your text describes how each of the items on the left contributes to defensiveness. As a computer programmer or systems analyst, what are some situations or times on the job when others would display evaluation, control, etc. toward you, thereby creating a greater potential for you to feel defensive? List a type of situation for each item. These are potential problems. On the right, list ways you could respond that would not increase the amount of defensiveness.

Are there times or ways in which you might perceive:

Evaluation
When working on a project for a user or client, comments are made to you such as, "You don't understand the accounting system our company uses."

Control
"You are the programmer, not the manager of this project; I'll decide what should be done."

Or perhaps you've tried to speak to as many employees as possible who have needs and concerns about the project you're working on. One supervisor says to you, "You need to ask me first before you go around talking to the accounting department."

Strategy

Users may appear to be trying to get you to solve problems that go beyond computer programming. They may appear to be blaming you for problems that are really personnel problems or internal communication problems.

Superiority

Although you have been hired to perform a job, others may speak to you as if they know more about your job than you do. Although he or she may have little understanding of the computer's capability, a user may imply he/she is superior to you in knowledge with a comment such as, "Where did you learn to code? We don't use that style here anymore; it's outdated."

Certainty

Users may use words like "always" and "never" when describing problems to you. Comments like "That will never work" or "Since you changed it, this program never does what we want it to," may trigger defensive reactions from you.

Neutrality

Comments that show no regard for your feelings or needs may create defensiveness. You have worked long and hard on a project and a client says, "We're just throwing out the part of the system you've worked on. We can't use it."

Legal Assistant Studies Student Worksheet

Your text describes how each of the items on the left contributes to defensiveness. As a legal assistant, what are some situations or times on the job when others would display evaluation, control, etc. toward you, thereby creating a greater potential for you to feel defensive? List a type of situation for each item. These are potential problems. On the right, list ways you could respond that would not increase the amount of defensiveness.

Evaluation

Control

Strategy

Neutrality

Superiority

Certainty

Legal Assistant Studies Instructor Notes

Your text describes how each of the items on the left contributes to defensiveness. As a legal assistant, what are some situations or times on the job when others would display evaluation, control, etc. toward you, thereby creating a greater potential for you to feel defensive? List a type of situation for each item. These are potential problems. On the right, list ways you could respond that would not increase the amount of defensiveness.

Evaluation

Attorneys under pressure bark orders at you and make constant use of you language, "You didn't. . . , you don't have . . . ," etc.

Control

You are told, "You have to do this first," and "You have to finish this before 5:00." You feel that your whole life is controlled by this case or attorney.

Strategy

As you are interviewing clients, you perceive an attempt to deceive you or get you to get away from your interview plan.

Neutrality

Lawyers, clients, and cases seem to be more important than your needs. You are expected to put your needs after those. You perceive a lack of regard, an indifference to your needs and feelings.

Superiority

Others in the legal community make remarks about you being only a paralegal, not having law training, etc.

Certainty

You've done the work on a certain brief and you know how it was constructed. You are told, "You will have to redo this."

RESPONDING WITHOUT DEFENSIVENESS
Computer Programming Student Worksheet

Receiving criticism is a part of many jobs. There are often times when we feel our self-concepts, our abilities, our worth as an employee or a person are under attack. Learning to deal with criticism in a way that doesn't contribute to more defensiveness is an important part of the job of a computer programmer or systems analyst.

Responding to criticism in a way that is hostile or defensive often creates an even more defensive climate. Learning to respond non-defensively can help solve a problem without added antagonism and without a defensive spiral.

Here is a specific situation. Write out as many non-defensive ways of responding as you can think of.

You have been working on a project for several days. You turn it over to your user who looks at it and says, "This isn't what I asked for." You feel angry, hurt, and confused. You feel defensive and want to say, "This is exactly what you told me to do." Instead, you try to create several responses that will work toward solving the problem without increasing tensions, antagonisms, or defensiveness.

1.   SEEK MORE INFORMATION.

Ask for specifics about the criticism.

Guess about specifics.

Paraphrase the critic's ideas.

Ask what the critic wants.

Ask about the consequences of your behavior.

Ask what else is wrong.

2. AGREE WITH CRITIC (FACTS OR CRITIC'S RIGHT TO HIS/HER PERCEPTION).

   Agree with or acknowledge any truth (validity of any part of critic's position).

   Agree with the critic's perception (critic's right to see the event his/her way).

Computer Programming Instructor Notes

Receiving criticism is a part of many jobs. There are often times when we feel our self-concepts, our abilities, our worth as an employee or a person are under attack. Learning to deal with criticism in a way that doesn't contribute to more defensiveness is an important part of the job of a computer programmer or systems analyst.

Responding to criticism in a way that is hostile or defensive often creates an even more defensive climate. Learning to respond non-defensively can help solve a problem without added antagonism and without a defensive spiral.

Here is a specific situation. Write out as many non-defensive ways of responding as you can think of.

You have been working on a project for several days. You turn it over to your user who looks at it and says, "This isn't what I asked for." You feel angry, hurt, and confused. You feel defensive and want to say, "This is exactly what you told me to do." Instead, you try to create several responses that will work toward solving the problem without increasing tensions, antagonisms, or defensiveness.

1. SEEK MORE INFORMATION.

   Ask for specifics about the criticism.

   What part of this project isn't right?

   Guess about specifics.

   Is it the _____?

   Paraphrase the critic's ideas.

   Are you saying that the whole way I've done this is wrong?

   Ask what the critic wants.

   What do you want me to do with it now?

   Ask about the consequences of your behavior.

   How will this affect the overall project?

   Ask what else is wrong.

   Is it just this report that is the problem, or are there some other things wrong that I should be aware of?

2. AGREE WITH CRITIC (FACTS OR CRITIC'S RIGHT TO HIS/HER PERCEPTION).

   Agree with or acknowledge any truth (validity of any part of critic's position).

   It's true that putting in a new system like this can slow production for a short time.

   Agree with the critic's perception (critic's right to see the event his/her way).

   "I can understand why you're skeptical about this new computer system. I know you got stung the last time some 'specialist' installed the software."

Legal Assistant Studies Student Worksheet

Receiving criticism is a part of many jobs. There are often times when we feel our self-concepts, our abilities, our worth as an employee or a person are under attack. Learning to deal with criticism in a way that doesn't contribute to more defensiveness is an important part of the job of a legal assistant.

Responding to criticism in a way that is hostile or defensive often creates an even more defensive climate. Learning to respond non-defensively can help solve a problem without added antagonism and without a defensive spiral.

Here is a specific situation. Write out as many non-defensive ways of responding as you can think of.

You have been working for an attorney who is under a great deal of stress. You understood that she wanted you to be working on a particular brief. You have worked into your breaks and have given this a lot of time and attention. This morning after barely greeting you, the attorney says, "That motion response is due today." You feel defensive and want to say, "Would you decide what you want me to work on and stick to it?" or "I've been working on what you asked me to do." Instead, try to create several responses that will work toward solving the problem without increasing tensions, antagonism, or defensiveness.

1. SEEK MORE INFORMATION.

   Ask for specifics about the criticism.

   Guess about specifics.

   Paraphrase the critic's ideas.

   Ask what the critic wants.

   Ask about the consequences of your behavior.

   Ask what else is wrong.

2. AGREE WITH CRITIC (FACTS OR CRITIC'S RIGHT TO HIS/HER PERCEPTION).

   Agree with or acknowledge any truth (validity of any part of critic's position).

   Agree with the critic's perception (critic's right to see the event his/her way).

COPING WITH TYPICAL CRITICISM
Computer Programming Student Worksheet

For each of the situations below, try to come up with eight different responses. Then discuss which response would have the best chance of reducing defensiveness and which response you think would be the best for each given situation.

1. "You just play at that computer all day. I don't see any benefit to the rest of us having you here."
2. "You really screwed us up. The old system was so much better. We could always pull up the information we needed. Now I can't get at accounts payable when I'm typing letters."
3. "You sure don't consider what's best for us in payroll. It seems like you just designed that new system for the convenience of shipping and receiving."
4. "This report never looks the way our CPA says it should."
5. "Since you're the new guy, you probably don't know any of our job control language."

6. "The programmers on the Accounting project say that your Inventory program files should be compatible with theirs."
7. "I'm not happy with the way this program calculates overtime pay; we don't do time and a half."
8. "Didn't you hear that the inventory control program is supposed to have a field for Reorder Point?"

1. SEEK MORE INFORMATION.

    Ask for specifics about the criticism.

    Guess about specifics.

    Paraphrase the critic's ideas.

    Ask what the critic wants.

    Ask about the consequences of your behavior.

    Ask what else is wrong.

2. AGREE WITH CRITIC (FACTS OR CRITIC'S RIGHT TO HIS/HER PERCEPTION).

    Agree with or acknowledge any truth (validity of any part of critic's position).

    Agree with the critic's perception (critic's right to see the event his/her way).

Legal Assistant Studies Student Worksheet

For each of the situations below, try to come up with eight different responses. Then discuss which response would have the best chance of reducing defensiveness and which response you think would be the best for each given situation.

1. A client you've been assigned to interview says to you, "You're not an attorney. You don't know how to handle my case."
2. A client says, "I'm just wasting my time and money with you. I want to talk with a lawyer, not some $5.00-an-hour paid help."
3. After turning in what you felt was your assigned job, the attorney says to you, "You were supposed to research this brief. This isn't even close."
4. You are writing a response to a motion to suppress physical evidence. The motion response is due soon. You need to talk to the case agent to get the information you need. When you get the case agent on the phone, she says, "I don't have time to waste with you."

1. SEEK MORE INFORMATION.

    Ask for specifics about the criticism.

    Guess about specifics.

    Paraphrase the critic's ideas.

    Ask what the critic wants.

    Ask about the consequences of your behavior.

    Ask what else is wrong.

2. AGREE WITH CRITIC (FACTS OR CRITIC'S RIGHT TO HIS/HER PERCEPTION).

    Agree with or acknowledge any truth (validity of any part of critic's position).

    Agree with the critic's perception (critic's right to see the event his/her way).